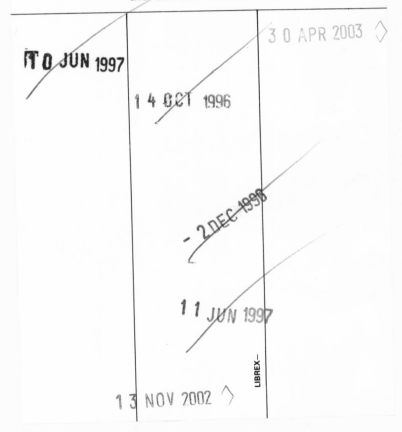

Books are to be returned on or before
the last date below.

1 0 JUN 1997

1 4 OCT 1996

3 0 APR 2003

- 2 DEC 1996

1 1 JUN 1997

1 3 NOV 2002

LIBREX—

TROUBLE SHOOTER Returns

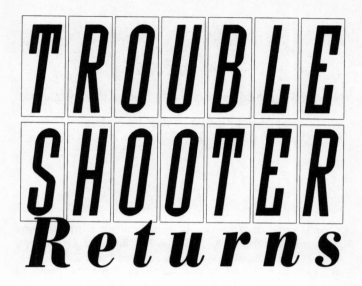

TROUBLE SHOOTER Returns

John Harvey-Jones

BBC BOOKS

FOR ABIGAIL

My adored granddaughter – a light-hearted companion

and friend on two of these adventures

BBC Books would like to thank the following for contributing photographs:
Jane Ashford, Alex Hansen, Barry Henson, Phil McCheyne, George Pope,
Justin Pumfrey, John Redman, Robert Thirkell.
Sir John on HMS ARK ROYAL: Crown Copyright, Royal Navy Photograph
Sir John at ICI: *North Eastern Evening Gazette*

This book is published to accompany the television series entitled
Troubleshooter Returns which was first broadcast in 1995
Executive Producer: Robin Brightwell
Series Producer: Robert Thirkell
Directors: Robert Thirkell and Michael Mosley

ISBN 0 563 37061 0

Designed by Gwyn Lewis

First published in 1995 by BBC Books,
an imprint of BBC Worldwide Publishing
BBC Worldwide Limited, Woodlands,
80 Wood Lane, London W12 0TT

Set in Monophoto Calisto by Selwood Systems, Midsomer Norton
Printed and bound in England by Clays Ltd, St Ives plc
Colour separations by Lawrence Allen Limited, Weston-super-Mare
Jacket printed by Lawrence Allen Limited, Weston-super-Mare

Contents

PART FOUR · TROUBLESHOOTER RETURNS TO WORK

Introduction

For as long as I can remember I have hoped that one day I will grow up and reach maturity, but I came to the conclusion, long ago, that I suffer from some sort of arrested development. I am, after all, in my seventieth year and yet I still feel as starry-eyed about the world around me as I remember being as a small boy, despite the almost unimaginable changes which have occurred to the world, to my country, and to me. More often than not I am surrounded by wise, sensible and mature people who appear to have no doubts about anything and seem to understand so many of life's mysteries which completely defeat me.

It may be that the omission of a period of adolescence, due to my wartime service, left a gap in the normal progression of a lifetime which I am still trying to fill. More positively, it may be that my continual fascination with what tomorrow will bring has precluded the process of reflection and looking back which must, I imagine, be a component of this complicated business of growing up.

However the years do pass and for some time now I have come to believe that people should cease playing an active primary role in business when they reach the age of seventy. I believe there are good reasons for this. Business is an enormously fast-changing pursuit and, no matter how flexible one thinks one is, thought processes do slow up and one tends to believe the experiences of the past are directly relevant to the problems of the present. Experience plays a role in terms of sounding warning bells or preventing mistakes, but I believe it is seldom the sole basis for charting the new, different and creative approach to the business problems of today.

Business is a young person's field and I believe that to hold on to prime positions of power after seventy is, without question, to block an opportunity for somebody younger, somebody who is (probably) less encumbered by memories of previous failures and certainly has more up-to-date technological skills. The pace of technological development, macro economic change on a massive world scale, and the endless changes in the aspirations, expectations and education of individuals, all require younger people to keep abreast of them. Although I can think of a small number of people who have continued to do outstanding work as business leaders in their seventies, I can think of rather more who have found it almost impossible to change and adapt fast enough.

The most common single reason for business failure is the inability of a company to adapt fast enough to the changes going on around it. It is necessary to reinvent the company continuously, and never to believe a consistently winning formula has been achieved. Business is a marathon rather than a sprint, and the company which is in front today is merely setting the pace for the competition from all over the world, the competition who strive continuously to overtake the front-runner. I cannot think of a single example of a company which has maintained pole position in its field in the world, year in year out. I have put forward these views over many years in all the companies in which I have served, and in all of them I have succeeded in writing into the statutes that no one, and especially no board member, should serve beyond the age of seventy. It was therefore clear to me, well in advance of the due date, that 1994, the year when I reached that magical age, would mean another change in my activities and another opportunity to seek to do things differently.

When I retired from ICI in 1987, just before my sixty-third birthday, I had already spent a lot of time discussing with my family, and thinking out for myself, what I wanted to do. Leaving anything, whether voluntarily or involuntarily, always creates a new opportunity and gives one the chance of moving on to new fields. The one thing which I was quite certain about was that I did not want to run another large international company: trying to repeat that experience would have been a bit like Oliver Twist asking for more and would, I suspect, have achieved the same result. So I planned to divide my working life into approximate quarters and to pursue four very different forms of activity.

I allocated a quarter of my time to non-executive directorships because I valued the chance to maintain a view of the evolving world through the eyes of international businesses, albeit not of the size of ICI. The second area I applied myself to was assisting the forces of education in Britain. The third I devoted to charities of one form or another, and the fourth to writing and other forms of self-expression.

By 1994 I had wound down my non-executive directorships and handed over my official positions at the schools with which I was involved, however I still maintain an active interest in those schools and try to give them some help where I can. I also maintain an active interest in education in Britain as a whole.

It was while I was trying to think how I would rebalance my life after passing my watershed year that the BBC suggested I might do another programme. After *Troubleshooter 2*, which in reality was *Troubleshooter 3* because I did two programmes in Eastern Europe in the period between the first and second series, my producer, Robert Thirkell, and I felt disinclined to continue with that particular approach to business programmes. We felt that the programmes were beginning to follow a formula and we wanted to take a different, more elastic, approach.

Robert suggested taking a look at some of the broader aspects of Britain's national life and the way things have changed over the years. Of course, every generation believes they have lived through periods of almost unbelievable change. I imagine that, by 1880, a man born in 1810 must have felt that the world about him had changed almost as much as I do today. I find it extraordinarily difficult to look back at life in Britain before the Second World War and trace the enormous changes that have taken place since then. In the year I was born, 1924, the maps of the world were largely coloured in the red of the British Empire. This was a world where peace was not kept by the United Nations, but primarily by the power and reach of the Royal Navy and where the suggestion that Britain should send in a gunboat was still both meaningful and possible. It was a time when the British still believed their education system, public schools and universities to be the best in the world, and that the great advances in British international competitiveness brought about by the Industrial Revolution still

3

seemed to place Britain in an unassailable position. It is the way that the values, power and prejudices of those days have affected the development of Britain and, in turn, influenced the lives and expectations of every single one of us which fascinates me.

Just as my own experiences have formed my current pleasures, values and motivations so, I feel, the past has played a major role in creating the sort of Britain we have today. During my lifetime Britain has gone from being a major power in the world, despite its relative size, to a country with the kind of influence that more truly reflects a population of 55.5m people in a world of 5292m people. This change has demanded major adjustments from the British and I believe our adjustment to this change in our circumstances, and our perception of ourselves, owes as much to the way we behaved in the early part of the century as it does to the increased pace of development of so many of the less fortunate parts of the world. Looking back with the perspectives of today it amazes me that in the 1920s we accepted what was, in reality, a totally disproportionate role in the world as our God-given right. We assumed that no force on earth could change the inalienable right of the British people to administer vast tracts of the world, and we believed that the institutions which we had evolved over the years to enable us to manage our own affairs could be grafted on, like budding a rose, to whichever country we happened to be involved with at the time.

When I look at the enormous civil service bureaucracy which has developed in India post-Independence, compared with the relatively small Indian Civil Service pre-Independence, I do wonder whether the British bureaucratic legacy was really as helpful as we believed it to be at the time. And when I see replicas of the House of Commons and its procedures in unlikely tropical countries, being administered by people with totally different backgrounds, histories and talents, I am amazed at the simplicity of the British belief in British institutions. All of this contrasts sadly with our current lack of confidence in the ability of Britain and its systems of government to adapt to the new role which events are forcing upon us, and yet despite our uncertainties we are still convinced that our systems are intrinsically superior to anybody else's.

4

Change has never come easily to us in Britain, except for brief periods in our history. The merchant venturers and sailors who scoured the world from Britain's shores, and the inventors, engineers and entrepreneurs who led Britain into the Industrial Revolution seem almost to have been an aberration in the normal flow of Britain's steady and measured pace of advance. Although the British have always derived great strength from their history and traditions, I feel that this reverence for the past hampers our ability to adapt speedily enough in a world where an ever-increasing rate of change appears to be the only certainty.

I feel that the past is meaningful to us primarily for what it means for the future. I have long been interested in the way that the various experiences of my life have contributed towards my perceptions and values and what drives me. During my entire life the pursuit of money has never been a motivating force for me, probably because I have always been lucky enough to earn what I needed to enable me to care for my wife and family, and to have choices about the way I have lived my life. I have never lusted after status symbols, I do not yearn to drive a Rolls-Royce and I can think of more things I will not do for money than things I will. But somewhere out of my past has come a great compulsion to keep going, and a real need as an individual to try to contribute to creating a better life for others where I can.

With all this in mind, Robert and I decided that it might be an idea to spend part of my seventieth year looking back instead of, as is my usual habit, looking forward, and that I might look at some areas of the past which speak to the future, both from a personal, and from a more general point of view. In a way a sort of *Troubleshoot* of Britain over the years, albeit from my rather specialized and individual angles of perception. Seventy is a good time to take stock of one's life and seventy years is a good span of time over which to look back at a country and the changes it has undergone; and gradually the programmes which now form the series *Troubleshooter Returns*, took shape in our minds.

Neither Robert nor I wanted the series to be one of purely self-indulgent reminiscence and the four programmes that we eventually planned look at the parts of our heritage which, through personal experience, have contributed to the formation of my values and my approach to life, but which have also influenced, to varying degrees, the way Britain is evolving as a whole.

We set our first programme in India, where the early years of my personal history and a large part of Britain's colonial history took place. We travelled to the place where my parents married, and where I lived as a young boy, and we looked at India, and several businesses in India, with one eye on the legacy that the British left behind, and which still persists, and the other eye on the changes that have happened in India post-liberalization and the end of the licence-raj.

Our second programme looks at British education, once again from both a personal and a general point of view. I believe that education is vital to the successful economic future of Britain and so we wanted to take a look at how British education – which has undergone so many changes – was functioning in the 1990s. And I wanted to test my fundamental belief that the failure of the British education system is due to a lack of expectation. The reason why so many young people leave school with so few qualifications is fundamentally because so little is expected of them at school. I wanted to discover if a school which currently lies at the bottom of the league tables could be turned round by applying this basic principle. My belief that everyone can do better if only more is expected of them is based upon my experiences in the Royal Navy – the Navy of my youth took people from every walk of life and lifted us all up to the same unbelievably high standard.

Our third programme concentrates – as you might expect – on the Navy where I spent nineteen years of my life, between 1937 and 1956. We revisited my naval past. First we went to Dartmouth, my old naval college, and then we went back to the Mediterranean (where I was sunk twice during the Second World War) to visit ARK ROYAL on operational duty off Bosnia. We also went to the Swan Hunter shipyard where I joined my first submarine, the TRUSTY, in 1944, and I talked to the First Sea Lord and the Ministry of Defence (MOD) to find out how the Navy is managing in the very changed world of the 1990s.

Our fourth and final programme in the *Troubleshooter Returns* series takes a look at the problems of industry in Britain. I revisited ICI in Wilton, near Middlesbrough, which I used to run, and found it much smaller than it used to be. I visited the Nissan factory in the north east

6

of Britain and discussed the problems they face, and I revisited several old *Troubleshooter* friends from previous *Troubleshooter* series, particularly Churchill Potteries who are trying to raise money from the City. And I talked to people in the Treasury and in the City about the needs of industry, and I tried to impress upon them how vital it is that they adapt in order to meet the needs of industry today.

Apart from the opportunity to revisit and reexamine some of my own formative influences, I hoped to learn something about the ways in which the places, institutions and businesses I visited are adapting to Britain's new role in the world and its changing economic possibilities.

As a nation we British seem to blame everybody except ourselves for the stresses and strains imposed on us by the massive changes we are going through, but I still believe that Britain is a marvellous country in which to live and grow up. Despite our lack of self-confidence and some deeply disturbing changes in the ways in which we behave towards one another, my belief in the basic decency of the British people remains undimmed. I continue to travel all over the world and have yet to find another country which beckons me or seems to offer the values that I find in Britain and that I hold dear. The values of tolerance, humour, concern for others and respect for the past seem to me to persist, even though they appear to be overlaid by more violence and less concern for our environment and countryside.

These journeys into the past and attempts to look a little further ahead have been a fascinating experience. Perhaps I should say that inevitably the journeys have been personal ones. The perceptions and ideas are mine but their origins are traceable within each of the four subjects which constitute the series. I hope that those who see the programmes and read this book will find that some of the ideas strike a sympathetic chord. I do not believe I know what others should do but I do believe that my experiences have some relevance, and if only such experiences could be shared more often we might perhaps find it easier to have a better and broader understanding of what needs to be done in the years ahead.

As always, I would like to thank the BBC, without whom the *Troubleshooter Returns* television series, and this book, would not exist. Filming in India was the first time I have ever spent a long period with a film crew, and I could not have been more fortunate. The crew became both friends and confidantes and Robert Thirkell, the series producer, who has been through a million ups and downs with me since the *Troubleshooter* pilot in 1987, along with his trusty assistant, Jane Ashford, whom I've also worked with since the beginning, were invaluable colleagues. Robert went to endless trouble selecting the crew for India. The cameraman, Alex Hansen, succeeded in finding beauty in the most unlikely places, and so determined was he not to miss anything which might enhance the film that he was out at dawn to catch the sunrise and could barely be dissuaded from going out in the evening to catch the sunset. His assistant, James Moss, was a tower of strength with endless good humour, and the sound man, John Pritchard, managed a technically difficult job magnificently, often working against the background noises of factories and rumbling machinery. Not only am I deeply grateful to all of them, but I have seldom enjoyed an exhausting trip more than I did in their company. We worked extremely long hours and it was a miracle to me that the crew unfailingly kept their commitment and good humour: the banter and joking never stopped.

I would like to thank Robert for his thoughtfulness and support, and I would also like to thank my second producer, Michael Mosley, for his invaluable help. I would like to thank, too, my editor, Heather Holden-Brown, for her continuously thoughtful comments and suggestions, and for her support and encouragement throughout the writing of this book. And, finally, I should like to thank Heather's colleagues, Angela Mackworth-Young and Martha Caute, for their efficiency and patience in the face of what can only be described as ever-changing deadlines.

PART ONE

1. Business in Bombay

First Impressions

If you want to be spoilt (and who doesn't?), India in the 1920s was definitely the place to grow up. One of the most endearing Indian characteristics, then and now, is unlimited adoration for small children, and that, combined with the fact that my boyhood time in India was the only period in my life when I lived with my parents in anything approaching a normal family situation, has left me with an abiding love for India and its people.

Although I was an ordinary middle-class kid, I was brought up in ludicrous style: we lived in a wing of the palace where my father was tutor and guardian to a young Maharaja. My father was charged with implanting upright British values (1920s-style) into the Maharaja, and, unfortunately, into me. He was doing what many of his British contemporaries in India were doing at that time: teaching British beliefs and British values to the Indians. And that's why I decided to begin this journey in India. I wanted to discover more about my earliest background and how it moulded me, and I wanted to see what the lasting effects – if any – were of the British attempts to mould India. I also wanted to revisit the parts of India which had loomed so large in my parents' lives.

None of us are immune to the influences of our heritage and in my case the strands which tie my forebears to India are almost too many to list. On my father's side the family went to India in about 1815. Successive generations of his family served in the Indian Army until the 1920s, when my father left the Army to pursue a freelance political career in India (as well as tutoring young princes in Dhar, Udaipur and Junagadh, he served on state councils). My mother's family were also

9

from India. Her father, having failed the exams which would have enabled him to continue his career in the Navy, sought the rip-roaring life of an indigo planter in Bihar. And my wife's background is also Indian, her father managed a cotton factory in a suburb of Bombay.

I left India before my world had expanded sufficiently to allow me to comprehend the vastness and variety of the country, but I have been lucky enough to return several times, and I always feel the same thrill. I never tire of India and each visit leads me to question and reconsider the values by which we in the West live our lives.

So it was with a sense of excitement and anticipation at revisiting familiar places and discovering new ones, that I landed at Delhi airport. I was expecting unbelievable crowds at the airport as on previous visits, but contrary to my expectations of a bazaar, interspersed with an occasional aeroplane here and there, the airport was a model of efficiency and even at 11.45 am, it was far from overcrowded. (When we left India things were rather more as I had expected them to be when we arrived, but our arrival was exemplary.) However, our first brush with Indian bureaucracy was more than up to the standards I had learned to expect.

The good thing about Indian bureaucracy is that the bureaucrats are polite, endlessly patient, and good humoured. The bad thing is that there is so much of it: every task has to be repeated, checked and rechecked. Despite having had every sort of injection and medical certification known to man, as well as a few I have never even heard of (what is Japanese encephalitis and what on earth is it doing in India anyway?), our progress through the arrival formalities was slow. But we eventually managed to extricate ourselves and were successfully reunited with our luggage – something else I had not expected – to be met by Robert's long-suffering BBC assistant, Jane Ashford, and our BBC Indian fixer, Jane Sabherwal.

After a quick snack I rushed off to change some money, and this proved to be a splendid example of the way things can be in India. I was handed a solid block of 10 000 rupees held together by thick, corroded, wire staples. (One of the staples was made of copper which, I suppose, represents progress, since it had not corroded.) The application of a Swiss Army knife and twenty minutes of hard work, plus

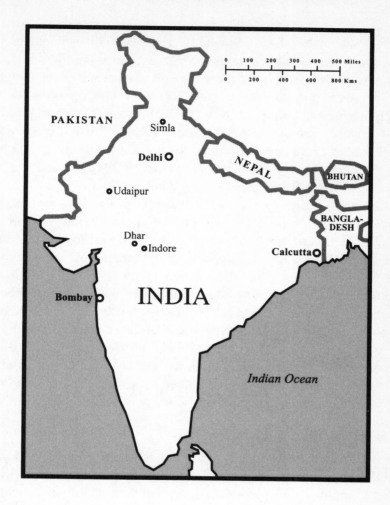

the near destruction of the top and bottom notes, eventually released my rupees so that I could actually use them. It is, in fact, common practice in India to staple blocks of rupees together, but it certainly adds to the potential for destruction of at least some of them.

I was very much looking forward to our journey through India, particularly because on this visit with the BBC *Troubleshooter* team, my twenty-year-old granddaughter, Abigail, was travelling with me. During the journey we had several opportunities to do things together and I hope that Abby returned to Britain with the seeds of a love for

11

India sown in her heart. She fairly bubbled with excitement one morning when we went shopping together in a bazaar, although she was absolutely horrified by the scale and persistence of the begging. She saw her first snake charmer, albeit a rather slow motion snake and a very desultory charmer, and we had a hilarious time trying to buy her Christmas presents for her mother because we found only one jeweller who could cope with credit cards. Abby was amazed at how low the prices were, even before we started to bargain, and she, like most Westerners, found bargaining difficult, at least at first.

During our Indian journey Abby was invited to an Indian wedding which, I have to admit, had me fussing about like an old wet hen because she had to travel some way away from us. I loaded her down with money and a lot of unhelpful, grandfatherly advice, (why is it that, to grandparents, grandchildren never really grow up?), but all was well and, except for a three-hour delay, Abby was where she should have been to meet us, and utterly captivated by the extraordinary experience that is an Indian wedding. She also began a love affair of her own, albeit it with a two-year-old boy (the son of the BBC's *Troubleshooter* research assistant in India, Jane Sabherwal), which endures to this day and, if for no other reason than to see how he is getting along, I hope that some day Abby will return to India.

HMY BRITANNIA in Bombay

We began our journey in Bombay where practically every Indian businessman I have ever heard of, and a good many high-level British business people, plus a surprising number of representatives from small and medium-sized British companies, were gathered for a series of targeted trade missions to coincide with UK Week in Bombay. The Indo-British Partnership Initiative (IBPI) were hosting a conference aboard BRITANNIA which I attended part of and met up with many old friends. However due to a severe case of British bureaucratic bungling we were not allowed to film the conference. The Department of Trade and Industry (DTI) wanted us to film the conference and so did the Ministry of Defence (MOD), but Buckingham Palace and the Foreign Office did not. I was to come across this sort of bureaucratic mismanagement throughout my Indian journey, and this incident

12

served to remind me that it was the British who bequeathed bureaucracy to the Indian nation in the first place.

I must confess to a real pang of emotion as I went aboard BRITANNIA. The Royal yacht was in impeccable condition, as you would expect, and every officer and rating looked as though they had just come out of the laundry. I was warmly welcomed aboard, since the old connection still means that I am looked upon as one of them. A nice feature of the Navy is that anybody who served there is automatically considered a life-long member of the club.

Douglas Hurd, the British Foreign Secretary, and Manmohan Singh, the Indian Finance Minister and architect of Indian liberalization, were at the conference and Robert Evans, the Chairman of British Gas, was chairing the British contingent. A number of working parties had been set up to study what Britain and India could do together, and they were to report back to Douglas Hurd and Manmohan Singh at this meeting.

Douglas Hurd spoke without notes, and talked about the misconceptions in India that Britain was over the hill, and the misconceptions in Britain that Indian bureaucracy was impenetrable. In his mind both views were incorrect, although I must confess I recognized an uncomfortable degree of truth in both cases. Manmohan Singh, who seemed to be almost a 'non-politician' (indeed his training is in finance and administration and not in politics), believed there was now a broad consensus of public opinion that India must look outward, and he was totally committed to flexibility in the labour market, which he hoped would come after the elections. He made a plea for assistance from the GATT signatories which he saw as vital if India was to have full involvement in world trade, but as far as this audience was concerned he was pleading to the converted, albeit a rather worried converted.

Then there were reports on the four key areas which had been studied: telecommunications, power, manufacturing technology and agriculture. At this stage, sound common sense and apparently attainable numbers seemed to disappear through the porthole. The sheer scale of what was required to produce an infrastructure which would jerk start the economy was absolutely mind-boggling. Power alone needs the equivalent of 6000 megawatts to be invested every year for the next twenty years, and while this was technically possible, I could

13

not begin to imagine where the money might come from. And this was only the tip of the iceberg. A further £3bn a year was needed to bring the telecommunications systems up to date, not to mention funds for improving the roads, ports and other vital necessities, if India is to become a world-class exporter.

The presentations were well-rehearsed but the whole thing felt like some kind of ritual square dance, with an invisible caller announcing the next steps. Nevertheless, while it was clearly going to be impossible to meet the total need, the sheer scale of the potential opportunity was made very clear. I found the discussion about food perhaps the most interesting of all. I am old enough to remember when the conventional wisdom was that there was no way India would ever be able to feed itself, yet here we were talking about food processing as a major export opportunity. Something like 15% of crops are lost between the fields and the marketplace, due to porous gunny sacks and rodent spoilage, and hardly any added value is put onto the foods. Such foods that are sold overseas go as raw material rather than finished items. But over and over again we got back to the main problem, which was how they could possibly attract the necessary finance. One of the Indians pointed out that the best chance would be if the Swiss bank accounts held by Indians could somehow be repatriated!

While these discussions were going on, BRITANNIA left the jetty in its marvellously silent way, with the crew wearing plimsolls to muffle the sound of their feet on deck. We proceeded at a stately speed from the jetty into the Bay of Bombay, where we stopped and rolled gently for about three hours while the discussions continued. During the question and answer session a number of really pertinent points were raised, largely by the Indians themselves, who saw this as a splendid opportunity to address their finance minister. As I had expected, the problems they raised were the exit strategy[1] from plants and businesses;

1. Exit Strategy: The ability to restructure and shut down plants even in the face of horrendous levels of unemployment. In India a plant can only be shut down with the agreement of the workforce, who recognize a good bargaining point when they see one. In reality therefore, the only way a plant can be shut is to pay very heavily for the privilege of doing so. This is one reason why plants in India continue to operate long after they would have been run out of business anywhere else in the world. It is a sad fact that in many cases it is cheaper to continue operating at a loss than to shut down one factory and open up elsewhere.

the shortage of ports; the ability of small and medium-sized companies to respond; and (greatly to my surprise) the problems of Indian lack of adherence to international agreements on intellectual property rights, particularly with regard to genetic engineering. The whole experience was a great introduction to my subsequent visits to some of the Indian businesses, and confirmed my conviction about the opportunities in India. The delegates I talked to after the conference uniformly felt optimistic that the process of liberalization was for real and India would, albeit haltingly, begin to move ahead to join the world from a commercial point of view. I came away from the conference with the belief that as long as the current government remains in power, the process of liberalization is here to stay.

In 1991, Manmohan Singh presided over reforms which, by Indian standards, were mould-breaking. Liberalization, as it is known, curbed the licence-raj (the system whereby Indian businessmen and women have to ask permission from Delhi about what, where and how to produce. They have to ask permission to import, and they have to ask permission about what technology they may use and with whom they might collaborate. In short, Delhi controls everything and individuals have no freedom to act on their own business initiatives.) Under liberalization, foreign investment is encouraged, economic reforms are being introduced and the licence-raj is being abolished.

Foreign investment in 1993–94 amounted to US$4.1bn, whereas in 1991–92 it was US$1.48bn. Recent foreign investors include Coca Cola, General Electric, Procter and Gamble, Morgan Stanley, Peugeot and General Motors. Import bans and duties have been cut and the rupee was made convertible on the trade account. The 1995 exchange rate is approximately 48 rupees = £1 sterling. However the Indian Government has not done as much as it could for the foreign investor who still faces bureaucracy on a stunning scale when he tries to sort out details with the state and local authorities on infrastructure, local taxes and related issues.

At a dinner later on in my journey, I had an extremely interesting discussion with the recently retired chief secretary of the cabinet, who pointed out that the bureaucratic system which has been applied in India is not a purely British one, contrary to what I thought. He said that the

15

Indian system had been heavily amended to include even more checks and balances, because of a basic lack of trust. And herein, I think, lies the problem. Whereas in China, foreign investment is now welcomed; in India, although it is welcomed in theory, in reality potential foreign investors must still wade through official processes of the pre-reform era which can take inordinate amounts of time and effort. I have complained often enough about what I see as the myopic attitude of the British Government towards what is necessary for industrial success, but when one compares their approach to that of Indian bureaucrats, it is as if the Indians have come from another planet. But I still feel that we British must take some responsibility: some of the seeds of Indian attitudes to business and wealth generation were sown by us, and they are, perhaps, one of the harshest legacies we British left to India.

I have long been saddened by the comparisons between the speed of self-improvement in India and that which has been managed in China. For twenty years I have believed that India should exceed China in every way, but I've seen so many false starts. The populations, geography and sheer scale of both the opportunities and the problems are almost beyond imagination in both countries. Yet India, which has been fully opened to the West, with a Western-educated middle class and intelligentsia, a democratic system, a relatively stable community and the separation of legal and political power, has made false start after false start in terms of economic growth. China, which has chosen the path of extreme communism, has leapt forward in the last ten years, and is now moving at growth rates which put India to shame. Foreign investors are now rushing to put their money into China, while large companies still limit their involvement in India.

The comparison seems even more incongruous when one thinks of the advantages that the Indians have over the Chinese in terms of doing business worldwide. Perhaps the most helpful legacy of British rule in India is the universal use of the English language amongst managers, administrators, the armed forces and so on. Indeed English is still almost the only language which enables you to communicate relatively easily in every part of the country. And English is the commercial business language. It is much more difficult to communicate with the Chinese, both philosophically and linguistically. India has always had the advantage of being a bridge: Indians understand both the Asian mind and the European mind. So what's not working?

I believe that the problems of India stem directly from many of the problems we have in Britain. The British lack of inner conviction that the customer really is king sometimes develops in India to an absolute contempt for the customer. And you're in dead trouble unless you believe that the customer is the most important person and unless you're continuously trying to improve your product and the way you make it.

Our problem in Britain is that our manufacturing base is too small, as it is in India. On the other hand if you look at it the other way round, the opportunity in India is still immense, and I have always believed in the tremendous potential of India. You cannot move on this continent without seeing the enormous needs that people have, the basic commitment, the ability to work hard, the patience, and many other virtues. One day, India will be a superpower. It is a country of almost 900m people which makes it an enticing potential market; it is the seventh largest country in the world by area and it is now the fifth largest world economy. There's a large expanding middle class (a reported 220m people) with a relatively high spending capacity, who are spearheading a consumer revolution in India.

There are, however, various flies in the ointment. India's literacy rate is below the rate at which economic success is usually achieved. With the exception of the oil-rich Gulf States, no country has achieved economic take-off without also achieving a literacy rate of 60%. India's literacy rate is still only 52%. Without better education India cannot hope to control population growth, which is currently running at 25% a decade (or roughly 2% a year), nor can it hope for economic take-off. And it is almost impossible to make anyone redundant in India and some employers still feel they must provide much more than employment for their employees. In a car plant I was later to visit in Calcutta, Mr Mano Pachisia who ran the plant, was responsible for a 2000-pupil school, a hospital, managers' and workers' housing, shops and temples. I questioned whether all this made sense in 1994. After all I knew that other factories in India provided none of these facilities and yet had a well-trained, enthusiastic workforce. But Mano Pachisia disagreed. He felt that housing and other facilities were needed to attract and hold the workforce. And Indian government ministers have postponed plans for extending employers' rights to sack redundant workers, something which is virtually impossible under current legislation.

However the economic benefits of liberalization are visible. Although inflation, which reached a peak of 16%, is still high at almost 11%, exports are rising rapidly, foreign direct investment is starting to flow and businesses are being forced to upgrade their product as the consumer, particularly the middle-class consumer, sees what the competition can produce and refuses to be taken for granted any longer. Middle-class Indians see better programmes on television, launched by private satellite television operators, and competition from privately-owned airlines has jolted Indian Airlines, the state-owned carrier, into introducing great improvements.

When we flew from Bombay to Calcutta, later in our journey, we flew with one of the new privatized airlines. We were also checked in extremely quickly and the plane arrived bang on time. East West Airlines was set up in February 1992 – with one aeroplane – by professionals with a travel-related background. They now run seven Boeing 737–200s and three Fokker 27–500 series aircraft, and they plan to increase their fleet in 1995.

The Bajaj Scooter and Motorcycle Manufacturing Company

My first meeting was with Rahul Bajaj, the founder and extremely rich owner of the Bajaj Scooter and Motorcycle Manufacturing Company. He used to run the Indian equivalent of the CBI. He was extremely vocal at the IBPI conference about how India should proceed post-liberalization, and he is an old friend of mine. He has, almost single-handedly, revolutionized Indian personal mobility, and he is the very best sort of Indian businessman. Although he has profited enormously from the protected Indian economy pre-liberalization, he is wise enough to see that the only way India can hope to obtain faster growth is to open up to world markets.

Rahul Bajaj has consistently supported liberalization. He is one of the founder members of a Bombay group of industrialists who are trying to influence the Indian Government's approach to liberalization,

18

and he looks forward to the day when Indian industry is able to compete on a world level. He pointed out various problems with the liberalization process, including the need to find a humane way to cut down on the large numbers of employees that exist in so many Indian industries (see the footnote on exit strategies on page 14), and the need for privatization of the inefficient public sector which accounts for nearly half the nation's capital, but only produces 27% of its output. But his fundamental attitude towards liberalization, like mine, was optimistic.

The Bajaj Scooter and Motorcycle Manufacturing Company is, amazingly, the world's fourth largest manufacturer of automotive two-wheelers and its largest three-wheeler manufacturer but, to give some idea of the scale involved, Honda produced over 4m two-wheelers to Bajaj Auto's 1m per annum and Honda's annual research budget is more than Bajaj's annual turnover. However, great excitement surrounded the imminent arrival of the latest Bajaj scooter model, which was to incorporate an electric starter for the first time. I could see that an electric starter would be a real advantage for middle-class Indian families driving off in their best clothes to a dinner party, and it is they who form the majority of Bajaj's customers.

A Bajaj scooter represents the height of ambition for most of India's young married people and practically all the middle class. They are built for ruggedness, ease of maintenance and fuel economy, to a 1960s Vespa design which has been continuously upgraded for better performance. Rahul currently exports some 4.5% of what he produces, mainly to Sri Lanka and Bangladesh, and he has recently been selling very cheaply into South America, but the old-fashioned nature of the cycle, coupled with its lack of any modern fittings, has confined Bajaj to those undemanding export markets.

The difficulty with the Indian protected economy has been that anybody with a permit to manufacture was assured of a speedy return on his investment. Because these permits were only granted for products which were plainly needed, market access was assured, and because the number of permits were limited, competition barely existed. Add to this the near impossibility of importing and you have a climate that ensures most Indian-made products could sell in India

19

for many years without reaching world standards of quality or design.

Post-liberalization however, the opportunities for exporting Indian-manufactured products, unless they are significantly modernized, are not good. At the moment Bajaj's export markets are some of the poorest and least developed countries who have, by definition, the least money, and if he wishes to export to richer countries, he will have to upgrade his scooters for those markets. Rahul knows this and he pointed out to me that India needs time to adjust its product mix and get the quality right before it can expand into world markets. However, since the mid-1980s Rahul has steadily increased his market share (Bajaj now holds 49% of the market) and the process of getting the quality and product volume and mix right is well under way. Rahul is also acutely aware of the widely-held overseas image of Indian-manufactured goods: that they are trashy and inferior.

There is a real problem here for Bajaj because extreme ruggedness is necessary for any form of transport to survive the near-lethal combination of Indian roads and Indian driving. Since the roads are always packed with every form of vehicular and non-vehicular transport, ranging from elephants, camels, bullock carts and horses, to pedestrians, bicycle rickshaws and scooters, high speed and a beautiful design are far less necessary than extreme manoeuvrability and some means of going from the top possible speed (about twenty-five miles per hour) to nothing at all at the shortest possible notice.

I understand that Bajaj's sales director thinks that they should make special models of their scooters for export to the developed countries, and maybe this is the way they should go. Bajaj needs to export in order to gain greater volumes, foreign exchange and the corporate confidence of knowing that their products are internationally competitive, but the model that sells in India could not compete in the developed countries.

Rahul then took me for a ride on one of his scooters. The BBC film crew had persuaded him, God knows how, to be filmed driving a scooter along the esplanade in Bombay, with me on his pillion (the indignities we suffer for the sake of the television camera!). I knew that he had arrived in a Mercedes, so I enquired, rather tentatively, whether he could actually drive one of his scooters. It wasn't quite such a stupid question as he thought it was, since in my ICI days I couldn't have operated an ethylene cracker.

Needless to say, his confidence in his driving ability suffered in front of the television camera when he could not get the carefully chosen model to start. Fortunately the Bajaj dealer, who was turning several shades of white at the failure of his chosen example to perform for the master, eventually got it started and Rahul and I set off in a rather wobbly fashion. I was more than a little concerned that the Bombay traffic would not have quite the same respect for a foreign camera crew as the British traffic seems to have, but when art calls risks have to be taken, and so we found ourselves weaving our way, safely as it happens, along the esplanade, while Jane Ashford and Robert Thirkell clapped their hands to wake clouds of somnolent pigeons . . . they said it would improve the look of the shot.

Darmilla Fashions

Our next call was to the textile area in a suburb of Bombay called Dadar. Textiles are extremely important in any emerging economy and I was particularly looking forward to this visit for two reasons. I wanted to see how the Bombay textile industry was faring under liberalization, and I wanted to revisit an area of particular personal significance. My wife's father ran a cotton mill in Dadar for many years on behalf of the Banerjee family, and my wife spent the first few years of her life living in an apartment near the sea front in Dadar.

We arrived by train from Bombay at Dadar Station, which might just as well have been Pinner, or any other suburban line from London, except for the sight of an extremely slow-moving elephant ambling gently through the traffic beyond the station, bearing its mahout and proceeding westwards on unexplained business.

The prospect of filming an Indian station with an Indian elephant in the foreground, and me on my way to what we, at that stage, imagined to be a modern factory, was more than the film crew could resist. Within seconds our government minder was dispatched to haggle with the mahout to ask how much it would cost for him and his elephant to reverse and walk past the station a couple more times. We soon discovered that deflecting Indian elephants from their intentions does not

21

come cheap, and that the mahout's poor and simple appearance was deceptive. He possessed the trading instincts of a Tesco's buyer and 'To deflecting one elephant: £15.00,' was later to appear in our accounts. But even for that magnificent sum there was no way the lady in question (for lady she was) would increase her stately amble. It took an age for her to return and walk twice round the roundabout so that we could film from every conceivable angle. But it was worth it. Robert's delight was tangible when he got, in one shot: an elephant, several thousand Indians, Dadar Station, and me climbing into an air-conditioned car.

Our first destination, the Darmilla Fashions factory in Parel on the way to Dadar, was located in the middle of an appalling slum, but even here the price of property was extraordinarily high. Bombay property prices are equal to Tokyo property prices: it costs over £1000.00 to buy a ten foot by eight foot shack here, with no planning permission or legal tenure. You can't rent easily in Bombay and you can't get a mortgage so you have to pay up front, and I wondered how on earth the incredibly poor people who were squatting in these appalling conditions, without water or power, raised this sort of money. It was totally beyond me.

Darmilla Fashions is owned by a husband and wife team, Urmilla and Darab Talyarkhan. They began with one unit on their present site, and each time they made enough money they built on more units until they achieved their present 7000 square feet. Darmilla Fashions makes ladies' clothing to order for British and European companies like Next, Principals, Oasis and Warehouse. They are a really successful niche market clothing manufacturer. Darab trained with Binder Hamlyn in Britain and he is a calm and gentle accountant and his determination to control detail contributes to an extremely successful partnership. Urmilla, his wife, comes from an army family. She is a colonel's daughter who started her career as a British Airways' stewardess. Both have a real grasp and understanding of the markets they are supplying.

Urmilla provides the drive and is prepared to take risks, while Darab manages the finances. They started the business in 1985 and they've expanded very fast. They are now producing up to 200 000 pieces a year, and they're making good margins. Their secret lies in their quality control. Darab personally inspects approximately 25% of the 200 000 pieces in their three production units in Bombay. I said that I appreciated that they had managed to do what a lot of Indian companies had failed to do, they had maintained quality as well as growing the business extremely fast, but I questioned whether it really was the best use of Darab's time to inspect so many pieces personally. He replied 'How else could I vouch to my customers for my products?' I tried, with little success, to suggest that there had to be another way.

Both Darab and Urmilla spend long hours at their factory, and so does their workforce. When I suggested that they recruit a professional manager to shoulder some of the load, their reaction was a mixture of unwillingness to delegate, a defeatist attitude that they would never find someone willing to commit to the business to the same extent that they were committed (they often work an eighteen-hour day), and a certain meanness: they were unwilling to pay the market rate for a top-flight manager. I found these attitudes difficult to reconcile with their own obvious commitment both to their business and to their workforce, but there is a business philosophy that exists in many family-run Indian companies which, perhaps, goes some way towards explaining their attitude.

The philosophy states simply that for each of your sons (it doesn't yet apply to daughters), you must provide a business. Since manhood in India is still measured by the number of sons you produce, it quickly becomes obvious that family businesses must grow at a fast rate, but for reasons not entirely connected with business economics. Urmilla has, however, decided not to have any children, and I suspect that Darab's unwillingness to pay for the calibre of management they require reflects his disappointment at not having a son to leave the business to, and therefore he is unwilling to make the necessary investment. I also suspect that the business is Urmilla's surrogate child, which is why she wants to see the business grow and grow, but precisely because they have no sons to whom to leave the business, Darab thinks that the business has grown enough. The business provides well enough for the two of them, and for their 'adopted family' (their workforce), so there really is no pressure, he believes, for further growth. They are going to have to resolve this fundamental difference of opinion if the business is to survive.

However, if the business does continue to grow, and I hope it will, they really must hire a top-flight manager or two, otherwise they will steadily find themselves working ever-longer hours. Darab and Urmilla have a geniune concern and affection for their people, but everyone works from nine in the morning until eight at night (or longer) every day, including Sundays. I spoke to the senior seamstress Elizabeth, who had started with them some twelve years earlier, and I concluded that she and her fellow workers had no set hours of work, they simply worked until they were tired. There are about thirty-eight workers at the factory and, to my surprise, they are a mixture of Muslims (nine), Hindus (twenty-five), and Christians (four). During the recent race riots in Bombay, Darab and Urmilla hid their Muslim workers and smuggled food and other necessities for their sustenance, at considerable personal risk. This is absolutely admirable, and may partly explain why the staff work such long hours, but it does not make business sense. An exhausted workforce soon becomes a sloppy workforce. Darab explained that he'd tried to persuade his workers to take Sundays off, but they had replied that they would only spend money if they weren't working.

I suggested that the production and quality control could and should be delegated (although both of them have problems with delegation), and that this would leave them free to work on the areas where they are each uniquely qualified. The combination of Urmilla's talent for selling and Darab's careful approach to running the business made them a very strong team. Darab claims their profits are higher than many publicly-quoted companies and they were particularly proud because they had just passed a routine inspection by the Next quality inspectors with flying colours. Yet, despite this, their response time is still twenty-eight weeks. I expressed total incredulity at this enormous time-lapse, which represents the period from receiving the order to dispatching it, and not to the customer receiving it. This is even more extraordinary when you bear in mind that they're supplying mail order companies who, generally speaking, wait until they receive their orders, and then and only then, do they buy the product. However Darmilla have not, so far, managed to reduce their response time, nor do they see it as being a very necessary aim. The problem is the decentralized nature of the textile industry and the number of stages a garment has to go through. The actual making up, which is the only stage done by Darmilla themselves, can be completed in four or five days once the cloth has been obtained, dyed and finished.

The longer I talked to Darab and Urmilla the wider the gap seemed between them in terms of the way they see the future of their business. Urmilla is determined to drive the business as far and as fast as she can. However Darab wonders what point there is in continuing to work as hard as they do. Darab dreams of diversifying into growing herbs in South Bombay as an additional business, but I pointed out that he would be leaving a high margin business, where they are able to charge nearly European prices by constantly controlling the quality of the product, for a business with no added value. They have no intention of integrating backwards by manufacturing or finishing cloth themselves, but they do recognize that they must develop their own supply chain before someone else does. In a way they have trapped themselves. I am sure they are driven as much by the need to keep their workers secure, as they are by any personal motives of material gain. They have everything they want including a nice house, their own boat, air-conditioned cars and as much champagne as they want, but they also work very long hours and, because the factory is open on Sundays, they find themselves working then as well.

I pointed out that a great many changes were going to have to be made quite quickly. I said that they must drastically cut their response time and face up to the problems of getting some management in, otherwise their ability to grow the business will always be limited by the sheer number of hours they and their workforce can put in, and no one can continue to work the sorts of hours they all work forever. I also think that Darab and Urmilla must strike a balance between her desire to grow the business forever, and his desire not to grow it any further at all. If they do not resolve these problems soon, a very successful business will, I believe, come to an untimely and unnecessary end.

S Kumars

Our next call was to the Shree Ram textile mill. As we approached it I wondered whether we had somehow been transported back in time. I

25

found myself looking out at the chimneys of textile mills that were exactly like the mills I'd seen in books on Britain's Industrial Revolution: our 'dark satanic mills'. I could have been in Bradford in the nineteenth century and I began to wonder whether the technology which Britain had transferred to India in the early part of the twentieth century had ever been upgraded. No modern mill has a chimney for a start and I was very doubtful about whether these mills could produce competitively. I was saddened by the architectural muddle of slums, ancient mills and modern buildings that was Dadar today, and I wondered what my wife would think if she could see it now. Perhaps it was better that she kept her earlier memories.

The Shree Ram mill is owned by the Kasliwal family who hail from Indore where I lived as a boy. The Kasliwal family business was founded by two brothers and, although they have not exactly retired, the main running of the company has now been delegated to the next generation of Kasliwals.

There are five Kasliwal brothers of the younger generation. Ambuj Kasliwal is in charge of textile exports; Wavij Kasliwal manages textile manufacturing; Vikas Kasliwal manages the Shree Ram mill and is in charge of future projects; Nitin Kasliwal is in charge of marketing and, with Vikas, future projects; and Mukul Kasliwal is in charge of the organization's finances.

The Kasliwal business currently consists of the Shree Ram textile mill, which is a composite mill where spinning, weaving and finishing are carried out; a hydroelectric plant at Maheshwar; a tyre plant in Pithampur, Dhar (where I also lived as a young boy) and at least two more textile mills in Indore. The Indore mills produce approximately 60% of output, the tyre business approximately 5% and the Shree Ram mill approximately 35%. The Kasliwals have recently launched a new issue of shares in their company, S Kumars Synfab, and they plan to grow and diversify the business into other areas. While we were in Bombay there were placards and posters everywhere advising people of the imminent issue.

The brand name for the textiles is S Kumars and the founding brothers developed the brand over a period of time. The brand now holds 5% of the Indian fabric market and is distributed through 25 000 retail outlets across India. The Kasliwals have increasingly backward integrated into manufacture although they were careful, at first, to pick up bargains and bankrupt properties only; and they have reinvested in new production facilities in Indore.

The five brothers are each trained in a basic skill such as science or accountancy, and they all hold MBAS from American and European business schools. So I was looking forward to visiting a really modern, well-run Indian company.

My face dropped when we arrived at the Shree Ram mill. I expected the Kasliwals to run a modern factory, and for the most part, as I discovered later, they do. But not this one. The Shree Ram mill was built like a massive battleship, with enormous stress-bearing walls supporting four stories. It was vertically integrated and relied upon gravity-feed to move the products through the various processes. In Britain, mills such as these have long since been converted into craft centres, museums and other modernized versions of the past. But here in Bombay, 5000 workers slaved away at every stage, from raw cotton through to the finished fabrics, in pre-Victorian conditions in a sweating, humid environment. I was horrified and I said so. The conditions at the Shree Ram mill were an insult to a skilled and dedicated workforce, and I couldn't see how the Kasliwals expected this business to survive, let alone compete, with modern technology elsewhere.

Vikas Kasliwal, Harvard-educated, and the member of the Kasliwal family responsible for this appalling mill, took me round. I immediately liked him and his brother Ambuj. Vikas is an accountant by training and his brother is a scientist. They were open, jolly, realistic, decisive, and very clear thinking. In fact the connection between them and the Shree Ram mill appeared to me to be merely accidental, so different were their views and theories from the practice which surrounded me.

We started off in the product showroom, which was the most cheering part of the visit. The materials were beautifully finished, textured and printed and there were polycotton, viscose and cotton mixtures on view. They were aimed at the middle market in India but also had very strong exports to the Arabian Gulf, Africa and Asian countries. The family's success is based on a decision taken in the late 1940s: to bypass the primary wholesalers and go directly to the second tier of consumer

27

outlets by branding their fabrics. The products were, it seemed to me, well-judged for their market, but I was still totally amazed that they could be produced at all, let alone economically produced, in this antiquated environment.

My amazement increased as we progressed from one ghastly 'black hole' to another. We went, via spinning and carding, to the top floor, which was packed with antique machinery from the 1940s and 1950s and housed in lighting conditions so poor that I wondered how it was possible for anything of quality to be produced. I was also extremely surprised to learn that there were few environmental controls, and that chlorine bleaching seemed acceptable on this site in the middle of Bombay, adjacent as it was to a fast-growing residential area.

The Shree Ram mill, I discovered, has a history of going bust, as owner after owner failed to reinvest. A bit like Britain these days, I thought. But the mill is now in a situation where it simply cannot make enough money to reinvest and recreate itself, and yet the market demand is there for S Kumars' products. The Kasliwals bought this mill in 1985 for, by their own admission, a song. The idea of a Kasliwal 'song' produced a vision of a purchase price so low that I began to wonder whether the value of the property (over £100 per square foot) might provide the solution to these terrible working conditions. The value of the square footage was more than modern machinery would cost, so I thought that the Bombay property boom might work to the Kasliwals' advantage.

Vikas told me that their productivity levels were poor. They had failed to get the union to agree to any more modern manning than one man to four machines. Even with such outmoded machinery, which requires constant attention, I realized that one man to ten machines would have been a more rational manning level, and I was amazed that they still managed to sell at a profit with these manning levels forced upon them.

Vikas and Ambuj were, obviously, aware of the problems at this mill and they explained to me that their future plans were to modernize, and to replace piecemeal, on the present site. We talked about manning levels and Vikas told me that they would be aiming, when all the modernization and productivity improvements were complete, to employ about 900 people on the site, instead of the current 5000. When I mentioned 600 as a more realistic number he roared with laughter and said he would let me know if they ever got near it. I was really horrified at the thought of them slogging their way through endless negotiations as each new piece of equipment was introduced. The Kasliwals are trapped between the labour laws (and the difficulty of making employees redundant in India) and the union (and their insistence on prohibitive manning levels). But the economic logic was inexorable. The Shree Ram mill simply could not continue in its present form. It had to be modernized or it would inevitably go broke once more, and in the process it would pull down the Kasliwals' profitability and hazard all employment.

The more I walked around the factory, the clearer I became about the very limited range of possibilities open to them. I decided that I would try to persuade them to shut down the entire factory and start again. They could sell the site for development and use the considerable cash the sale would realize to set up with new plant and machinery on a new site. I thought they should offer reemployment to the best of the workforce, thus retaining at least some of the jobs.

However, my Indian industrial education was not yet over. The weaving shed brought me to the point of despair. I had not thought ever to see anything like it in my life; it really offended me and quite upset me. It was like a Victorian print of the Industrial Revolution, with enormous belt driven shuttle looms crammed together into one vast, sweating shed. Ragged workers in shorts and tattered sweatshirts watched the shuttles fling and clatter in noise levels which made conversation impossible. The heat and the dirt and the noise of the machinery, which was endlessly breaking down, graphically illustrated the term 'sweatshop'. Vikas explained that they had been trying to compete only in areas where modern looms have to work slowly, and they had been relying on the fact that they were carrying no capital costs to provide the margin. But they had now reached the stage where there was no way that the quality or the margins could be pushed further. No matter what the Kasliwals did, the weaving shed was doomed and he thought it would be gone within eighteen months. From my own point of view I felt that tomorrow would have been better than eighteen months. I found the whole place an affront to human dignity, even though the workforce were proud of their skills and their ability to keep the entire antique set up moving.

It was all horribly allegorical. The machines were almost all made in Britain between 1935–45, and many had been exported during the Second World War when Britain was still the world leader in textile machinery. I was staring at a repetition of what had happened in Lancashire and Yorkshire, when failure to reinvest had trapped mill after mill into chasing volume and low margins, only to find that they were pushed further and further down until reinvestment was no longer a possible way out. At least the Kasliwals had a chance of escape. The value of their site would enable them to set up elsewhere with modern machinery, and their control of the market and their ability to buy in product meant there would be little problem in managing the transition while the new plant was being built.

Despite the inexorable economic logic of my argument for the immediate sale of this antiquated mill, Vikas argued that their responsibility was to keep people in work as long as possible. My own view remained that they were perilously close to the stage where they would lose the whole thing unless they reinvested soon and, with the enormous growth rates that were forecasted, they needed to have the capacity to meet future demands both in quantity and in quality. I felt that I had made some progress in persuading Vikas of the dangers of step-by-step reequipment on the existing site, but that he was by no means convinced of my argument.

We went to have lunch with the rest of the family. The youngest brother, Mukul, was the Finance Director responsible for S Kumars' market entry. I asked the Kasliwal brothers why they had decided to go public, even though the family still controlled 70% of the equity. I worried about the pressures that public ownership would place upon them, since they claimed they had never had any problems raising finance. The two older brothers, the founders of the business, replied that it was partly a matter of fashion and partly the necessity to have a public quote in order to have their dynastic ambitions taken seriously. Prakash claimed that pressure from the institutions producing the credit, combined with flexibility for their growth strategy, had been the prime driving forces. He was undoubtedly the most international of the brothers, with many European friends and a broad view of the combination of business and financial pressures necessary for the future. I really liked the whole Kasliwal family. Their generally tough and practical approach to business combined with their (mostly) forward-looking policies makes them just the sort of business family India needs for the future.

The conversation around the luncheon table could have been held in any international textile business. The perennial subjects that pre-occupy all those in the industry were discussed: GATT, the multi-fibre agreement, the North American free trade area and so on. I seized the opportunity to press my point to the whole family about the dangers of step-by-step reinvestment on the Shree Ram site. I believed they would never get the necessary changes of attitude amongst their work-force, nor the willingness to adapt, if they did not start everything anew, and I said that the ability to adapt and change were the prerequisites of a modern operation.

The two founding fathers were quite clear that they wanted to create a Kasliwal dynasty to rival that of the Birlas and the Tatas (two of the largest, most powerful, successful, influential and rich Indian family-owned industrial empires), and that their aim was to build up at such a rate that each of the five sons would eventually have five businesses of their own which they, in turn, could pass on to their sons when the time came. This was the flip side of Darab Talyarkhan's pessimistic belief that there was no point in trying to expand Darmilla because he and Urmilla had no sons to pass the business on to.

I continued pressing my point about the sale of the Shree Ram mill and I was delighted to hear the fathers say to the sons that they felt I had a point, and that the sons must reconsider their concepts. But I was not very optimistic that they would act on what I had said. The difficulties of shutting down factories in India are large (see footnote on page 14), and although the Kasliwals listened very carefully to my advice about how to break the news to their workforce and involve them in the process, it seemed to me unlikely that they would follow it. Nevertheless, I felt that I had managed to stir some consciousness of the difficulties that S Kumars would face if they pursued their current policy, but now all I could do for the moment was sit back and wait until we met once more in Indore, later on in my Indian journey.

At the end of my visit to Bombay I felt that I had seen some of the best, and some of the worst, of India. The Shree Ram mill was the worst, but the optimistic plans outlined for India's future at the Indo-British Partnership Initiative (IBPI) conference aboard BRITANNIA, combined with Manmohan Singh's ideas for further liberalization, represented the best. And I personally left Bombay with a greater understanding of some of the problems facing India as it moves forwards into the twenty-first century, not the least of which is the dynastic approach that drives so much of Indian business. It made me thank my lucky stars that I hadn't had a child for every business I'd been responsible for while I was at ICI . . .

But now I am about to embark on a much more personal quest. I am going to Udaipur in the heart of Rajasthan, where my father was once guardian and tutor to a young Maharana.

2. Indian traditions

The Maharana of Udaipur and The Lake Palace Hotel

I was looking forward to seeing Udaipur once more, and I was particularly looking forward to meeting the Maharana of Udaipur, Shriji Arvind Singhji Mewar whose father, Shriji Bhagwat Singhji Mewar had been one of my father's protégées. When I was six I was sent from Dhar back to school in Britain. My father, Mervyn Harvey-Jones, later moved to the State of Udaipur where he became tutor and guardian to Bhagwat Singh. Because of this connection I felt as though I was about to meet a distant relation and, as is always the case with such meetings, I found myself wondering whether we would have anything in common. I was looking forward to discussing our fathers just as much as I was looking forward to discussing the Maharana's businesses.

I hoped to gain a better understanding of my own father from the Maharana, and I hoped to meet some people who might still remember him. I wanted to find out more about how he had been regarded, and what sort of legacy he left behind. My father devoted practically all his adult life to the service of Britain in India.

The present Maharana of Udaipur is the seventy-sixth Maharana, and he comes from a line that stretches back over 1400 years to 566 AD. Until the dispossession of princes in 1971, seventy-four generations of the Mewar family had been warriors and rulers but, thanks to Bhagwat Singh's foresight, when dispossession came the Mewar dynasty, almost alone among Indian princely families, had managed to keep enough property to maintain a fair approximation of their former lifestyle. But Bhagwat Singh did not intend to hold onto the Mewar properties just for their own sake; he planned to convert one of the Mewar palaces,

33

the Lake Palace, into a hotel. He realized that hotels would provide the vital source of income necessary for his successors as they made the difficult transition from a dynasty of ruling princes to a dynasty of commercial businessmen.

The first hotel, The Lake Palace Hotel, has generated enough money since it opened in 1963, for the Mewar family to expand. There are now six hotels in the group, but it is The Lake Palace's beauty and photogenic nature that has generated worldwide publicity: it has become a symbol of India and of Indian beauty for tourists throughout the world.

I was met at Udaipur airport by Om Singh Chauhan, one of the Maharana's representatives, and by Major Durga Das who had recently retired from the Indian Army Cavalry to take up the post of ADC to the Maharana. Om was the very model of a British public schoolboy and Durga Das could have been a British cavalry officer from forty years ago. He was immaculately turned out, carried himself in an unmistakable military manner and treated me in a fashion which could only be described as overly respectful.

Om bustled around organizing the collection of our baggage and generally acting as though he was in command of Udaipur airport. I discovered that this assumption of stately power pervaded the Maharana's staff and offices, despite the fact that the position of the Maharana of Udaipur is no longer a constitutional one. The Maharana no longer receives any money from the State nor has any official position and so, these days, he depends for his heritage upon his personal popularity, and the success of his business.

I was swept from the airport into a Mercedes – an extremely rare sight in India due to the 300% import tax levied by the government. The Mercedes was driven by the Maharana's personal chauffeur who had a similarly martial air to Durga Das, and was immaculately dressed in whites, with a red beret. A flag fluttered from the bonnet of the Mercedes and the Maharana's arms, the Sunface of Udaipur, were displayed prominently on the badge plate. If this was how a Maharana who has been shorn of all his State revenues lived, I wondered what it must have been like in my father's day. However, despite the magnificence of the car, we cut no ice at all on the road to Udaipur city

34

and we moved in typical Indian style, weaving through a throng of pedestrians, bicyclists and livestock of every sort, with whom we shared the road.

We saw the blaze of lights from the Maharana's Shivnivas Palace long before we arrived there. Not only were the walls of the palace floodlit, but the whole building was outlined with strings of lights, rather like a fleet review. We wound our way endlessly up the steep palace drive, saluted along the way by smartly uniformed soldiers in sentry boxes who turned out to be members of the Maharana's security force. When we finally reached the courtyard we were greeted by a further blaze of lights: not only were there all the lights of the nearby Lake Palace Hotel, but also the lights of the BBC camera crew who had set up to record the moment of my arrival at the Shivnivas Palace. As the car arrived in the palace courtyard, to my amazement, the pipes and drums of the Maharana's band burst into a welcoming skirl. The band was twelve strong; I could barely have had a more awe-inspiring reception.

When I finally met the Maharana himself, he proved to be very different from my expectations, which were mostly founded upon the book of the Royal Family of Udaipur, and contained a picture of him wearing full ceremonial Indian uniform. In reality Arvind Singhji Mewar was grey-bearded, well-built and wore a beautifully tailored Nehru jacket. He leaned upon a gold-topped cane, without which he was seldom seen, and his greeting was warm and full of genuine interest: it did feel somewhat like meeting a distant relation. Arvind's English was perfect, both in intonation and in his use of colloquialisms. Yet, despite the warmth of his greeting, he appeared to guard his position and his power jealously, and was watchful for any sign of disrespect.

We began by talking about our fathers, and the more we talked the more it appeared that his relationship with his father, Bhagwat Singh, my father's protégée, mirrored my relationship with my own father to a frightening degree. I already knew that my father thought that Bhagwat had been his greatest personal success in terms of his development as a surrogate British gentleman: he had been an excellent shot and quite fearless, with many dead tigers to his name. He had also

35

been a county-class cricketer, an excellent hockey player and a first-class rider and polo player.

When Bhagwat Singh went to Mayo College (set up by the British to educate Indian princes), he was accompanied by my father, an Indian guardian, a string of polo ponies and a large personal staff, all of whom were under my father's control. Bhagwat Singh was a great success at Mayo College and Arvind was very proud that his father had been awarded the Viceroy's medal for the best all-rounder. Bhagwat's values had been formed almost entirely by his experience of Mayo College, and by my father's tutelage.

Like my father, Bhagwat Singh placed duty before everything; before family, commercial interests, personal proclivities and certainly before personal enjoyment. Both my father and Bhagwat were totally reserved, private people who believed it a terrible weakness – if not a sign of total loss of manhood – to show any emotion. Bhagwat virtually ignored his son, just as my father had ignored me. Indeed there was a period of many years during which there was no contact whatsoever between the present Maharana and his father, however, in the last years of Bhagwat's life a rapprochement occurred which, sadly, was more than happened between my father and me.

I explained that I had hardly known my father and that much of my youth had been spent in a fruitless quest to become the sort of son I thought he wanted. This led to my continual attempts to be a credit to him by 'fighting a good war', working for Naval Intelligence after the war, and so on. Arvind and I agreed about the central paradox of all this: we had both been brought up in the same way, we had both had the same values instilled into us, and we were both successful therefore, logically, we should both bring up our own children exactly as we were brought up in order that they too should achieve success. But to bring up children without showing a flicker of interest in them, nor any feelings for them, was quite beyond both of us.

Arvind's elder brother, the crown prince of Udaipur, did not succeed his father to become the next Maharana because he filed a suit for legal separation from the family during his father's lifetime, in 1983. Consequently he had voluntarily debarred himself from succeeding his father. Under Indian law, if you legally separate from your family you

36

cannot become the head of the mainstream family. Therefore the seventy-fifth Maharana, Bhagwat Singhji Mewar, had no alternative but to pass on the mantle to Arvind Singhji Mewar. The eldest son became an MP in Udaipur.

Before Arvind succeeded his father, he was sent to a Chicago business school to learn the hotel trade. Arvind now not only runs his businesses, but he is both the temporal and spiritual leader of the people of Udaipur. He would like to maintain these traditions for his son to inherit (Arvind has one son and two daughters), but I wondered whether the local authorities might become jealous of his ability to maintain so many of the traditions of his royal household without their assistance, and if so he would tread a difficult path. As we talked I began to realize the complexities of the manifold roles Arvind is trying to fulfil. He still wishes to maintain the paternalistic tradition of the Mewar household, together with a place in the affections of his people, despite the lack of any form of constitutional position.

The State of Udaipur was once divided into the equivalent of sixteen Duchies and the sixteen 'Dukes', some of whom are members of the Mewar family, still call upon Arvind on official occasions. He is also reviving the traditional festivals, which give him an opportunity to show himself in a public role which the State cannot deny him. He is deeply concerned about whether the role of the Mewar family can be maintained, and he is haunted by the fear that he, as the seventy-sixth Maharana, might be the last.

The problem Arvind faces is a common one for all royalty today: does he maintain his position by remaining remote and therefore apparently different, or does he seek broader exposure to the public? There is also the difficulty of satisfactorily explaining to his people that it is the economy of Udaipur State that ultimately benefits from his hotel operations, because the tourists who stay in his hotels spend money locally. He also feels a certain pressure to maintain employment for the people of Udaipur.

We finished our discussion and Arvind invited us all to join him for dinner. The evening was both physically and emotionally surprisingly warm and I felt greatly for Arvind and his problems. I reflected on how difficult it must be for a Maharana to be personally honest with himself in such a situation, but an awful lot of the show and attention of the royal household did look a bit like a personal ego trip to me.

The next day we progressed around the lake at something less than walking pace, aboard a magnificent barge. It was a sort of Indian galley propelled by several very leisurely oarsmen who manned their large sweeps standing up, with no stroke or helmsman to guide them. We went up the steps to the poop deck, which was lavishly endowed with cushions on which we sprawled in what I hoped was a suitably dignified Mogul manner, and were served a very un-Mogul breakfast of orange juice and Danish pastries.

While we progressed round the lake I endeavoured to understand the commercial logic of the whole business and how it was run. The evidence of the success of the Mewar family's business venture was all around us: we could see the Lake Palace Hotel, the Shivnivas Palace Hotel and the Fateh Prakash Palace Hotel in all their glory, but it was also evident that the royal traditions were still intact. I was very concerned about how it was all being financed. I struggled to work out what depended upon what. I wondered whether the maintenance of a royal lifestyle was really necessary for the tourists.

One of the snags which was immediately clear was that everyone deferred to Arvind in his triple roles as head of the Royal Family, religious leader, and commercial managing director of the hotel business. Nevertheless he claimed that he spends very little of his time running the hotel business and that the overwhelming percentage of his time and money was devoted to maintaining his royal responsibilities.

As we talked it became apparent that Arvind was full of ideas and ambitions for the expansion of the commercial side of his business. He wanted to start his own airline in order to increase the tourist potential in Rajasthan, which he felt was not being properly exploited because of the poor standard of air service. He'd thought of developing a golf course and of building a villa complex in some woods on the far shore of the lake; he'd thought about building a recording studio for top pop stars and of developing conference facilities in the Shivnivas Palace Hotel, and he wanted to split his hotel group and put one half into partnership with The Oberoi Group (a major Indian hotel group), and then go for a public flotation. He also wanted to terminate The Taj

Group's contract (another major Indian hotel group) to manage The Lake Palace Hotel, which they had held since 1971.

But I was still grappling with the essential paradox of the whole enterprise. The more successful the hotels are, the more the economy of Udaipur benefits, and I know that business is done differently in India because labour is cheap and employers are strongly driven by the desire to provide employment, but nevertheless they've got to provide real jobs that actually contribute to the effectiveness of an operation and to the economy as a whole. There are also Mewar family trusts that support, amongst other things, three major temples and hundreds of smaller ones, and a separate trust that supports a 1200-pupil school in Udaipur.

I suggested to Arvind that in order to lower his overhead, he could have fewer cars (he has a garage of cars ranging from Cadillacs and Mercedes to the ubiquitious Indian-manufactured Ambassadors and Contessas); and he could get rid of the band and scale down the numbers of his security guard. I also said he could scale down the total staff by about 40% or 50%.

I pressed Arvind gently and he acknowledged that the commercial argument for much of this expenditure was fairly weak. He readily acknowledged that the band could be dispensed with but that the band played regularly for hotel guests and could therefore be considered a tourist attraction, and Arvind remarked, rather charmingly, that although the band could be dispensed with, from a personal point of view it would be a pity to see it go. I could not help but warm to his attitude and wondered whether I would be as ready to shut down a band, if I had one, as I was suggesting he should be.

Arvind is obviously extremely ambitious for further expansion of his group and he is thinking about developing outside Rajasthan. (He has already bought The Gorbandh Palace Hotel in Jaisalmer.) I asked whether any attempt had been made to measure the impact of the tourists on the State of Udaipur, and whether any estimates existed of the impact on GDP of his own activities. I felt that these would be useful numbers both politically, and to justify the way he was going about things. Like everything else in Udaipur there are plenty of concepts, but very little real data to back them up.

When we had finished our breakfast voyage around the lake, I went to tour the household and look at the Mewar organization while Arvind went on to handle the day's routine tasks. Om Singh Chauhan, who had met me up at the airport, took me round and showed me how things were run. Om was twenty-five, gold-earringed, and a Daly College (India's equivalent of Eton) educated graduate of the Ness Wadia College of Commerce in Poona, and the Poona Institute of Management and Research. He had recently been appointed Manager of Sales and Marketing for the Maharana's central office. Om reported, albeit with a great deal of deference, directly to Arvind. His background, and his time at Daly College, meant that his attitude was more British than any British public schoolboy's. The Poona Institute of Management had filled his head with all the necessary business jargon, but he had little business experience and I think he viewed my visit with some trepidation. However he was keen, enthusiastic, and loyal to the Maharana, and if those qualities could do the trick, there was no doubt that Om could deliver.

I asked Om for a copy of the organization chart which was rather reluctantly produced, and which turned out to be a clear model of how things should not be run. There were no profit centres, everything appeared to be a cost centre, and it all ended up in an enormous line, reporting directly to Arvind. With a sinking heart I started my tour, visiting the boats department, project office, archives, personnel office and the charitable trusts office in the process. Everywhere it seemed that the same story applied: there was almost total control of authorization of expenditure, and I found little control of the dynamics or the financial rationale between different activities.

I visited the newly opened Fateh Prakash Palace Hotel with the manager, Simon Shekhar. The Fateh Prakash Palace was a beautiful hotel but, by British standards, it did not have nearly enough rooms, and the room charges per night of US$100.00, although obscene by Indian standards, were exceedingly cheap by international standards. The Fateh Prakash's manager was unable to influence visitor numbers, since those were controlled by central reservations, and when I asked central reservations how they optimized their visitors and what knowledge they had of the variable opportunity cost for

40

different rooms, they seemed unfamiliar with these concepts.

After my morning of research I felt that Arvind's current management would have difficulty taking over the running of The Lake Palace Hotel themselves. To my certain knowledge The Taj Group used international standards of control and, for all its faults in style, was clearly focused and managed. No one in Arvind's organization seemed to be able to provide me with any real numbers for the turnover of the whole business, however Arvind had recently suffered a severe loss when his company secretary and chief legal advisor, who also seemed to have doubled as his finance director, was killed in a recent Indian air crash, and this tragedy no doubt contributed to the lack of available figures. It was thought that the turnover might be of the order of £4m and by doing a few rough calculations it seemed to me the maximum potential of the business might be about £5m turnover, with a profit of about £1m, if the business was tightly run, but these really were wild guesses.

I found it difficult to calculate the cost of maintaining the royal traditions, although part of the benefit of the band, the security force and so on could be justified to the hotels, I felt that the rest of the costs had to be justified either against the maintenance of the royal household, or as a sort of social service, providing work for his subjects, the people of Udaipur.

That afternoon, Arvind drove me to Shikarbadi, a former Mewar hunting lodge which occupies a very special place in his heart. It is also the royal polo stud, and the lodge was Arvind's own home before he inherited from his father. Shikarbadi has recently been turned into a rather unique sort of hotel with luxuriously equipped, richly furnished, tented rooms. When we arrived at the gates of the royal stud, an escort of lancers and sword-carrying officers formed up in front of, and behind, our Cadillac. Arvind was rather more accustomed to such pomp and ceremony than I was, but I felt sure my father would have taken it all in his stride.

My father used to hunt tiger here and Arvind had arranged for me to meet two of the retainers who had worked for his father, and who had known my father during his years in Udaipur. They were the head Shikari, who used to lead tiger hunting expeditions for my father, and the cricket coach, both of whom were indispensable members of any self-respecting Indian royal household. The head Shikari, Dhabhai Tulsinath, did not really have a great deal to tell me about my father and most of the his stories were of the 'There I was beating the bushes and suddenly this mighty snarling beast soared out at me,' variety. However the cricket coach, Mr A. R. Naidu, who is in his seventies and had been the coach for the all-India team at one time – the time, incidentally, when Udaipur State produced half of all the test cricketers in the Indian team – had obviously been a very close colleague of my father's and he gave me a photograph of the Udaipur team with Bhagwat Singh, himself and my father, wearing an appropriate pith helmet, walking off the field. Mr Naidu spoke of my father as a very stern man and told numerous stories which made my flesh creep. He told of him frogmarching an accountant, who had failed to obey orders not to work on a Sunday, out of the office, and of his anger with anybody who smiled when talking to him. Surprisingly however, Mr Naidu also claimed that my father could be sensitive with his staff, and was a splendid man to go to if anybody had health or personal problems. He never fired anybody, considering it his responsibility to put things right, and Mr Naidu said that he always thought of my father as a sad and frustrated man, but nevertheless someone who knew the value of every man. My father apparently hated leaving Udaipur at the end of his contract, and he showed considerable affection for Bhagwat Singh, whom he was very proud of, and whom he called his son. At the end of the day he was frequently joined by Mr Naidu in his bungalow for a couple of scotches and soda, before turning in.

I asked Mr Naidu whether my father ever mentioned me and he looked embarrassed and eventually said that he had no recollection of my father ever having spoken of me at all. This, sadly, confirmed my views about my relationship with my father. I was sunk twice during 1942, while fighting the war in the Mediterranean, something which I would have thought worthy of at least a passing comment. This confirmation from Mr Naidu that my father had not even mentioned me in connection with those events saddened and angered me: I was forced to accept the fact of my disinheritance.

Later I gave Arvind my report on his business situation and offered such advice as I could. He did not appear very interested in what I had to say, and I felt rather as though he was humouring me by allowing me to show my paces. Nevertheless I was determined to have a go and I summed up by saying that I accepted and admired the niche market position which had been established for the group, and that I understood his wish to manage The Lake Palace Hotel himself, but I felt that that could only be done when he had much better financial and management systems in place. He had to be clear that once The Lake Palace Hotel was within his own control he would have to face up to very heavy branding and international advertising costs, if he was to maintain the image. Attractive though the group was it would not be able to sell itself and I felt it was an absolute necessity to appoint a managing director with a financial and systems background. I told him I would sound out Arthur Andersen and one or two other international management consultants and put an appropriate one in touch. I subsequently discovered that Arthur Andersen had a good deal of experience in the hotel business and so I arranged for them to contact Arvind, having warned him their advice would not be cheap.

I told Arvind that I was strongly opposed to the idea of an airline, but highly supportive of putting money into conference facilities, and I cited some examples of similar investments which had worked very well in Britain. If the conference facilities were of a high enough quality they, in turn, would attract the necessary airline traffic into the State.

I explained that I was deeply concerned about the lack of direction and target setting for his managers. Om had excellent potential but insufficient experience to cope on his own, and I had real concerns about the loading on Arvind himself. I sympathized with the conflicts between Arvind's feudal and his commercial role and pleaded with him to reconsider the idea of going for a public placing. I wanted him to avoid going public because I foresaw the unresolvable conflict that would inevitably develop between the funding of the calling and duties of a Maharana, and the funding of the commercial interests. Plainly, how he spent his money was entirely up to him, but he needed to be totally clear what was serving a commercial purpose and what was not. He really needed to look at the whole business the other way round. Everything that was spent over and above the base commercial cost of running a fully competitive hotel system should be justified either as a contribution to his regal role and his religious responsibilities, or as a contribution to his personal lifestyle. Arvind listened politely but I am not sure I was really making very much impression.

The final goodbye took place that evening, when I was invited to a farewell tea with Arvind. It was as British as many other things in Udaipur had been, with cucumber and tomato sandwiches and Battenburg cake served on beautiful china, overlooking the lake. Both of us became quite sentimental.

My final feelings were of warmth and sadness for Arvind. He was treading a lonely and difficult path, trying to retain a nonexistent position on behalf of a family tradition which had run its course. However I also saw that Arvind felt the sense of duty and responsibility to his calling that had been drummed into his father by my father. The difficulty is that these feelings of duty and responsibility, although necessary, are not enough. They must be accompanied by the most efficient, modern, competitive and flexible approach to business, and he's having serious difficulty with the latter. I was sad to leave but the visit had been a fascinating journey back in time. I felt I had gained more of an understanding of what had made my father the way he was. He had plainly been greatly admired in a rather lonely, professional sense, but nowhere had I found any signs of real affection for him. And, as I said at the beginning, the relationship between Arvind and his father mirrored, almost exactly, the relationship between myself and my own father and this seemed to me to be Mervyn Harvey-Jones's legacy to the Indian dynasties whom he had served. It hardly seemed a worthwhile memorial for a lifetime of committed service to Britain in India, and on the whole, I felt that this journey around my father had been sad rather than jolly.

Daly College, the Indian Eton

If my father, in his small way, had left a British legacy to India, then Daly College has left a much larger British legacy. I wanted to find out if the College was still run along the British Victorian lines that it used to be, and I set off to find out. Daly College is in Indore, and another of my father's protégées, Bahadur, the Maharaja of Dhar, was educated there. I knew Bahadur reasonably well, although I was five years his junior, because we lived together as a family in Dhar.

Daly College was founded in 1884 and named after a British lieutenant general. It was one of three or four Colleges set up specifically for the training of Indian princes (one of the others being Mayo College, where Bhagwat Singh was educated). In the 1920s, when Bahadur joined, there were between fifty and seventy-five pupils at Daly College. Now there are more buildings and there are 1100 pupils. We drove up to the College which looked exactly as it had done in the 1920s, the only perceptible difference was that the cricket nets were on a slightly different part of the grounds. When I visited Daly College the head-teacher was a former cavalry man from the Poona Light Horse, named Colonel Kak, who, like others I had met, had left the Indian Army because he felt the conformity was too restrictive.

The objectives of Daly College have changed little as far as I could see. The primary emphasis is still on character building in classic British terms. The school is still very much one for the *élite* although, despite the fees, there is no attempt at individual tuition. It is coeducational, aiming for 60% boys and 40% girls, and the age range is from five to seventeen years old. All the teaching is done in English and the aims of the school are not to achieve the highest possible academic grades, but rather to turn out 'future leaders'.

Certainly the boys and girls were well-scrubbed and uniformed, in their light blue tops with dark blue trousers or skirts. Apart from the rather inappropriate nineteenth-century Mogul-British architecture, we could have been at any pre-war British public school. The BBC had managed to find Rajen Singh, who had been at Daly College at the same time as Bahadur. He told us that Bahadur had never really fitted in at the College. Rajen Singh was one of the first 'commoners' to attend the College and he told us that he had found the whole place a masterpiece of snobbery. Many of the teachers were British right up until the 1950s, but in Bahadur's day the main concern was about how many gun salutes each prince had (in those days the superiority of an Indian State was measured by how many gun salutes it merited), and how many tigers they had shot. The discipline had been Dickensian, lateness being punished by doubling round the fields carrying a rifle over your head. Physical training in the mornings and sports in the afternoon had been compulsory for everybody, and Bahadur had never fitted easily into this environment.

Rajen Singh said that his time at Daly College had trained him to be a playboy, but despite his cynicism about the College, his sons, nephews, grandsons and granddaughters had all followed in his footsteps and attended the College, even though he was more and more doubtful of the relevance of the College to the needs of modern India.

Rajen talked at length about Bahadur, whom he had seen only two days before his death from a heart attack in 1980. He felt that Bahadur had totally wasted his life, appearing less and less in public and staying in his palace alone, or with his favourites. For a man whose only interests had been music and, sometimes, tennis, I can barely think of a harsher treatment than my father's tutelage, followed by having to take part in the rituals of what was effectively a British public school.

After meeting Rajen and talking to Colonel Kak, I stepped out of the front door of the College to see, of all unlikely things, our original Buick, which I remembered so well. One of the few photographs I have from my time in Dhar is of me, aged four, wearing a solar topee and standing in front of our Buick – and here it was in running order complete with a turbaned driver, a mechanic on the running board, wooden wheels, mica windows and canvas hood. I was totally over-whelmed to see this relic of the past, which still sported the old Dhar number plate that I remembered: Dhar 2.

I was taken on a tour of the playing fields where everything I saw was very reminiscent of St James's and the Abbey School in Malvern, of which I was chairman. The girls' teams were playing hockey and the cheerleaders and supporters on the touchline were exact replicas of the girls at Malvern. Meanwhile I could hear, above the excitement of the girl supporters, the steady thump of ball on bat from the cricket field on the other side of the building, where the pavilion rivalled that of any British county club.

Rajen believed that the colleges for princes had been part of a British conspiracy to make the princes dependent upon and obedient to the British, and I think he may have a point. Rajen thought that the whole intention of Daly College had been to eliminate individuality and induce a pattern of conformity which the British felt comfortable with.

Nevertheless he was the first to give credit for the good things that were taught: honesty, integrity, language, and the responsibilities inherent in leadership. His sons were more critical of the system, believing it stifled creativity and encouraged yesterday's values and a backward-looking approach. India's needs for the future, particularly in business, are flexibility, courage, vision, sensitivity and imagination, not qualities emphasized at Daly College. Despite all this, the sons and daughters of middle-class India are still sent to Daly College, and when I asked why, they replied that it was the done thing and a considerable sign of success, and their parents felt that the contacts their children would make at the College would be useful to them later in life. What a very middle-class British approach to education!

The Maharani of Dhar

I said farewell to Daly College and went on my way to visit the bungalow where I lived with my family when my father was tutor and guardian to Bahadur, the Maharaja of Dhar, in the 1920s. Although I was greatly looking forward to meeting the Maharani, Bahadur's widow, I was somewhat apprehensive because I knew little about her, or her relationship with Bahadur. When I had last visited Dhar I had been unable to find our bungalow, but now I recognized it as soon as we approached. When I lived there it had had a massive forty-acre compound which occupied the whole of one side of the town. Practically all of that had been sold for housing, but enough garden had been kept by the Maharani to ensure that the bungalow was still secluded. The sentry boxes were still there although, of course, there were no longer any sentries, but as soon as we swept into the drive I recognized everything as though it had been yesterday. The veranda, which in my time had been open, was now enclosed between pillars, and a rather ugly extension had been built on to the wing my parents had used, but other than that the house was unchanged.

Mrunalini Devi Puar, the Maharani, greeted me warmly and showed me around, although I barely needed it. Even the furniture was the same, still the up-to-the-minute 1920s Waring and Gillow stuff I remembered, and mostly in the same positions; the two vast stuffed tigers my father had shot sat erect and on guard in the dining room in exactly the same places, and except that the punkahs – the vast ventilation flaps which were suspended from the roof – had been replaced by electric fans, and running water had been installed, nothing had changed and I felt as though I was in a timewarp.

One wing housed my father's study, with separate bedrooms for himself and my mother and an adjoining bathroom. In the centre of this wing was a large domed dining room with a sitting room in front, and the whole was surrounded by the veranda. A second wing had been occupied by me, Bahadur and Manka. Manka was Bahadur's Indian companion and the same age as him. The bathroom and bedrooms were still just as they had been, although the bathroom had modern fittings. In my day a staff of between 150 and 200 people had been employed to keep my father and mother, myself, the Maharaja and Manka in the modest style to which we aspired, and the compound had had an entire village of its own, with a laundry and a shop.

I got on splendidly with Mrunalini, the Maharani. She was a daughter of a prince of Baroda, one of the largest, and richest, Indian states, and her marriage to Bahadur had been an arranged one. She was married at seventeen in strict purdah, and she told me she could not see a thing during the ceremony, and that she was miserable both before and during the entire ritual. The marriage did not work out and within a year Mrunalini returned to Baroda. Although they did not divorce, Mrunalini never spoke ill of Bahadur. I was very young when I knew Bahadur, but he'd always seemed to me to be a rather effeminate boy who was even more terrified of my father than I was. I think, now, that the same characteristics in my father that made him good for Bhagwat Singh, or at least not too harmful, particularly the emphasis on sport, were probably fatal for Bahadur, who needed affection and gentle encouragement, neither of which were exhibited by my father. According to Mrunalini, her husband was a sensitive man who was not particularly interested in any sport except tennis. In Mrunalini's view, Bahadur felt rejected many times. He was adopted by the Dhar royal family who, having no sons of their own, followed the Indian tradition of adopting a cousin to succeed. Bahadur therefore felt

48

rejected by his natural parents first of all, then by his adoptive parents who handed him on into my father's exceedingly unsuitable care, and finally, when my father moved on to another job, he left Bahadur thrice rejected.

Mrunalini told me that although Bahadur had often spoken of my father, he had done so with respect rather than affection and she felt that both Bahadur and my father had been sad and unfulfilled people. She knew, however, of his affection for my mother. She said that in his later years, Bahadur had become a recluse, and she thought he had probably taken to drugs. Personally, I suspect that he may have been gay and therefore I cannot imagine anyone worse suited to become his guardian and tutor than my father, who would have made strenuous attempts to eradicate any signs of sensitivity, rather than allowing Bahadur simply to be himself. Mrunalini said that Bahadur did very little with his life and she agreed with me that my father had been entirely the wrong man to bring him up.

We had a marvellous Indian lunch and Mrunalini and I talked endlessly. She told me that Baroda was her main home, but that she visited Dhar for about two weeks every three or four months. She told me that she had had a dreadful time settling the death duties when Bahadur died in 1980. She was left with the bungalow, which she was determined to hang on to, but was bitter about the treatment meted out to her, and to other princely families, by the Indian state.

I felt a great rapport with Mrunalini and I hoped this meeting would be the beginning of a long association. It would be difficult not to respect her. She survived an ill-suited and, I suspect, unconsummated marriage and yet maintained her tranquillity, warmth and values. She broke with the princely tradition in order to follow her own career, and she has developed a considerable position in the academic world in her own right. At the age of thirty-eight Mrunalini took a degree (having finished her schooling when she was only sixteen), followed by a PhD. She is now the Chancellor of The Maharaja Sayajirao University of Baroda, which has over 35 000 students in residence, and is one of the largest universities in the world by student population standards.

Mrunalini went to a great deal of trouble to show me a number of photographs of Bahadur at various ages, including one of him looking very slick and sleek in corespondent shoes, and she also showed me the photographs of their wedding. When I left I said that I very much hoped we would meet again, and I left my childhood home with mixed feelings.

Dhar itself brought back so many happy memories, but I felt extremely sad about my father's contribution to Bahadur's already difficult life. He made it even more difficult. Until Independence British civil servants educated many Indian princes and, in my opinion, the British values and opinions that they inculcated into the Indian princes only served to confuse the princes. In those days the British believed unswervingly that their values and views were superior to anyone else's and this rendered them inflexible and severely resistant to change.

I was left pondering the traditions that we British so blithely bequeathed to the Indian nation, and that, in the case of Daly College, the Indian nation has hung on to. Daly College seemed to me to be an anachronism: the emphasis on games and on conformity are completely at odds with the needs of modern India. That sort of training is a Victorian training, and it was my father's training. I think that it not only harmed Bahadur, but it also, probably, harmed my father, and in a wider sense, I believe that it has harmed Britain.

In my view it is time for the people and the institutions – both in India and in Britain – who still pursue these outmoded ways, to take a long hard look at themselves and think about how to change. For change they must, otherwise we will turn out yet another generation of conformists who are trained to run the empires of the 1880s, rather than a new generation of individuals who are trained to run the businesses of the 1990s.

3. Travelling Indian roads

Hindustan Motors Ltd : the engine plant

My next call was to Hindustan Motors. Under the licence-raj there were only two main licenced car manufacturers in India: Hindustan Motors Ltd (HML), and Premier Automobiles Ltd (PAL). Since deregulation competitors have entered the market, and I wanted to see how Hindustan Motors was faring, post-liberalization.

I began by visiting Hindustan Motors' engine plant at Pithampur on the outskirts of Dhar which, in my boyhood, had been nothing but jungle. Now it has been transformed into a brand new industrial area, known locally as the Detroit of India. The Pithampur industrial estate is part of a government scheme to start up a new industrial belt in Central India. Practically everything seems to be made here: tyres, plastics, trucks, films, edible oils, chemicals, you name it, the Pithampur estate produces it. But despite this diversity of production, concepts such as buying in, just-in-time delivery, low inventory operation, and so on are still almost unknown.

The Hindustan Motors' plant looked absolutely splendid, both architecturally and visually. The cladding was aluminium to reflect the light, and the roof was high to give ventilation. The surrounding grassy area was irrigated and maintained by a contract gardening company, and 40 000 trees had been planted with a further 60 000 planned. The trees diverted the wind and absorbed the heat; the cladding deflected the heat and the irrigated lawns prevented the dust rising, so that the whole working environment was remarkably pleasant and the temperature inside the factory was at least 5°C lower than that outside.

The factory was first considered in 1985, assembly began in 1987 and the machine shops began operating in 1992. I thought that if the inside was anything like the outside, this visit was going to be an absolute treat: a complete contrast to the Kasliwals' 1890s sweatshop in Bombay. The engine plant at Pithampur, from the outside anyway, was absolutely up to international standards. I asked what had decided Hindustan Motors to locate their new and most modern investment some 1000 miles from the ultimate end point of their products in Calcutta, and I was told that there were sizeable tax advantages, but the attraction which had really swayed them was the guarantee of an uninterrupted power supply due to the new power stations that had been built locally and specifically for the purpose.

Ramesh Rath, the Vice President of Hindustan Motors, met us and so – to my horror – did all the senior managers. It was 3.00 pm on a Sunday yet everybody was working, partly – it must be said – in order to fit in with the BBC filming schedule, but in India, as I had already discovered, working on Sundays is not unusual. Management and workers wore the same uniform, made by S Kumars (whose Bombay factory I had visited), and all of them wore name tags on their breast pockets. And there was an apparently inexhaustible supply of garlands: I have never felt very much at ease being garlanded, and on this occasion I was completely at a loss. I was given three garlands when I arrived, followed by more at regular stages of our visit, until I thought I was going to have to feel my way around!

The effusiveness of Ramesh's greeting was embarrassing. Later he showed me the paperback edition of my book, *Making it Happen*, which had plainly been read and reread, annotated and underlined, until it was almost falling apart. During my visit to the engine plant most of my comments were greeted with a recital of some relevant paragraph or passage of my thoughts from the late 1980s. I fervently hoped that their adherence to my, by now rather distant, thoughts and ideas had proved fruitful.

Despite Ramesh Rath's volubility he is a professional, go-ahead, concerned manager. He is also an engineer, and plainly a good one. Ramesh is intensely proud of everything that has been achieved since 1992: he was personally responsible for the development of the engine plant at Pithampur. The plant employs about 385 people of whom no less than 180 are in managerial and technical positions. Ramesh's very first action on arriving at the Pithampur factory was to contact all the schools in Dhar and the surrounding areas, and to appoint a technical training manager. The manager combed the schools relentlessly to locate, at an early stage, the people he felt could be trained to operate in the entirely different way they had in mind, as Ramesh explained, 'the Harvey-Jones way'. (I said he was effusive.) In addition to selecting and coaching the boys (for there were hardly any girls employed in the plant) at their schools, the technical training manager also arranged for the schools' curriculum to be changed and adapted to meet the needs of Hindustan Motors more closely. The chosen workforce – the cream of the schools of Central India – went through progressively intensive training before they were finally employed at Hindustan Motors. And even then their induction period lasted over three months, and 20% of all labour time is training time.

I met a number of employees who had come through this very far-sighted and expensive manning system, and I could well understand Ramesh's enthusiasm. However, much of the credit for this achievement should go to C.K. Birla himself. (The Birla family have a controlling shareholding in the giant Birla group which owns Hindustan Motors.) I asked Ramesh what instructions he had been given by the Birla family and he told me that there had been just three. First, there was to be no compromise on quality, which was to be world class. Second, the plant was required to be world competitive, not only in quality, but also in productivity, and third, the factory should be landscaped.

My first impressions of the plant suggested that Ramesh was fulfilling all three requirements, but I was dismayed to find when we went inside (after even more garlanding), that less than a third of the whole space was occupied by machinery; that the current level of production was only 6000 engines, against the breakeven point of 10 000, and that the capacity of the plant was 15 000 engines.

As happens so often, they had not reacted fast enough to the collapse of their sales estimates, having invested in too much plant and over-estimated their potential growth. The machine tools had been bought wherever they could purchase the most modern and effective equipment, however they pointed out with pride that they had designed and made some of them themselves and that an increasing number of the machine tools came from India. But the plant was built to manufacture an engine designed by the Japanese Isuzu company, and this engine had originally been intended for installation in an Isuzu car. The Indian Government refused Hindustan Motors permission to make the Isuzu car, so, in an attempt to increase their market share, Hindustan Motors adapted the engine to fit both the Ambassador and the Contessa Classic – Hindustan Motors manufactured cars – but inevitably the numbers of engines required are far lower than originally forecast and when I looked at the space, the overcapitalization was obvious.

The Ambassador would be instantly recognizable to anyone my age: it closely resembles the 1950s Morris Oxford. In the 1950s when British cars dominated world car markets, Britain sold its Morris Oxford technology to India, and the Ambassador was born. Hindustan Motors are relaunching the Ambassador, equipped with the adapted Isuzu engine, and it is hoped that the new model, to be called the Ambassador 1800 ISZ, will boost the Ambassador's sales, thus loading up the engine plant at the same time. The new engine will produce more power and thus be able to run air conditioning. There is also a diesel-powered Ambassador and Hindustan Motors hope to replace the Morris diesel engine with their own unit, which would also produce more power and operate more smoothly.

Hindustan Motors have also developed a three cylinder engine for greater fuel economy, and are working on an LPG (liquid petroleum gas) model, with the taxi market in mind. They have also reverse engineered a diesel engine in line with Isuzu's, and when Hindustan Motors eventually sent the drawings of the engine to Isuzu themselves, the latter, to my amazement, agreed that Hindustan Motors could produce the diesel engine and had sent their own drawings for comparison. In the reverse engineering process a number of improvements have been introduced, largely to cope with Indian suppliers and conditions. I told them that I'd present them with a gold cup if they managed to produce an electronically-controlled two-stroke engine within the two to three years that they planned to produce it. All these innovations are attempts to get out of the rat trap they find themselves caught in, through lack of basic demand.

The engine plant's main costs are interest charges and the cost of bought in materials; the labour content was calculated to be 10% of total cost. I thought this was a remarkably low labour content even though labour is cheap in India. Their main effort was targeted at driving down the costs of their bought in materials. They aimed to reduce those costs by 15% in the next two to three years, primarily through developing Indian suppliers. The difficulty here is to maintain quality standards. Plainly when assembling an engine the quality of the end product is only as good as that of the poorest quality constituent piece, and I understood both their insistence on quality and their problems with maintaining it. They have developed a large number of test rigs for components, many of which are extremely simple, but since they have been purpose designed, they can test every bought in component quickly and efficiently.

The plant was well-run and there were very few people visible which is always a good sign. The work progressed at a steady and reasonable rate and all the working practices had obviously been carefully designed. There were signs of excellent production engineering every-where, unencumbered by the shortage of capital. All the machines were computer- controlled and there were a lot of very flexible machine centres. The safety record was first class and the material flow was logical and sensible, as indeed it should have been with so much extra space available. The pride and enthusiasm of the workforce shone through everywhere, despite the fact that the plant was losing money. They aimed to match Japanese productivity, and many sections were within 10% of what they thought the equivalent Japanese level of effectiveness would be. In their view, however, the plant was, overall, something like 30% behind the Japanese equivalents, but the whole plant was spotless and they hoped to qualify for ISO 9000 soon (the International Standards Quality Certification for manufactured goods which is the international equivalent of BS5750).

The metallurgical labs had state-of-the-art instrumentation and were certainly some of the best laboratories I have seen anywhere. These labs were really the key to the development of local Indian suppliers, the factor which offers both the greatest single cost saving, and also, in the long term, the most secure business basis. The investment has already more than paid for itself by the results they have achieved in increasing the quality of their suppliers, but there is still a tremendous amount of underused capacity available throughout the factory and, although I knew that C.K. Birla has always insisted that Hindustan Motors should not supply any other car company (and I can understand his wish not to give anybody else the advantages of this highly efficient outfit), I thought they should look seriously at the idea of turning the various functions into self-standing profit centres. In this way they could undertake general engineering for other companies, self-supply more equipment, and become individually profit responsible, all in one go.

I was full of admiration for everything that had been done at the plant, but it seemed to me that the peril of their financial position was not sufficiently appreciated by the people down the line, although I had no doubt that Ramesh was very much aware of the potential dangers. There were signs of the usual syndrome in large companies, that 'they' – i.e. the bosses – would not allow any harm to befall this jewel in the crown. But fundamentally the engine plant depends solely upon the car division in Calcutta to provide them with the vital extra loading they need, and the more I walked around, the more convinced I became that they must do more to help themselves. And I discovered that they were carrying four months' stock, which is far far too much.

It was very late by the time we got to the training centre where all the management were gathered to hear my views on the plant. I was able to praise them sincerely and tell them what a pleasure it had been to visit a factory which was so plainly aiming for world standards. I tried to emphasize the financial downside of their situation, suggesting that they were insufficiently aware of the potential profitability of the individual sections of the business, and that I thought they were also looking upon cost reductions as a target, rather than an absolute necessity. I was concerned that the organization lacked an integrated computer system for financial and management control, and I said that I thought they should build other things for other companies in order to load up their plant. I told them that I was worried by their dependence upon the competitiveness of a car that had been designed in the 1950s and, in the case of the Contessa, a 1970s Vauxhall Victor design, and

I was worried about the ability of these cars to maintain a market position. I said that unless they reached their breakeven point of 10 000 engines, and progressed from there to their capacity of 15 000 engines, a tragic waste of a wonderfully modern space and a dedicated and well-trained workforce would inevitably occur. However I was extremely pleased to be able to tell them that the Hindustan Motors' engine plant had convinced me that it was possible to set up modern world competitive businesses in the remoter parts of India. I told them that my next call was to the Hindustan Motors' car plant in Calcutta where I would reiterate these points.

Although it was nearly 2.00 am by the time I got to bed, I found myself more optimistic about India's potential and its ability to compete than I had been at any time so far. I was looking forward to seeing the Calcutta car plant, and to explaining to Hindustan Motors in Calcutta my ideas for taking their engine plant into profitability. I fell asleep pondering the fact that Hindustan Motors were manufacturing engines based upon a Japanese design on a site where, not that long ago, there had been nothing but jungle. A sign of progress, I felt.

A conclusion from the Kasliwals

Before I left for Calcutta I had one more meeting, in Indore, with Vikas Kasliwal. The Kasliwals own textile factories in Indore and it was a great relief to me to discover that these Kasliwal factories were modern ones. I wondered what the Kasliwals had decided to do about their antiquated Shree Ram mill in Bombay, and I have to admit that I was not particularly optimistic that they would have done anything much.

I was amazed, therefore, to hear Vikas telling me that the whole family felt they owed me a debt of gratitude. My visit to the Shree Ram mill had polarized their thinking and they had spent some time discussing the views I had expressed. Vikas told me that I had created a commotion in their minds.

Vikas also told me that the family had looked at the idea of shutting down the Shree Ram mill in the past, and my views had finally tilted them over the edge. After my visit, the Kasliwals decided to close the mill and, once they had made the decision, they saw no point in losing any time. The Shree Ram mill had been closed down. I was absolutely delighted and not a little shell-shocked by the speed of their actions, particularly since, as Vikas and I agreed, speed is not a well-known Indian (nor a well-known British) characteristic.

Vikas told me that he had also taken my advice about breaking the news to the workforce himself. Meetings had been arranged with their 5000 staff over a period of two days, and Vikas had spoken at every meeting. He told his workforce that the Kasliwals had decided to sell the old factory and use the money to rebuild in a better location, with brand new machinery. He also told them that employees who were unable to move to the new location would be bought out. Vikas told me that their new site would operate with just 800 employees.

I knew that this direct approach to employees was a first for the Indian textile industry, and I was delighted to hear that the meetings had gone extremely well. I told Vikas that I was quite sure that the difficult decisions they had taken would bring long-term improvements, both for their workforce and also for S Kumars. It is far better to have 800 secure jobs based on world competitive technology with the potential for growth, than 5000 jobs in a business that is essentially doomed. They were planning to have the new plant ready by the end of 1995, and Vikas asked if I would perform the opening ceremony. I assured him that I would be honoured to do so, should it prove at all possible. I was truly thrilled to know that the old factory was going to be replaced. My visit to the Hindustan Motors' engine plant had shown me that it is possible to build and run plants up to the highest world standards in India, and now the Kasliwals were about to follow suit.

The changes that the Kasliwals had in mind could only be beneficial for India. Brand new equipment would increase their export opportunities and enable them to start off with higher quality products and better paid people. But I was still worried about the S Kumars' view of the Indian market. On more than one occasion they had told me that their product was too good for the Indian market, and I could not help feeling that they would do better to try to lead taste up market, rather than serve down to price points. I told Vikas this and, as usual, he took it on board. This meeting left me more than a little shaken, but absolutely delighted by the effect of my advice and the speed of its implementation.

Sir John taking breakfast with the Maharana of Udaipur on a barge on Lake Pichola.

OVERLEAF The barge passing the Lake Palace Hotel.

ABOVE The bungalow in Dhar where Sir John lived with his family when his father was tutor and guardian to Bahadur, son of the Maharaja of Dhar, in the 1920s.

OPPOSITE ABOVE A picnic with Rajen Singh, a friend and contemporary of Bahadur at Daly College.

OPPOSITE BELOW The Buick used by Sir John's family in Dhar in the 1920s.

OVERLEAF View of Simla, in the foothills of the Himalayas, where Sir John's parents met and married.

Portrait photograph of Sir John Harvey-Jones at Clifton College

Hindustan Motors Limited: the Calcutta car plant

We arrived in Calcutta to find dense crowds crammed into cafes, watching television sets that were visible from the street. India was playing South Africa at Eden Gardens, and India's passion for cricket could not have been more evident. The crowds in the street leapt, groaned, cheered, jumped and exclaimed at every ball. India won by two runs in the last over and no one could have doubted the victory for the whole of Calcutta erupted with fireworks, explosions and rockets. When we were collected by Mano Pachisia, the Executive Vice President of Hindustan Motors, the following morning, he treated us to a ball-by-ball description of the match as we drove up the banks of the Hooghly on our way to the Hindustan Motors car plant.

Hindustan Motors' two main car products are the Ambassador, based on a forty-year-old Morris design, and the Contessa, based on a twenty-year-old Vauxhall design. The Ambassador is seen as the workhorse of the middle classes, whereas the Contessa, which has air conditioning, is seen as the up-market, luxury car. Premier Automobiles' best-seller (Hindustan Motors' sole competitor until liberalization) is based on a thirty-year-old Fiat design. Since liberalization, both companies have lost market share (more of which later), and I was therefore extremely interested to see what innovations Hindustan Motors had introduced in the manufacture and design of their cars in order to hold their own against the competition.

It wasn't a great start. We arrived at the car plant to find that the entrance was through a bazaar and under some railway lines, and once we were inside I was amazed to find that the site was massive. This is the site I referred to on page 17, where the employer felt he should provide so much more than employment for his workforce. As we passed the 2000-pupil school, the hospital, the managers' and workers' housing, the shops and the temples I felt sure that Mano Pachisia, who runs the plant, was wrong in his assumption that all this was necessary to attract and keep a workforce these days. After all I had just come from the same company's engine plant which provided few of these facilities and yet had a well-trained, enthusiastic workforce. It occurred to me that the family-oriented attitude of Indian business people, both in the immediate family sense, viz the Kasliwals desire to create businesses for all their sons, and in the wider sense, viz Mano Pachisia's paternalist provision of all life's essentials for his workforce, must change if India is to be commercially successful in global terms in the twenty-first century.

We called in at one of the temples and made a pooja (a prayer) which I felt was rather necessary since Robert, our producer, had developed an intractable case of 'flu that morning which manifested itself in a series of major eruptions when things didn't quite work out the way he wanted. Inside the temple there was an extremely sensible Hindu exhortation recommending self-discipline, self-control and tolerance. I pointed it out to Robert with some delight, and it seemed to have an effect since the subsequent eruptions settled into minor rumblings.

Mano Pachisia, who is an accountant by training, explained the layout of the factory before we went inside, and I attempted to summarize my concerns about the business situation at the engine plant and its total dependence upon the car plant. Mano explained that the loading on the engine plant would be 12 500 pieces and when I queried this vast increase, he explained they were planning 6000 engines for the Contessa, another 6000 for the Isuzu-engined Ambassador, which would sell at a considerable premium, and 500 diesels for the ordinary Ambassador. This all seemed optimistic and unlikely, and I was concerned about what would happen if the expected sales failed to materialize. (In the event the engine plant produced 7000 engines for the Contessa and for the Ambassador and 700 diesels, making a total of 7700 that year.) We boarded a Hindustan Motors' manufactured vehicle called a Trekker, which resembled a motorized golf cart, to begin our tour of the factory.

Our first stop was at the foundry and, once again in India, I wondered which century I was in. This foundry made the foundry where I did my engineering training at Dartmouth in the late 1930s look modern by comparison. Everything was hand poured, there was no instrumentation and the only automation I could see was a single mould transfer line, which crackled and grunted erratically. Although they were very proud of their quality control they still have a 14% reject rate which is absolutely hopeless, and the system, which appeared to be

60

rudimentary in the extreme, was run by a rather uninterested looking, shabbily-dressed Indian supervisor. The manager of the foundry, who was extremely bright, had obtained permission to seek work outside in order to load up his shop and he had even managed to achieve an export order. But one of their major problems was hopeless overmanning. The entire factory employs 12 000 people but they intend to reduce total manpower by about 2000 over five years. They had already instituted a three-year freeze on recruitment and they had even looked at the idea of buying people out to hasten the demanning process, but could not make the sums work out. Despite the appalling productivity problems there wasn't any real sense of urgency or concern. Everywhere I looked I saw exhausted, old-fashioned machinery, heavy overmanning and questionable organization.

It was a relief to leave the foundry, but the press-shop proved to be even worse. The presses were American, European and Japanese, but the dyes were original (they were old when they were bought secondhand from the British Motor Corporation and Vauxhall). Even the most cursory examination showed me that the body panels being stamped out were all different, and the next stage, the assembly shop, looked like a vast game of spillikins and it was difficult to discern an assembly line at all. All the bodies were spot-welded by hand and a considerable amount of bashing and hammering was required to make anything join to anything else. I found it all the more amazing that the Ambassador had such a reputation for strength when everything depended upon these sweating welders with their ancient hand-welding techniques and a lump hammer.

The paint shop proved to be equally antiquated. Each Ambassador was given a single coat of primer – sometimes in the dipping tank – and two top coats, but covering the cars with paint seemed as much a matter of luck as of judgement. I cheered up a bit when I discovered that they were about to invest in a new dipping tank, but during the whole of my visit to the Hindustan Motors car plant, I did not see a single computer on site and no systems were evident anywhere at all. Cars used to be built like this, but I could not see how Hindustan Motors could possibly compete in the expanding Indian market, let alone in world markets, if they continued like this.

And still I hadn't seen it all. The final inspection bay was quite incredible. There were no white-coated inspectors flicking the occasional duster. The main tools of the Hindustan Motors' inspectors appeared to be seven-pound hammers and two-foot wrenches. The final inspection bay was more like a final rectification bay and the cacophony of hammering, thumping and bumping that went on in order to force recalcitrant bits of car back into shape, was mind-boggling. However, it did occur to me that if the cars could take this sort of beating, then they'd be able to stand any Indian road ... but anything farther from modern standards of quality would be difficult to imagine.

I was then taken to the Research and Development (R&D) department in conditions of great secrecy: the BBC cameras were excluded. Interestingly enough the R&D department were collaborating with both Lotus and Ricardo International Plc in Britain, but the majority of the work of the R&D department seemed to be designing new panels and other external pieces. The R&D department's latest venture was the development of a new bumper which, as well as being more effective, will save them 200 rupees per car (roughly £4). This is obviously a good thing, but it's not the fundamental work of an R&D department who should be working on designs for new models rather than designing new pieces for old models.

The Hindustan Motors' car plant must be the most old-fashioned plant I've seen in many many years, and there is very little that I can say in its favour. I did discover that they carried the smallest amount of finished stock that I'd seen in a car factory for a long time, but that was probably because daily production numbers were relatively small.

The plant produces approximately eighty-five Ambassadors and fifteen Contessas a day which, by international standards, is low. They also make 3000 Trekkers a year and they have signed a deal with the American giant, General Motors, to make a version of the Opel Astra (the Vauxhall Astra) in Baroda. However these figures are still far too low. I told Mano Pachisia that I felt they were trapped. Their main competitive advantage was the fact that they had no capital cost but equally well they were not making enough money to justify reequipping. I felt the actions they were taking were far too slow to resolve their problems within any sort of reasonable financial timescale.

I emerged from the Hindustan Motors' car plant extremely shaken by its antique nature, but not as shaken as I was about to be when I drove an Ambassador around Hindustan Motors' test track. Needless to say I was equipped with a top of the range, Isuzu-engined, air-conditioned Ambassador, the ultimate dream of most Indian executives. The whole experience was surprising. The steering was light and positive and the lock was quite good, the clutch and gears were excellent, and the foot brake would quite literally have stopped a tank (which was probably just as well from time to time). The less appealing features of the car were the negligible battery capacity and the handbrake, which was weak. However the test track was simply unbelievable. It was made of Indian pave, loosely linked by pot-holes, and even by Indian standards the track was mind-bogglingly awful and I had some difficulty surviving three laps. All Hindustan Motors' cars are tested on this bottom-shattering road to simulate the life they'll lead on Indian roads. It was certainly the worst Indian road I have ever been on, and I could not help wondering how many cars had fallen to pieces on it. I was told that the redoubtable Ambassador could manage 10 000 laps on this track before it collapsed!

If you order a new Ambassador in India there is a four-week delivery period and the majority of cars are driven to the customer, so the delivery mileage might be as much as 2000 or more by the time you receive your new car. And amazingly Britain is importing Ambassadors. Since 1992, the London-based Fullbore Motors Ltd have brought a few dozen Ambassadors into Britain for assessment, demonstration and testing, and they have redesigned the Ambassador to ensure that it meets the European Union (EU) regulations on exhaust emissions, defrosting capabilities etc. The response to Fullbore's initial advertisements in motoring magazines astonished Fullbore's joint partners, Mark Owen-Lloyd and Jo Burge. It exceeded their most optimistic expectations, and now that the testing and redesigning process is complete, Fullbore Motors expect to import between 200 and 300 Ambassadors between February and December 1995 at an approximate retail price of £6850.00. They are also negotiating the sale of their multi-point fuel injection system back to Hindustan Motors, so that, when the time comes, Hindustan Motors will be able to comply with future Indian exhaust emissions regulations.

There's no doubt that the Ambassador is a rugged car and I must admit to feeling rather enthusiastic about it after my test drive. It may be that there is a place for it in other parts of the Third World. The Ambassador is the stuff of every Indian car driver's dreams and the good news is that it is cheap, at least by European standards. It currently retails for approximately £5500.00 and is probably the simplest car in the world today. It's easy to repair and it's tough. And in a country like India where there aren't great streams of service stations, it's invaluable to have something you can repair yourself with bits of wire. High hopes were pinned on the relaunched model, and I read an article by a Japanese journalist who reckoned that the Ambassador was the right car to impress your girlfriend with, and every Indian I have ever come across says that the Ambassador is virtually impossible to destroy.

At lunch I met Mr A. S. Narayanan the new Executive Vice President in charge of all plants for Hindustan Motors. He was seeing the Hooghly plant for the first time. I pressed on with my concerns about their lack of urgency and was greeted with the predictable reply that the Birla family was rich enough to face the losses and in any event the government would not allow the closure of the Hindustan Motors' plant. This seemed to me to be more or less the argument British Leyland had once put forward, only to be subsequently closed down, so I tried to warn Mr Narayanan that I thought they could be in for a rude shock.

I said that the Calcutta car plant was one of the only remaining vertically integrated car plants in the world, car manufacturing everywhere else being an assembly job. I told Mr Narayanan that they could make a start by demerging the individual units and making them self-standing, and I said that I was convinced that, even making the cars in their present fashion, things could only be improved by more than halving the numbers employed (from 12 000 to around 5000), and if they endeavoured to change to an assembly system the numbers employed could go down significantly lower than that. I stressed once more that, as well as the short term question of stemming the losses, the real question was the longer term strategic problem of how to utilize the engine plant at Pithampur. I told him that I had considerable doubts about Hindustan Motors' ability to sell the 30 000 cars they were claiming for the year and that, even with the new engine, it would take time to relaunch the revised and improved Ambassador. Mr Narayanan appeared to agree with me on many of these points.

I had been asked to speak to about seventy of the middle and senior managers, pointing out that the role of the car plant was to be a cash cow to raise enough money to justify investment in new plants and new models. Despite a fairly passionate address, the only questions I was asked were along the lines of how could they compete with this technology, these unions or this history, with no capital? By this time I felt pretty sorry for Mano Pachisia and the new executive vice president who had to rely on this already defeated bunch of managers. The executive vice president told me he agreed with my comments but thought there was insufficient management will to tackle the problems that lay ahead. I told him I feared they would probably have to get rid of some of the managers in order to achieve a new and sufficiently energetic approach to the problem because their products face stiff competition in post-liberalization India, chiefly from Maruti Udyog Ltd (MUL), whom I was to visit before I put my final thoughts on Hindustan Motors to C.K. Birla himself.

Maruti Udyog Ltd (MUL)

Jane Sabherwal and I went to visit the Maruti car plant without Robert whose 'flu-induced eruptions had reached force ten on the Thirkell Richter scale and, thankfully, forced him to retire to bed with a compote of pills contributed by the crew.

Maruti Udyog Ltd was established in February 1981 and was then owned 100% by the Indian Government who, after the liquidation of Maruti Limited (a private company), acquired its assets and formed Maruti Udyog Ltd. This government-owned company established a joint venture with the Suzuki Motor Corporation and today Maruti Udyog Limited is owned 50% by the Indian Government and 50% by Suzuki. It is based in New Delhi.

Maruti began production in November 1983 with a production facility of 100 000 cars a year. We met the Managing Director, Mr

Bhargava, who was, I thought, an inspired choice to manage the Maruti plant. He had been a career civil servant and was marked out as a high-flyer but, like so many people I've met who have served with the Indian Army, he had become dissatisfied with the Indian Civil Service when he worked in the Cabinet Office. Mr Bhargava had been involved with Maruti from the very beginning and was responsible for the initial market survey which showed that only a small, cheap, urban car could produce the necessary volume of 100 000 cars a year. He had then led a worldwide search for a partner, culminating in the choice of Suzuki.

The result of Mr Bhargava's market research was an 800cc mini-car which, when the order book was opened, received its 100 000 orders instantly, and which is now by far the largest-selling car in India. Maruti also manufacture a five-door hatchback, the Maruti YE2, with a one-litre engine. Trial production of the YE2 began in April 1993 and by the end of 1994 Maruti had manufactured 6335 YE2s, 1649 of which were exported to Europe under the name Suzuki Alto. At the moment this car constitutes a very small percentage of Maruti's sales, but due to its popular 800cc mini-cars Maruti's passenger car market share is currently 72.7%, and the capacity of the Maruti factory was increased in 1994 by 70 000 units at a total investment cost of US$218m.

Hindustan Motors and Premier Automobiles have lost market share to Maruti Udyog mostly because they continue to manufacture cars with obsolete designs and technology. In 1991 the vehicle division of the giant Tata Group, the Tata Engineering and Locomotive Company Limited (Telco) launched two passenger cars to add to the competition; previously they had only made trucks. Telco launched the Sierra and the Estate and have entered into a joint venture with Mercedes, so Hindustan Motors face further competition from them and from Premier Automobiles' link with Peugeot and Sipani's link with Rover (to manufacture a version of the Rover Montego).

Hindustan Motors' current production capacity is 45 000; Premier Automobiles is also 45 000 and Telco's passenger vehicle production capacity is 20 000. In the year to March 1993 Maruti sold 121 626 vehicles compared with Hindustan Motors' 21 897, Premier Automobiles' 17 388 and Telco's 3908. Maruti have, self-evidently, achieved pole position by a long way.

The philosophy of the Maruti plant has been to produce Suzuki-designed cars in India, and to 'Indianize' the production. Over time, the Japanese content of the 800cc mini-car has fallen from over 80% to between just 4%–5%. This accounted for the surprising lack of robots in a brand new plant: robots are employed only where consistency of quality is unobtainable through hand work. At every stage they had done the sums to decide whether rigorous quality control of work practices and cheap labour was more effective than automation. The plant employed approximately 4500 people to produce its expected 1995 volume of 200 000 vehicles. Nevertheless, the labour costs were less than 2% of sales. Moreover, because of the lack of robotization the capital costs were intrinsically lower than other comparable car plants. The major problems have been achieving consistent work practice. Like my friends at the Hindustan Motors engine plant in Pithampur, all the other things, such as single dining facilities, uniforms, approachability, involvement of management and so on were much in evidence, but consistency of quality was a constant battle.

Maruti have also had the same problems in improving the quality and consistency of Indian suppliers. For example, no Indian supplier was able to produce the required quality of steel. It therefore had to be imported from Japan and, since the appreciation in value of the yen, from Germany. The quantities of steel were too small to justify investment in a mill by Maruti themselves, or to encourage any other Indian company to take the risk of trying to build up demand elsewhere. In Mr Bhargava's view, Indian manufacturers are still looking for no-risk, guaranteed-return investments. He said that the Maruti plant was still only turning a 2%–3% return on capital, although the suppliers were doing much better. Despite this poor return, Maruti had succeeded in self-financing almost all its expansion, so the cash flow situation must have been pretty healthy.

The Maruti plant was an eye-opener. It was as modern and competitive in its own way as the Hindustan Motors' engine plant and the philosophy behind the whole business seemed to me to be very appropriate for the future of the Indian car industry.

Conclusions

My final meeting was with C.K. Birla. I felt that I owed it to Ramesh Rath at Pithampur to make sure that his messages got through to the highest level I could reach. I had not seen either C.K. or his father for many years, although I had met them on previous trips to India in my ICI days. C.K. thanked me for the visits I had made to the Hindustan Motors plants. He told me that he had heard what I had said to his managers, and that my comments had been viewed by Ramesh Rath and Mr Narayanan as thought-provoking and most helpful.

I began by complimenting C.K. on the Pithampur plant and his own contributions to it in terms of insistence on world competitive manning, quality and environmental conditions. I then said how worried I was that the heavy overcapitalization and underutilization of Pithampur must be costing the company a substantial sum of money. I was concerned that they were banking on Calcutta for their salvation and I was not sure this would be forthcoming. C.K. agreed that Pithampur could only make money when working three shifts, and that the loading on the factory was absolutely vital.

Secondly I said that although I thought the management at Pithampur was excellent, I was not clear whether they had the headroom to do things like seeking other work, especially export work. I was worried that there seemed to be no one with the responsibility for loading up the plant. I told him I believed the laboratories and quality control department should be a separate profit centre, which would be of great value in raising the entire standard of manufacturing in Central India, as well as making money in the process.

My third worry was the Calcutta car plant, unless changes could be made much more quickly than the present management were contemplating. They were relying on the riches and good nature of the Birla family, coupled with what they saw as the government's determination to make sure they did not go under. They did not realize the necessity of cutting costs in order to survive.

C.K. said it was a pity I had not had time to visit the Bangalore plant which manufactures heavy equipment. He said that it was a very different cup of tea with state-of-the-art technology. It had been loaded up on flexible machining orders and was making money already. But he did agree that more urgent action must be taken in Calcutta, and said this was the basis on which the new Executive Vice President, Mr Narayanan, had been appointed. He still believes the old Ambassador will last a further ten years, and he has great faith in the relaunched model, but he is primarily relying on the link with General Motors and the introduction of the Opel Astra, which is being built on a brand new greenfield site in Baroda. C.K. was fairly conservative about market growth. He estimated that in India overall the car market would grow to no more than 500 000 cars within five years. He expects that his customers will want to trade up, so the Contessa and the Astra will eventually be the top of the mark Indian produced cars. He took my point about the possibilities of exporting the existing Ambassadors and Trekkers to Third World countries and said he was going to try to develop this opportunity. He also promised to think about allowing Pithampur more autonomy.

I left C.K. feeling concerned and sceptical. I hope the relaunched Ambassador takes off, but I must confess, even with growth of the Indian car market, I still doubt Hindustan Motors' ability to load up the Pithampur engine plant on the basis of the relaunched Ambassador alone. I was told later that the engine plant are going to be allowed to take in work from elsewhere – and that they certainly need to do – but how Hindustan Motors balance the investment in the engine plant with some future model, is, I think, the very big problem which they have to resolve strategically.

A sad postscript to this section is that I learned that Ramesh Rath died on 6 April 1994 of a cardiac arrest. I know that his death is a tragic loss to both Hindustan Motors and to all those who knew him, but most particularly to his family.

4. Simla: the beginning and the end

India and the British: Britain and the Indians

My last port of call, the final destination on my Indian journey, was Simla in the foothills of the Himalayas in Northern India. It was really rather a fitting final destination because it was also, in a sense, my first destination: my parents met and married there. I haven't been back since I was four, and as I gazed out at the magnificent countryside through the train window, I wondered what Simla would be like and whether I would recognize anything. I was really excited about returning.

Simla remains cool in the baking summer months when the plains smoulder in the heat and dust. In the days of the Raj the British administration came to Simla every summer. They brought their offices with them as well as all their personal paraphernalia. They also brought their attitudes and their traditions. Of all the places I revisited in India, none was so evocative of early twentieth-century Britain as Simla.

We travelled, slowly, on the Delhi-Kalka express. Indeed, if this speed was the way an express train travelled, I wondered what on earth happened on a slow train. But at least the lack of speed gave us the opportunity to see the breathtakingly beautiful countryside, and we arrived at Kalka, in the foothills of the Himalayas, in the early evening. We transferred to two Ambassadors for the remainder of our journey up to Simla. The edge of the road disappeared vertically into the valleys below us as we climbed ever higher towards Simla, and the houses along the way were built in the most precarious fashion, cantilevered out over the drops. There were pines everywhere, the like of which I

70

do not remember ever having seen before. As a keen gardener I know that many species of pine originate in the Himalayas, but I had not realized that there was such a vast range.

It was a brilliantly clear evening and Simla sparkled in the night sky as we drew near. Our hotel, The Oberoi Clarkes Hotel, looked like a transplanted British bungalow cantilevered out over the side of a precipice, proudly sporting stockbroker Tudor half timbers on the front. Robert, who had travelled on ahead, greeted us with warm samosas and cold beers – both most welcome – and a report that the Thirkell 'flu epidemic was over. We sat in the lounge overlooking the valley and exchanged news and brought each other up to date until, at about 1.30 am, we took to our beds. My room contained Waring and Gillow's best 1930s furniture and had a rather neglected feeling. It occurred to me that it must have looked just the same, although less neglected, in my father's day.

The next day our first stop was to organize some photographs in Mr Bindra's photographic emporium which was built in 1937. It seemed to me that nothing much had changed since then; Mr Bindra's photographic equipment dated from 1938, and his window was filled with photographs of stiff, grimacing, impeccably dressed, emotionless British army officers and civil servants and sturdy-looking Anglicized Indians, all wearing tweeds and, in some cases, Trilbys. Most of the photographs had been taken in the 1920s and 1930s.

Mr Bindra began in this business at the age of eleven and, despite his aged appearance, he turned out to be a mere fifty-one. It appeared that Mr Bindra was Simla's society photographer: the David Bailey of Northern India, but the most modern photographs he had on display must have been taken in the 1960s. However he was still able to pay the rent on one of Simla's most fashionable streets, so something was bringing in money. After sitting in front of Mr Bindra's camera (the like of which I have only seen before in the Science Museum) for an age, we were eventually promised our photographs later that day.

We then went to the market place where everything hummed with excitement and activity and I was in my element. The market place was like any Indian bazaar, except that the streets were about four feet wide with shops cantilevered out above them and steep, rickety staircases leading to the upper levels. Some of the buildings appeared so unstable that at any moment I expected to see the whole lot slide down the mountainside. There was a solid mass of bustling, chattering Indians everywhere, and there was barely room for a hand cart, or a well-loaded Sherpa, to negotiate the steeply inclined, narrow streets.

We then walked on up from the market place and found ourselves in a street that was so unlike the bazaar we might have walked into another world. We stood on a British high street: it could have been the high street in Ross on Wye. And this street, perched as it was right at the top of India, struck me as an apt allegory for the relationship between Britain and India during the years of British rule. A piece of Britain had been, as it were, parachuted in, and once there it had made no attempt to blend in with the culture of its landing place, rather it had simply superimposed its own culture. There was a Post Office and a theatre called the Gaiety Theatre, and lamp posts that must have been transplanted straight from Britain. And, to me, the worst of it all was that in the days of the Raj the Indian people were not allowed up here. I thought that spoke volumes more than anything else possibly could about British attitudes, in those days, to the countries they ruled and to the peoples and the cultures of those countries.

But whenever I visit India I also always feel extraordinarily nostalgic, and therein lies the paradox. I have a deep and abiding love for a country which I might never have known if my countrymen had not once ruled there, but in which my countrymen did not always exhibit the most sympathetic behaviour. The contrast between the wide asphalt street that I stood on, with its half-timbered stone buildings, its town hall and shops with plate glass display windows, and the higgledy-piggledy but vibrant bazaar with its hundreds of tiny shops and some shopkeepers selling directly from the pavement, could barely have been more poignant, nor more illustrative of the differences of approach and attitude of the two cultures.

I looked down the high street. At one end stood the church where my parents were married, and at the other end stood the Grand Hotel where they conducted their courtship. We walked along to the Grand Hotel, which is now an Indian Civil Service holiday home, but I had no difficulty picturing the band playing for a tea dance and my father and mother, dressed in their best, striving awkwardly to communicate with each other. I felt them both very close to me throughout the whole of my time in Simla, and the process of filming began to seem rather like a series of interruptions.

The tremendous contrasts between the Simla of the British and the Simla of the Indians left me with very mixed feelings, and my many conversations with professors and industrialists and men and women of influence in India during my journey, left me feeling pretty unhappy about some of the legacies left by my forebears. Things like the seemingly impenetrable bureaucracy, and the attitudes to education. The reinforcement of the class system and the attitudes to business. All of these things have hindered India from taking its rightful place in the world, and I think it's very possible to argue that the British did as much harm to India as they did good.

Indian bureaucracy is directly inherited from the British, and the British handed on the civil service conviction that administration is the highest form of service to one's country. One of the professors I talked to said that there is a strong inherent Indian urge towards the bureaucratic approach which was merely reinforced by the British but, whatever the origins, bureaucratic administration doesn't create wealth. In fact bureaucrats tend to think that the creation of wealth is corrupt, but a surfeit of bureaucracy puts the brakes on enterprise and wastes, indeed deadens, innovation.

Another British legacy, the British public school system, has been, I believe, more detrimental to India than it has been beneficial. Daly College and Mayo College are, in their own ways, just like Eton. Every Indian who leaves Daly College thinks he is a superior being, and there is a lingering belief that what matters is who you know, not what you know, which, in my opinion, is a decidedly unhelpful attitude for the creation of successful businesses.

The British class system has inhibited the British over the years, and its arrival in India undoubtedly reinforced the Indian caste system, to the detriment of both countries and of both cultures. I think many people in both countries are trying to pull down class barriers, and certainly if I look back over my life, social mobility has totally changed in Britain. But I still believe that as long as class, or caste, retain even

73

the smallest influence in British or Indian societies, economic growth will be inhibited.

And then there is the contempt for commerce and wealth creation, and indeed for industrialists themselves, which exists in both countries. In the days of the Raj any businessman, no matter how distinguished, was considered a boxwallah (a pejorative Anglo-Indian term for a commercial European person), and was expected to be inordinately grateful if he was allowed to sit at the same table as an army man, or an Indian Civil Service man. Indians learned from the British that industrialists were lesser beings and civil servants were superior beings. Although I don't think this attitude exists amongst ordinary people in Britain, or in India, any longer, I still think that there lurks, within the British establishment, and within certain elements of Indian society, an inner conviction that people who earn their living as I do are inferior to people who earn their living in the professions. It makes me angry and it makes me sad for both countries, after all, the economic health of both countries is carried on the backs of the poor devils who actually make and sell things, isn't it?

It seems to me that in India, and in Britain, economic success is not seen as the linchpin that it is. Economic success means a better future for all Indians and all Britons, but it has been looked upon as something which is almost irrelevant when measured against political problems or the pursuit of bureaucratic control. The fact of the matter is that the ability of countries to make choices and to improve the lot of their citizens depends totally upon their economic success. And that is why I, for one, am proud to be an industrialist.

And what, you may be wondering, do I consider to be the beneficial legacies that the British left to the Indians? Well, there are some, and they are valuable. The British introduced an honest, if cumbersome, administration system which India needed badly, and they gave the Indians the use of the English language which is a priceless commercial gift today. The British introduced a secular state and the rule of law, and even if the adversarial system tends to be slow, it is, generally, the fairest form of law.

But now I feel that the task facing Britain and India is to change the things that need to be changed. There are real similarities between the two countries because Britain and India wear common shackles: the shackles of bureaucracy and class, or caste, and the shackles of disdain for the creation of wealth. It is time for both countries to break free from these shackles and to move on into the modern world.

India: into the twenty-first century

We travelled back to Delhi by train, through achingly beautiful country-side, to catch our aeroplane back to Britain. As we travelled I thought about the businesses I had visited and the difficult move away from protected markets and a protected economy that India has begun. I must confess to feeling rather more cynical about the speed at which India can adjust than I did at the beginning of my journey.

I came to India believing, quite sincerely, that the first twenty-five years of the next century would be India's time. I have put my timing back on that, as indeed all timing is put back in India, whether it's the time an aeroplane is due to depart, the time a meeting is due to start, or the time that it will take India to achieve a competitive place in world markets. India is running to try and catch a departing train: much of the rest of the world is roaring away, and India is starting from a long way behind. India must achieve an absolutely frightening rate of change in order to establish the necessary growth patterns. And India needs very high growth. The population of India increases by 2% per annum (although, frighteningly, with the exception of 1981, every Indian census since the beginning of this century has shown a decline in the number of women as against the number of men), and this 2% increase means that nobody can become properly richer unless 5% economic growth, or more, is achieved. And to make a dramatic impact on poverty – the enduring facet of India – double figure growth is preferable, and for a long period of time. This has happened elsewhere in the world, so it can happen in India and the Indians are capable of it. The question is will India and the Indians choose to make it happen?

One of the impediments to Indian economic success is that India is about families, and extended families, rather than about a country. The primary loyalty for most Indians is to the family and their secondary loyalty, which comes quite a long way after their primary loyalty, is to their country. Now I don't suppose that Britain is full of people who

75

wake up every morning and run up a Union Jack but, nevertheless, I think that if most Brits felt that something was good for Britain, by which they meant the majority of people in the country, they would rally to the call. I am less clear that that would necessarily happen in India. I feel that there's no overriding conviction in India that the well-being of India is necessary for the well-being of everybody in India, and if I am right about this, then this attitude will continue to pose considerable obstacles to India's economic success.

I also believe that Indians don't understand profit in the sense of it being an absolute prerequisite for economic success. Rather, they believe profit is merely for the aggrandizement of the individual. But without economic success, nothing can be done to improve the lot of the Indians. Indian people care desperately about their fellow humans, so, if you're a manager in India, you are continuously being torn between the needs of the 'family' and the economic needs of the business. Thus I saw businesses where they had been unable to take the decision to make employees redundant, but I also saw Vikas Kasliwal manage this difficult process, proving that it is not impossible, even in this family-oriented culture.

Another problem that India will have to overcome along the road to economic success is the attitude – still sadly prevalent in Britain as well – that the customer is somebody to be worked down to, rather than led upwards. Indian customers particularly don't yet know what is available on the wider world markets, but it should not be assumed that just because a person doesn't have the opportunity to buy, for instance, a radial tyre, that he, or she, wouldn't buy one if they could. In Britain, as in India, there is a lack of inner conviction that the customer really is king. We British have only recently come to the conclusion that business is all about pleasing the customer, but in India, as I have mentioned before, there is, sometimes, a dismissal of the customer which borders on absolute contempt, and this must change.

India's fundamental economy is still agricultural. Seventy-five per cent of Indians work in agriculture, and the only way that they can hope to improve their lives is through greater industrial success and adding value to the crops that they grow so abundantly. One of the professors I talked to believed that India's immediate future lay very largely in agriculture, and adding value to agricultural raw materials for export, as well as making massive infrastructural investments.

India, from having been unable to feed itself, is now an exporter of agricultural produce on a vast scale. In 1992–93 India exported 6bn tons of agricultural produce at a value of 58bn rupees, but the products can only get to world markets through greater use of industrial processes, so industrialization is the key to giving India the choices that it needs. The future of India depends upon getting the services and the infrastructure delivered at effective costs and in effective ways. India must become able to attract the best in the world to invest.

India's manufacturing base is too small, just as it is in Britain, and the challenge facing both countries is the massive restructuring of our industrial bases. The British have been doing this for some time, but there is still further to go, and amongst those I encountered on my Indian journey, I met many who were deeply concerned about the time it will take to restructure the Indian industrial base. The question in India is how quickly the Indian industrialists can adapt, because if India is really to join the world community fully, then India must be able to earn its living overseas.

Amongst the women I met, there was concern that the position of women in India has barely changed over the years, and they told me that there were hardly any women in business in their own right. I was slightly surprised to hear this, but it is obviously one of many problems that must be overcome if India is to move ahead.

There are also too many Indian firms in which the workforce are looked upon purely as pairs of hired hands, as opposed to people who can contribute. This reinforces the link between literacy and economic success, and education and economic success, that is so necessary. India must strive to reach the 60% literacy rate that is required for economic take-off.

The highlight of this Indian journey has been to see some Indian plants, sadly too few of them – but at least some – that are up to internationally competitive standards, such as the Hindustan Motors engine plant. Such plants prove that India is more than capable of competing with the best in the world, and unless you're up with the best in the world you aren't anywhere in the world.

Many of those I met felt that the total adoption of all British systems in 1947, after Partition, had been a great mistake. British administrators had merely been replaced by Indian administrators, and the opportunity to create a totally new approach to the management of India had been missed. But I felt, as well as an ever-abiding love and continuous fascination for India, continued optimism for the future. I'm convinced that liberalization is necessary for India; there's no doubt that a lot of the damage done here is due to having been economically isolated from the world for so long. But the sheer scale of the task of changing attitudes in India (Indians are, in a way, as entrenched and conservative in their views as the British) is monumental. Bureaucracy is resistant to change and I think India faces a tough time ahead, however I remain optimistic for India's future.

The abilities of India's people, with their hard-working, cheerful, tolerant approach, coupled with the unquestionably high standards of their professional managers, should enable the country to soar away once the right conditions are created. The absence of these conditions mirrors the British experience in many ways, and is a reflection of so many of the problems we have been struggling with. The potential size of the Indian market and demand is so enormous that once India opens up to compete with the best, it will be a formidable force in the world. But for the first time since I have been concerned with India in an industrial sense, some things are beginning to go right. The changes of attitude, not only on the part of the politicians and the general public, but on the part of business people themselves have been immense. I hope India will be able to seize the opportunities that lie ahead, and that things will improve at a faster rate than they have done in the past.

The journey around my father

We allowed plenty of time to catch the aeroplane back to Britain which, in the event, was just as well. The hordes of people that I had expected to be at the airport when we arrived in India and had not found, were now here in their thousands as if to make up for my disappointment at their earlier failure to appear. There were people absolutely everywhere since no Indian ever leaves his homeland without his entire family coming to see him off, and we could barely get our cars within sight of the departure terminal and, as it was impossible to find a porter, we manhandled our baggage ourselves. But once safely aboard our aeroplane it was with a great pang of sadness that I watched India recede into the distance once more.

As we left India behind I, inevitably, found myself thinking about my father. I felt I knew and understood more about him and what drove him than I had ever done before, and thinking about him made me realize, yet again, how much we are the products of our upbringing and our beliefs. My father was a man of the utmost integrity and honour, but he lacked any real warmth towards anybody and the things for which he is remembered by those who worked for him in India are his sternness and his lack of friends. He was respected but he was not loved by those who knew him, and I consider that a sad thing.

I reproached myself less at my inability to reach him, for nobody else seemed to have been any more successful. I grieve for him, however. He spent a lifetime of totally dedicated service to creating completely the wrong values and approaches for India's future success.

I used to be driven, at least while I served in the Navy, by a belief that if I proved myself to my father I would somehow earn his attention, if not his affection. But, as I discovered on this journey, my father lived totally by his own ideals, and one of those was never to show any emotion. His ideals also required one to shoot everything that moved, be brilliant at games and always to keep a stiff upper lip. Undoubtedly these ideals harmed my father as they have, I believe, harmed Britain. On reflection, I consider it a lucky escape that my father did not bring me up so that these ideals were not drummed into me as they were into the hapless princes of Dhar and Udaipur. My father's ideals – which many people in both countries still abide by – are utterly contrary to the flexibility and the sensitivity that is so necessary for communication. Without communication neither the British nor the Indian nations can hold out much hope for future success at any level.

Onwards and upwards

Now I want to revisit some of the other formative parts of my life and see how they've changed, and whether they have changed fast enough to enable us British to earn our living in a very very changed world.

79

PART TWO

5. Back to school

Education is the foundation, the bedrock upon which a country builds its economic success. Its importance cannot be underestimated and yet I feel there is something very wrong with the state of education in Britain today. The majority of pupils in this country leave secondary school far less well-qualified than those of our major economic competitors, yet we spend more on education as a percentage of GDP than, for example, the Germans or the Japanese but their percentage of school leavers with no qualifications is markedly lower than ours. Quite apart from the economic implications, this is a tragic waste of Britain's potential.

I'm an industrialist and all my working life I've been worried about the relevance of British education and British educational systems to our economy as a whole. The battle today is an economic one and it can only be won by people who are really well-prepared, really well-educated and whose potential is used to the fullest. I am convinced that the British educational system does not give all our youngsters the opportunity to achieve their potential, and that is why I wanted to take a look at British education as part of this series of *Troubleshooter* programmes.

I believe passionately in the value of a good education and since I retired from ICI eight years ago, I have devoted a considerable amount of time to education. Among other things I have been chairman of the governors of St James's and the Abbey School, which my granddaughter attended, and was chancellor of Bradford University for six years. I have also spent some time with a headteacher who has been trying to turn round a tough, failing comprehensive: the school had a falling roll, bad academic results and low morale.

I wanted to visit a variety of today's schools in order to form some sort of judgement about their relevance to the changing economic world in which we British find ourselves, and also to find out whether schools are internationally competitive in the same way that industry and business has to be. In a world where everything is changing faster than we are accustomed to, and where Britain is getting left further and further behind, it is our ability to learn new skills, our willingness to embrace change and our belief in our own capacity to be the best in the world, which will be the keys to the future of our country. I believe the role of schools is to build up the self-esteem and self-confidence of the individual so that they are able to adjust and cope. Certainly in the world of industry people can only do what they believe they can do, and fundamental self-confidence and self-belief is, I am sure, nurtured at school. The difficulty is that our education system seems dedicated to demonstrating that anybody who cannot pass exams is in some way a failure.

The area I know most about and where I am most concerned is secondary schools. During the course of filming I visited a variety of comprehensive and public schools. I also talked to some of those who train the teachers and some of those who are undergoing teacher training, but I began my *Troubleshoot* of British education by paying a visit to my old prep school.

Tormore, the school from hell

I have travelled all over the world and experienced both the Arctic and the Antarctic and yet for sheer biting, blinding coldness, my memories always go back to Upper Deal in Kent. As a boy of six, newly returned from India, I was abandoned here at a school called Tormore. My mother, whom I adored, returned to India to be with my father and I found myself in a totally alien world for which my privileged upbringing in India had prepared me very badly. My parents are long dead and I shall never know on what basis Tormore was chosen. I assume, like so many other things in those days, it was through some form of old-boy network – and yet there were very few sons of expatriate parents at Tormore in my day. It was a residential, bossy, preparatory school, with about sixty young boys, and I was miserable there.

My return to Tormore was a unique and unforgettable experience. The school had closed down some time in the 1960s when it amalgamated with a school called Betteshanger School and eventually, in 1980, that school became Northbourne Park School. After Tormore's old buildings were vacated there had been an arson attack ... presumably by somebody who felt much the same way as I did about the school ... The grounds had been sold for housing development and now the remaining shell of the building was to be pulled down and it was to this happy occasion that I had been invited. In fact I scored a double first. Not only did I have the opportunity to knock down the prep school I had so hated but I was also able to drive a demolition bulldozer for the first time in my life. I almost forgot the bitter, biting cold in the excitement of both experiences. I placed the grab over the edge of the dormitory where I had spent my first miserable night at the top of the building, freezing under my only reminder of home, my Tibetan hand-woven rug. The dormitory came down and the demolition of the entire building took less than an hour, by which time all that was left of the school was a pile of crumbling rubble. I was delighted.

In my day Tormore was a typical middle-class preparatory school for boys and the headteacher, Frank Turner, was an archetypal headteacher of the times. He had been awarded a well-deserved Military Cross (MC) during the First World War, had played cricket for Hampshire, and had a love, in almost equal parts, of the classics (Latin and Greek) and beating small boys. He obviously felt he was ideally equipped to produce future leaders of the Empire and those who would have the opportunity of becoming the social, technological and political leaders of the country from the 1950s onwards. The school and its curriculum marched firmly into the future with its eyes set inexorably on the past. Art and science were considered unnecessary for the cricket-playing, Latin-quoting leaders of the future world, and discipline was fierce but arbitrary. Indeed I found the notoriously rigorous

82

discipline of Dartmouth and the Royal Navy an absolute relief from the unpredictability of matters at my prep school. The headteacher's love of inflicting corporal punishment was reflected at every level in the school. Bullying was rife and at least half the boys in my time crept around in terror of being beaten. Moreover boys aged ten, eleven and twelve were encouraged to beat younger boys. What they lacked in physical ability to inflict lasting harm, they more than made up for in enthusiasm and lack of judgement about the amount of corporal punishment which could be administered. I loathed and detested my years at my preparatory school and even at the time it seemed to me to have little relevance to what I might do later in life. It was a very very bleak period.

Tormore trained boys for a world which had already gone even when I attended the school in 1930. To be fair however (which I find difficult with an institution I hated so much), it did inculcate a habit of work and concentration in me which has proved invaluable in later life. Also, because I fitted in so badly with my fellow boys and found it so difficult to make friends, I took refuge in reading. Although the school seemed to me to lack warmth and concern for the children in its care, it did have a massive library with all the favourite boys' authors of the day, and I read them all.

I am glad to say that Northbourne Park School, Tormore's successor, is as different from Tormore as it is possible to be. I met Michael Webbs, the Deputy Headteacher, and when I talked to the youngsters I had an immediate impression of the changes. The pupils at Northbourne Park obviously had plenty of support and encouragement both at home and at school, and I was cheered to see that the remnants of the miserable Tormore had ended up incorporated into such an enlightened school. The children had no hesitation in telling me how much they liked the school and the education they were receiving seemed to me to be highly relevant to today's world.

But what of other less fortunate youngsters who attend less well-endowed schools? What are their chances of achieving success in later life? Unless *all* of our people can give of their best, Britain will be a sorry place come the twenty-first century. I set off to find out how some of Britain's secondary schools were faring and I began with one in Bristol.

83

Lawrence Weston School

It was a bitterly cold February morning when I left home to pay my introductory visit to Lawrence Weston, the school which was to occupy so much of my time in the coming year. I had been told that this school was the worst school in Avon: it had the lowest record of academic achievement in the whole area (the percentage of A to C passes at GCSE in the five core subjects was 6% as against the national average of 50%), and the numbers of pupils had fallen continuously from 1100 to the present, quite inadequate, 270. However, as so often happens, these statistics told only part of the story. Lawrence Weston estate, which lies to the north west of Bristol, is a relatively new industrial estate developed in the 1960s in the days of hope when we were all confident that we were building a new world. At that time the area experienced an unprecedented rate of expansion in the aircraft, chemical and metallurgical industries. The demand for skilled people to man these industries grew every day.

The Lawrence Weston estate was set up as a completely self-sufficient area. Shops and churches were built as well as semi-detached and detached housing and low-rise blocks of flats. The estate was spaciously laid out in keeping with the best theories of the time and there was plenty of greenery. The whole area nestles in the lea of a hill and is only a few miles from Clifton, a middle-class Bristol suburb, and within ten miles of the heart of Bristol itself. At the time, it must have seemed a triumph of the planners' art.

When Lawrence Weston school was founded, there was an almost evangelical determination to build something better for the future. Many of the hopes of the area were put into the school itself and such was the feeling of optimism that other schools were quickly drawn in to the estate. A Catholic school called St Bede's had been founded almost adjoining Lawrence Weston school. But it wasn't just the staff who were convinced that they were creating something which would last. The parents were involved and determined to obtain the best for their children and the feeling of growth and endless expansion created a tangible feeling of optimism.

But things have changed since those halcyon days. The area has suffered continual retrenchment as the industries concerned sought to

84

cope with intensifying world competition by decreasing numbers and increasing productivity. New investment left long ago and most of the businesses are fighting for their lives. As the numbers employed in local industries have gone down, their original owners have left to seek their fortunes elsewhere. Most of the inhabitants were of the same sort of age when they moved onto the estate in the 1960s, and they have now reached middle age and their children have moved away. As more and more of the original families left the estate, the council moved single parent families in. But what might have been an ideal solution for a small number, speedily became a trap. As the sources of employment in the area fell and single parents found themselves miles away from alternative employment, things became more and more difficult for them and the whole mix of society on which the Lawrence Weston school depends for its children has altered radically. Added to that, the Lawrence Weston estate has become synonymous with crime, drugs, joy-riding, ram-raiding and widespread unemployment. The taxi driver who took me from the station to the school said that both the area and the school had such a bad reputation that he certainly wouldn't consider sending his children to Lawrence Weston school.

Chris Lindup took up the post of headteacher at Lawrence Weston in 1991. He had arrived at the school almost fifteen years ago, and spent eight years as deputy head and three years as acting headteacher. When he took over as head, he was conciliatory and he sought consensus. He is an unusual headteacher in many ways and the struggles over which he triumphed in his personal background give him both a sympathy and an understanding of the problems faced by the pupils at Lawrence Weston. Chris was brought up in impoverished circumstances in Mill Hill, North London, and seemed set for a life of failure. He failed the eleven-plus and was unsuccessful at school, but he was, by his own admission, lucky enough to come across teachers who gave him a second chance at believing in himself, teachers who encouraged him to achieve. Gradually he found himself doing better until, after studying at the Open University, he went on to obtain a masters' degree in the management of education from Bath University. He taught in the North of England and subsequently at an approved school in the Bristol area before joining Lawrence Weston.

85

Chris's approach to his job is entirely in line with my own ideas. He understands the distressing family circumstances that many of his pupils face, and believes that his primary job is to provide a stable background for them and to build up their self-belief and self-esteem. If he can achieve that he believes the exam results will improve, but in the meantime he is faced with an academic rating system which considers schools on the basis of their exam results, rather than on longer-term objectives.

For some time Lawrence Weston was faced with closure and although that threat is past, things are still difficult. Forty per cent of the children at the school receive free meals, which means that 40% of their parents are unemployed, and the school has become an eleven to sixteen-year-old school rather than an eleven to eighteen-year-old school. Chris Lindup freely admitted that he and his staff were not sure how best to motivate their pupils. They had not, so far, succeeded in finding the internal switch that would turn them on and make them want to succeed. In his attempts to find solutions to the problems at Lawrence Weston, Chris had approached an organization called the Pacific Institute. The Pacific Institute is an American organization that runs courses aimed at elevating self-esteem. Chris hoped that by putting his staff through the Pacific Institute course they would, in turn, be able to raise the youngsters' self-esteem.

The school itself was a pretty standard 1960s-built secondary school in reasonable repair and fairly clean and tidy. I entered the building and received some pleasant surprises. The walls were covered with examples of the pupils' art and the general feeling was warm and cheerful. I met Chris Lindup and joined the school at assembly. I was impressed. The pupils were relaxed, smart and attentive and discipline was plainly good, but perhaps this was not altogether surprising because there was a very high staff to pupil ratio. Twenty three staff for the 270 pupils, a ratio that most schools would give their eyeteeth for, although not as a result of such a drastic decline in pupil numbers as Lawrence Weston has suffered.

I began my tour of the school and sat in on several classes. I also talked to the pupils and I was struck by the difference between the relative enthusiasm and optimism of those in Year 7, who had just joined Lawrence Weston, compared with those who were preparing to leave. Most of the youngsters liked the school, although they had rather mixed opinions of the teachers. Everyone spoke glowingly of the English teacher, Jane Phillips, and everybody liked English. Lawrence Weston's results in English were slightly below the national average, but far better than most of the results in the school, proving that it is possible to turn in the results if the teachers are dedicated and the aims are high enough. But when I asked a few of those who were preparing to leave Lawrence Weston what sorts of jobs they were planning to get, I found their answers heartbreaking and distinctly dispiriting: it was as if, at this young age, they had already lost hope. One young man didn't know what he was going to do, but he thought it wouldn't be much and when I asked him why, he replied that it was because he hadn't done well at school.

Many of the young leavers I spoke to were longing to leave the area and hated Lawrence Weston as a place. I then met the three top performers. All of them were loud in praise of the special support they received at the school and I attributed their successes to the high teacher to pupil ratio. Somewhat to my surprise, despite their success they said they had no problems with the other children. There was one boy who was aiming to be a scientist and had obtained an entry to university, and twin sisters, one of whom wanted to be a doctor and one a lawyer. They attributed their success to the support they had had from their parents which they felt most of the young people lacked. Not only were the three of them the school's academic stars but they were also on the prize-winning basketball team, even though the twins are quite short. Their view was that anybody could get what they wanted from the school and that the problems really lay with the personal drive and ambition of the individuals. This was a particular problem for the low achievers because there were not enough tutors to push them on despite the numbers of teachers, and too many of the teachers did not believe that the young people were capable of more. None of the young people I spoke to had any feeling at all about Chris as a leader of the school.

People are not born hopeless, but the young man who didn't know what he would do for a job when he left Lawrence Weston felt hopeless, and as I sat in on some of the classes and observed some of the teachers,

I began to get an inkling about why he had not done as well as he might at Lawrence Weston. I was assigned a guide for my tour of the school called Leah. She was extremely realistic about the school and notably honest in her responses. She felt that she had done reasonably well at the school and was delighted to have a clear idea of what she wanted to do next. She had recently been inspired by a school visit to France to study tourism and follow a career in the travel industry.

First we went to Peter Muddyman's maths class. Leah confided that maths was undemanding and boring. Leah's view was born out by the maths results which were poor, and a few minutes in the class showed why. The class of fourteen year olds were being laboriously taught to draw a straight line graph to demonstrate the exchange rate between pounds sterling and Portuguese escudos. The few pupils who actually bothered to draw the graph drew it within minutes, while the majority were uninterested and not really trying. But since these same pupils do relatively well in English, I could not help feeling that the whole class was being allowed to move at the speed of the slowest pupil.

Peter Muddyman has been head of maths at Lawrence Weston for fourteen years, but when I suggested that the problem he'd set his class had been solved by some of them in about five minutes, and therefore the task was too simple for them, he said that his pupils had an inbuilt feeling that they weren't going to be able to understand maths, so whenever he starts something with them he likes to begin with a simple concept so that they can build on that concept step by step and with certainty. When I asked him what he thought of the Pacific Institute initiative, Peter said that he and the rest of the staff were aware that something was going on, but he did not seem at all clear as to precisely what the initiative was. I left the maths class feeling depressed at the listlessness of the whole thing and quite sure that most of those youngsters were capable of much more than was being asked of them.

My next call was to the Physical Education (PE) class. Huw Rees, the PE teacher, has been at Lawrence Weston twenty-three years and by contrast with Peter Muddyman, he refused to be cowed by Lawrence Weston's poor reputation and was always looking for ways that his pupils could win at something. The basketball team had recently beaten the local grammar school and he had introduced trampolining on the basis that anyone can do it, even unathletic people. He even persuaded me onto one of the trampolines and I must say that I'm still not sure who came off worst, the trampoline or me! Later on I met Becky who, thanks to Huw Rees's initiative and encouragement, had reached competition standard in ice skating. Huw was convinced that more could be made of the youngsters and also that the school could bounce back. He thought the real problems derived from the decline in the neighbourhood and the autocratic leadership style of the previous headteacher. I found it really inspiring to find a man who had given more than twenty years of his life to the school – the last ten in almost continuous decline – who still believed in the youngsters and in the possibility, and indeed desirability, of turning the school around.

Next I met Julie Coulthard who teaches food sciences. Julie was longing for a new initiative and a new start, but she told me that she was afraid to hope for it in case she was disappointed. Julie has been at the school for almost fifteen years and she told me that when she first came the school had a buzz, the parents were involved and supportive and she had really looked forward to coming to work. Despite the school's current limitations, of which they were all so conscious, her class produced a range of excellent goodies: cream *éclairs*, chocolate *gateaux* and biscuits. Julie told me that despite the poverty in the area there was no difficulty in involving the children and no difficulty producing the ingredients and many of them were surprised at their own success. However, most of her pupils had little ambition other than actually to get a job. The idea of a career appeared to be an almost impossible dream and aspirations were low. Julie said she sometimes felt overwhelmed by the serious social problems that the pupils in the school faced, while at the same time her task was to try to educate them to the best of her ability. The more I travelled around Lawrence Weston, the more I worried about what seemed to me to be the low levels of expectation that pervaded the whole place.

Next I met Dave Perryman, one of the science teachers. Dave is widely respected in the school, but when I asked him what he thought of Chris Lindup's initiative he said that he didn't know what it was because although Chris had made a lot of noise about democracy, nobody had been involved and indeed nobody knew when, or even if, anything was going to happen. He also said that he'd been over-whelmed by the work involved for the recent course changes required under the national curriculum and preparing his pupils for their SATs (statutory assessment tests), and that he hadn't had a chance to think about the future of the school. Since the introduction of the national curriculum all teachers have been under tremendous extra pressure, but Dave seemed to me to be particularly despondent.

The children who join Lawrence Weston are, on average, eighteen months behind in reading capability which obviously affects their per-formance in other subjects, but despite their low levels of academic achievement, the school is a friendly place. However I felt as though I had just met the members of a defeated army who knew, and worse, accepted their fate. The teachers were, on the whole, good professional people who had lost hope and the pupils, except for the brightest and the youngest, were underperforming.

I'm a great believer in finding out what parents think, so the next stop was the local cafe. There I asked two single parents who lived in the area what they thought of Lawrence Weston. They complained bitterly about the drugs and crime in the area, and said that most of it was committed by thirteen to eighteen year olds, most of whom were the very children Lawrence Weston school was trying to educate. Neither of them had been prepared to send their children to Lawrence Weston. One of them had been educated there herself and didn't think much of the experience. Both parents were ambitious for their children and concerned about their schooling. One was putting her son into the local Catholic school, St Bede's, and the other wanted to get out of the area altogether but so far had not succeeded.

I went on to meet Phil Chard, the chairman of Lawrence Weston's governors, at a local factory: Britannia Zinc. Phil is the very best sort of rather old style trades union man: decent, concerned, determined to serve the community but, like most working people, he was worried and concerned both for his job, and for the future of the school. His daughter was a former pupil of Lawrence Weston. Phil had become a governor about six years ago when the school had been threatened with closure and had played a major part in the campaign to keep the school open. There had been links between Britannia Zinc and the

90

school from the very beginning and even in these straitened economic circumstances, Britannia Zinc still sponsored the school and helped in a number of ways. They took pupils for work experience, produced spare equipment and so on. Like others, Phil saw the school as being the heart of the estate and believed that if it was to go it would be a disaster locally.

Phil told me that there are something like eleven schools in the north west Bristol area and that at some stage or other, all bar two of them had suffered the same problem of falling rolls. But he said that Lawrence Weston's numbers were the worst affected when they were singled out for closure. Phil also recognized the need to revive the popularity of the school, but he was curiously uninformed about Chris's new initiative and tended to back Chris uncritically without wishing to be involved in what the idea was.

It was time to go back to Chris Lindup and tell him what I felt. I have to admit I wasn't much looking forward to it. When I met Chris this time, he seemed to me to be extremely defensive. He was pinning everything on the new initiative and really did not want to hear any criticisms. However I pressed on with my points because I knew Chris's heart was in the right place and I knew that he fundamentally agreed with me that as long as children are believed in and endlessly encouraged to believe in themselves, they can achieve extraordinary things. But I told Chris that I feared some of his staff would not buy in to his initiative at all, and without a united staff the initiative would probably fail.

Chris said that he thought there was a shared view amongst his staff of the way forward, but I protested that when I had asked his staff about the Pacific Institute initiative and about the school's objectives they had neither produced a shared view, nor known about any precise objectives. I was not entirely convinced by Chris's initiative myself and I suggested to him that it would be better to set a series of limited but achievable objectives, rather than put all his faith in one single solution. For instance, I suggested that he might make one of the school's objectives that everyone should be in school uniform by, say, the beginning of the spring term (the juniors are already in uniform), and that another objective might be that the school would increase its roll by fifty pupils per year; another might be that in three years' time Lawrence Weston would no longer be bottom of the academic league tables. I also said that when each of these targets was achieved, all concerned should be congratulated heartily and publicly: their success should be loudly trumpeted both inside and outside the school. When success is emphasized people feel that they are getting somewhere and anyway nothing breeds success like success. To create the feeling of winning you must measure achievements and improvements, otherwise no one will know whether things are getting better or worse, and the chance for aspirations to grow will be missed.

Chris agreed with some of what I said, but not all. I think he had genuinely expected acclaim and cheers for his initiative and was concerned at what he saw as an unjustified and unwarranted barrage of criticism. I realized that it was unlikely that he would ever change his basic consensus-seeking style of leadership, but I hoped at least that I might be able to sharpen the edges a bit and help him to gain more confidence in his own abilities to manage a change programme.

I pointed out to Chris that there was a big gap between his expectations for the school and his staff's expectations about what could be done. Many of the teachers believed that they were doing the best they could with the materials they had and some felt that their primary responsibility was merely to keep the youngsters off the streets. Chris said that everyone was working very hard and doing their best, but I pointed out that it was not a matter of working harder, it was a matter of working in different ways to raise the self-esteem and aspirations of everyone. The starting point had to be a change in the attitude of the staff and I didn't think that the Pacific Institute should be called in to begin that process, I thought that Chris himself should begin it. I also said that the teachers did not demand enough of their pupils and so the pupils were bored. I was sure that the pupils were capable of far more if they were only encouraged to produce more.

I repeated to Chris some of the comments I had heard about the school from outside, and Chris said that he knew the school needed better marketing, and that the motivation of both his staff and the pupils must be addressed, but he felt that his staff were a team, albeit a team that was unfocused. I said that a team that was not focused was not a team and that that was the heart of his problem. I repeated that he must get as many of his staff on board as he could, and I reiterated my argument about going for incremental change by setting and communicating and getting agreement upon achievable targets whose successful attainment should be recognized and praised. I also said that I agreed with him that better marketing of the school was a must, but that the achievement of some obvious and beneficial changes would inevitably make them all feel more positive about themselves and therefore more confident about marketing themselves.

I left Lawrence Weston worried about various things. Chris's most urgent problem is clearly to get more parents to send their children to his school, but I'm pretty concerned that if the headteacher hasn't persuaded all his teachers to buy into his dream then he has a bigger problem on his hands than he realizes. I have no doubt at all that this school can be dramatically improved, but in order to improve they must (a) know where they're going and (b) be reasonably sure of how they're going to get there.

My next call was to a school of a very different kind indeed.

6. Same era, same age : worlds apart

Clifton College

I crossed the Avon from Lawrence Weston school to Clifton College, a well-known public school in the heart of Clifton, one of Bristol's middle-class suburbs. Both Lawrence Weston and Clifton College are coeducational and both are secondary schools, but there the similarities end. Clifton College was founded in the nineteenth century and is housed in beautiful buildings in a wonderful setting. It has a superb academic record and affords its pupils every possible advantage, and although approximately 20% of Clifton's pupils are on scholarships and so don't pay full fees, the remaining 80% cough up £13 000 per pupil per annum (1995 figures) for the privilege. Public schools don't come cheap.

Although my education at Dartmouth was considered the equivalent of a public school education, the curriculum was specialized so that the passing out examination at Dartmouth was very different from the matriculation exams which, in 1940, were the last exams taken prior to university. It also differed because Dartmouth was run along naval lines with naval discipline and the naval skills of signalling, engineering, basic seamanship and boat handling were obviously of prime importance. The result is that I know very little about the classical public school. My experiences of private schools have been on a rather smaller scale. I was chairman of the governors of my granddaughter's girls' school in Malvern: St James's and the Abbey school. At that school the new headteacher, Elizabeth Mullenger (who came to us with a brilliant background in state education), and I set out quite

94

deliberately to change some of the values which had been prevalent in the school when my granddaughter joined. In particular we developed strong links with state schools as we were both aware that, in some respects at least, the academic achievements at our expensive boarding school did not stand comparison with the best of the state schools. Our school concentrated on trying to develop the whole child (St James's school motto is 'endless encouragement') and our objective was to make sure that every girl left us feeling she had achieved something. However, one of our aims was to teach our students that they were enjoying privileged access to an educational system for which their parents were paying dearly, and that this privilege carried with it responsibilities.

I chose Clifton College because it is within a stone's throw of Lawrence Weston, and yet the two schools are worlds apart. Clifton is the alma mater of the poet, Henry Newbold; the infamous First World War General, Douglas Haig, and the comic actor, John Cleese. I felt that any school that could produce such a diverse group of old boys must have something special going for it. Clifton is almost a caricature of everybody's idea of how a public school should look: there are choristers, cloisters, competitive sports, a splendid chapel and the pupils wear distinctive uniforms. The place reeked of affluence and privilege although it must be said that Clifton has a reputation as a down to earth, liberal public school whose aim is to enable each child to develop as an individual rather than as a recognizable product from a particular background. The school is proud of the fact that whereas you can often tell an Etonian or a Harrovian by the way they look and behave, Cliftonians are themselves: a public school image is neither imposed upon them, nor do they seek to acquire one.

Public schools are a very British phenomenon: *élitist* and successful. Practically all those educated in the public school system go on to further education of one form or another, and although they're few in number, people educated at public schools occupy a disproportionately large number of positions of power in modern Britain. I spoke to a group of 'A' level students and we discussed their ambitions and aspirations and how they felt they had been prepared for their future careers. They were an interesting bunch of young people with strong opinions on every subject you could think of, but the more they talked the more I failed to recognize the world they described. I felt that they were in for a severe shock when they finally emerged from the rather prolonged chrysalis stage that private education and university represents. If we are to compete with the best in the rest of the world it seems to me important that a significant proportion of the natural leadership of our country, no matter what their background, should wish to enter the wealth creating sector. But this was far from the thinking of my sample of students.

Lawrence Weston had disturbed and disappointed me because of the lack of ambition and aspirations of its pupils, but these young people at Clifton had no doubt whatsoever that an interesting, secure and professional future lay ahead of them. What worried me was that none of them seemed to have entertained, for a moment, the thought of a job in industry or manufacturing. It certainly wasn't perceived as a glamorous profession: one young man even went so far as to say that his idea of working in industry was of a whole lot of people designing toilet lids. They dismissed industry as a potential employer because, for them, Britain's industry barely exists anymore anyway. They felt that Britain's manufacturing base has been all but destroyed and that all that exists now are the service industries. I wondered whether they'd thought about what Britain – the world's fourth largest exporter – was exporting, but they felt that there was nothing wrong with exporting ourselves as a service-based economy.

Only one individual amongst them wished to become an engineer, and even he thought he would be unlikely actually to earn his living in engineering but would probably move on to the financial side of things. Two of the group wanted to become diplomats, which they thought of as a more exciting and challenging opportunity than industry, one wanted to be a journalist and another to study history and then become a writer. There was a potential doctor and I'm sure there were future accountants and future lawyers. When we discussed wealth creation, all of them thought about it in terms of financial services or computing; none were remotely interested in manufacturing as such. So it looked unlikely to me that any of the money that had been spent on their education stood much chance of being ploughed back into Britain's economy in the form of wealth creation.

The deputy head, Richard Bland, was as depressed as I was that so many old Cliftonians end up either as lawyers or accountants, rather than business people or entrepreneurs, Britain already produces ten times more accountants than Germany and Japan combined. Britain doesn't need more accountants, what it needs is industrialists and manufacturers. However, to be fair to these students, one obvious reason why they are so uninterested in industry is because of their lack of exposure to it. Civil servants, academics and lawyers come to talk to them about possible future careers, but industrialists don't. And that means that industry isn't projected to them as something in which they might become interested. Britain's school leavers don't really know what a job in industry entails – a fact that I've been bemoaning for years. Britain's industrialists ought to visit schools, often. The irony of all this is that the headmaster, Mr Monro, began his career in industry and has made special efforts to try and encourage industrial links with Clifton College. There are work experience schemes and youth enterprise projects, but none of this seems to have made any impact on the hearts and minds of the youngsters I spoke to.

We moved on to other topics and some of them said that they felt that although Clifton provided an excellent education and phenomenal facilities and resources, it nevertheless fostered a degree of arrogance in the pupils and did not equip them with any real grasp of the problems faced by the majority of the people of Britain. One of the girls told me that she had been shocked by a friend of hers who had asked her if it was true that pupils in the state system were not intelligent enough to take GCSEs, and one of the boys told me, without any sense of irony, that of course, with his background, he would never be faced with the danger of being out of work. Many believed that their responsibilities towards society were merely to do the best they could for themselves and have a clear idea of what they wanted to do. Curiously their confidence came from the idea that Britain had become a more meritocratic society and that, therefore, their excellent education would, in itself, ensure that they rose inexorably to the top of any field they happened to choose.

I felt that Clifton College was not preparing its pupils for tomorrow's world. There was certainly no lack of self-esteem and there was a touching conviction that Britain would remain rich and therefore be able to offer them plenty of opportunity. They mostly believed that they would find their way through life effortlessly, thanks to the chances they had been given at this early age. Depressingly, they may well be right, but if they are it does not seem to me to bode well for the future for our country. As an industrialist I am constantly aware that we are fighting for our survival not only against the best of the developed world, but also against the hungry, energetic, well-educated and determined efforts of highly intelligent people in the Third World, who are resolved to better themselves and their countries. And I have met very few people from Japan or Singapore who are so certain that the mere accident of birth, combined with a good education, would automatically enable them to achieve their ambitions and lead the sort of life to which the young people at Clifton aspired.

I found the stated aims of Clifton – to develop self-belief and the capability of every pupil so that everyone believed they could tackle new ideas and achieve something in life – very much in sympathy with my own view of what education should be about, but in this case the whole thing seemed to have boiled over. These young people were going to face a whole series of rude awakenings before they achieved their ambitions and, worryingly and almost without exception, the products of this privileged background saw themselves as working in the service industries or administration of one sort or another, rather than the actual 'muddy-booted', demanding, but infinitely necessary battle for our economic survival.

It seemed to me that neither Lawrence Weston nor Clifton College were preparing their young people for the tough competitive world which they will all face when they leave school or university. No one seemed to have the attitude that we need to fight the economic battle for Britain, and I found the discussion about industry with the students at Clifton shattering. Their acceptance that British industry is in terminal decline and the feeling that they had no part to play in the reversal of this decline was very depressing indeed. It's hugely important for Britain to create more wealth and we need more of the brightest of our

98

youngsters to apply themselves to these problems. In other countries industry still attracts the best, but in Britain it seems that nothing's changed. British public schools produce bankers and judges and lawyers and accountants; they don't produce industrialists.

However I was cheered by the thought of my next call to a comprehensive near Nottingham. I hoped I would find rather more of Britain's future industrialists there.

Garibaldi School

I have been in touch with the Garibaldi school near Mansfield, in Nottinghamshire, for about six years. The headteacher, Bob Salisbury, took over in 1989 when the previous head retired and he found himself with quite a few problems on his hands. Bob came from a school in an affluent Nottingham City suburb and he was well aware that he would face quite different challenges at Garibaldi. The school had a reputation as a rough school (it had an annual vandalism bill of £42 000, and it had been set on fire on two occasions giving rise to the local saying: 'Red sky at night, Garibaldi's alight'). The school roll had fallen drastically from the original 1100 pupils to a mere 500 and, among the remaining pupils, there was a high level of truancy and bullying was rife. Not surprisingly Garibaldi's exam results were poor. And, as if all that wasn't enough, this area of Nottingham – which is coal country and was once prosperous – has been economically devastated by the closure of 90% of its pits.

Bob Salisbury contacted me after he'd read my book *Making It Happen,* because he felt that the things I was saying about leadership and management in industry could also be applied in a school. We had many discussions about the possible ways forward and I suggested, among other things, that in order to compensate for what I saw as the likely decline in public sector funding, he should think up inventive schemes to fund the things that needed funding which would benefit both the school and the organization from which the extra funds came. I was also able to offer Bob support, encouragement and the occasional bit of advice which a head so often needs. It is extraordinary to me that there is so little specialist training and support for heads in what is a lonely, difficult and terribly important job. Plenty of people tell them what they're doing wrong, but not many are around to help them to put it right. However I understand that the Department for Education (DFE) has plans to change this. A mentoring system for heads called Headlamp will bring new heads into contact with established heads. The DFE plans to spend some £5m on the scheme which will be voluntary and free to the heads, and the hope is that most heads will want to take advantage of the scheme.

I have kept in touch with Bob Salisbury over the years and I was looking forward to seeing for myself what he'd achieved at Garibaldi. I had brought Chris Lindup, from Lawrence Weston, with me on this visit in the hope that Bob's enthusiasm would prove infectious, and that seeing how Bob and Garibaldi had triumphed over such similar problems to the ones faced by Chris and Lawrence Weston would fill Chris with hope. There are quite a few parallels between the schools, for example, one of the things that Garibaldi and Lawrence Weston had suffered from was that both their previous heads had attempted to convert their schools into grammar schools and had signally failed in the attempt.

Garibaldi was built in the late 1960s to accommodate 1100 pupils and it is situated close to a large council estate and very close to a number of coal pits. When Bob was appointed he knew that the original culture of the school, which had been one of control, where people were not allowed or encouraged to show initiative, needed to be changed as fast as possible, and that he must also find ways to sell the school, both within the area and outside. Bob was lucky enough to gain the support and help of the managing director of the local Mansfield Breweries, who adopted the school and helped in all the subsequent changes. But before Bob took any action at all he sent a questionnaire to everyone in the community and everyone involved with the school. He sent it to the teachers, the pupils and the parents, and he sent it to industrialists and community leaders in order to find out what they felt needed to be done. Then he began to talk to them all and not until then did he began to make his changes.

Bob Salisbury's beliefs are very close to Chris Lindup's but his approach is far more radical and risk-taking and the result is that Garibaldi has been transformed. Despite the continuing loss of jobs in the area the school's roll has increased to over 850 – almost double what it was when Bob arrived – with attendance of more than 98% on a regular basis and an almost nonexistent rate of truancy. And the amount of money Bob has had to spend on repairing vandalism at Garibaldi is now so small that it no longer even features in the accounts. Bullying has virtually ceased and the school is now a dynamic, creative and innovative place where the students believe in themselves.

The school is now firmly anchored in the community and the amount of money Bob has managed to attract to produce additional facilities is mind-boggling. The school has won every imaginable sort of award, including many that seem extremely unusual for a school. It became the East Midlands Company of the Year for 1992 and has also won the Chartered Institute of Marketing Award, a Modern Languages Award, an IBM Excellence in Management Award and it continues to be recognized as a place to watch.

Bob began by insisting that the pupils, whom he wished to be called students, should be treated with dignity and respect. They had previously been banned from the school buildings at breaks and at lunchtime for fear of the damage they would cause, but Bob believed in placing the responsibility for not damaging the buildings directly on the students themselves. Bob explained to the students that he and the staff would like to be able to treat the students as adults and that they needed their help in the whole process of change at Garibaldi. Bob explained that the staff were looking to the students to help iron out any problems which might arise, for instance when they were allowed to remain in the classrooms during breaks. Bob has changed what he described as a punishment culture into a culture of trust and innovation, where the greatest possible sin is inertia and students are encouraged to have a go, even if it does not work out. At Garibaldi now, even if what you try to do doesn't work out, you are given a pat on the back for having a go. The students are treated, in Bob's words, as fully paid up members of the human race. They are also constantly encouraged and stimulated by certificates and awards for every possible achievement.

Bob introduced targets for all the staff and tried to find ways of raising their individual capabilities and more fully utilizing their particular skills. He introduced a fortnightly newsletter which is written in a breezy style and circulated to all the pupils, parents and others interested in the progress of the school. Bob spoke to everyone and anyone in the area who would listen: miners, the chamber of commerce, local education officers, the local newspaper, and anybody else he could reach. He produced a five year plan and introduced regular SWOT meetings with the parents, where they analyze the strengths, weaknesses, opportunities and threats for the school. This last struck me as a particularly brave and unusual step. Early on Bob and his colleagues wrote a list of factors which would indicate to them when the school was winning, and although the list started with improved examination results as its number one, it also covered such items as the students' behaviour outside the school, links with feeder and receiving schools and employers, community involvement and so on. Although he had initially planned for a five year period, in reality they achieved most of their five year goals within three.

As well as changing the culture of the school Bob cultivated links with local companies so that the school could raise the money they needed in order to have the freedom to do the things they wanted to do. The school became the East Midlands ticket agent for Alton Towers – the school makes a commission on every ticket they sell – and they currently earn more than £20 000 a year in commissions. The school has also received other donations from Alton Towers which has enabled them to refurbish their sports hall.

Bob also used the buildings and space he has at Garibaldi to attract sponsorship and set in train a process of renewal and rebuilding which I found almost unbelievable. He has set up a conference centre which is hired out to businesses for a daily charge, a new sixth form room, and a new library. Sponsorship from the National Union of Miners (NUM), the Union of Democratic Miners (UDM), and British Coal enabled the school to build a computer room and they had a home computer pilot scheme for pupils with special educational needs. The Italian Embassy was approached and they sponsored an Italian teacher in honour of the school's name and even Garibaldi biscuits were donated by the manufacturer. One of the major suppliers of school furniture produced, for free, a technology room, a language room and a science lab which are used as showrooms, and a host of other initiatives are in train. However the school's success has not just been in raising money, practically all parents now turn up at open evenings and private sessions to discuss their children's progress. They have what Bob claims to be the best music department in the whole country, with a sixty piece concert band, two rock groups, a female jazz band and dozens of individual instrumentalists, and the school's football team reached the all-England semi-final a year ago. All of this has been achieved from a run-down school without any additional state support, purely by leadership, imagination, example and switching on and supporting every member of staff and every student.

Bob appointed one of his deputies specifically to determine what training was necessary for the teachers – partly by working with them in their classrooms – in order for them to achieve a higher proportion of their capability. This makes an interesting counterpoint to a recent Nottinghamshire survey which said that 96% of headteachers felt they made full use of the expertise of the staff, while 96% of the staff said they felt underutilized and were not given enough opportunities. At the very beginning of Bob's tenure as headteacher, in-service training for the teachers included a course on how to communicate with the parents. And Bob runs an appraisal scheme at the school. He has an hour and a half's interview with each of the teachers once a year to discuss their specific targets for classroom and personal performance as well as the targets for the whole school. All these are monitored throughout the year by the evaluation team who are always ready to take any steps which are deemed necessary to help teachers. The process of motivating the teachers had been handled very slowly at first and the first year's appraisals were more of a comfortable chat than a target-setting meeting, but they have recently taken a much harder turn. The teachers themselves see appraisal as an essential part of their own career and personal development now, and Bob pointed out that he felt it was vital to be absolutely open about what he was expecting. He explained that a considerable amount of in-service training for the teachers was to ensure they were able to take full advantage of the new freedoms he introduced, once he had dismantled the hierarchical controls of his predecessor.

Chris Lindup and I attended Garibaldi's morning staff meeting which was a revelation in itself. Practically every member of staff had something to report or some event they wished their colleagues to know about. The atmosphere was racy, informal and involved. It was reported that one of Garibaldi's students had been chosen to represent Nottinghamshire in the all-England Physical Education Championships in Telford. The new intake of 180 children and their parents were coming in over the next two weeks to meet their form teachers, so that when they actually started at the school they would not feel lost and would know people. A transfer curriculum had been introduced and was discussed with the feeder primary schools who now all did exactly the same work from Easter to October, so the new students joined Garibaldi without a break in their academic work.

Bob believes strongly in public acknowledgement and praise and there were examples of pupil and staff achievements all over the school, including the entrance hall which was plastered with all the awards the school had won. He and his school are living proof that constant acknowledgement and praise encourage achievement. Bob was still pressing for change but now he finds that at least half the new ideas stem from the staff, the pupils or the parents themselves. It was as a result of one of these suggestions that Bob had opened the sixth form to adult membership, and when I went to visit them later in the day I met a number of miners studying subjects with the normal sixth form pupils, to the evident benefit of both groups.

I left Chris to discuss matters with Bob while I went to talk to some of the students. All attested to the lively atmosphere and that there was so much going on they could barely keep up. They also commented on the way the teachers themselves – even those who had been there for fifteen or twenty years – had changed and found a new enthusiasm and informality about the way they worked. Certainly every pupil in the school knew the headteacher, who was accustomed to walking in at breaks and dinners and sitting in on classes. Another big change from the students' point of view is the atmosphere at break times. Before Bob's time, breaks had been characterized by gang warfare between the different houses. This had ceased when the house system was abolished. Yet another dramatic change was that most students now stayed on until sixth form to go to university. I was also shown the new sports hall, which is being built at a cost of £400 000, £200 000 of which had come from the European Union (EU), but this figure had to be matched. Bob, unstoppable as ever, was already well on the way to raising the other half of the money from the local technical college. I was amazed he could even contemplate the project because the area is not a rich one and many of the parents and local businesses are coping with their own financial struggles and hardships.

The youngsters who had just joined the school were the same optimistic, bright-eyed little creatures I had met at Lawrence Weston, but there was one major difference: they almost all said that maths was their favourite subject. On the whole maths is not taught well in Britain, we compare unfavourably in its teaching almost everywhere, even with developing countries such as Taiwan, so to find a school where maths is considered an exciting subject was a pleasant surprise and, fired with curiosity, I went to sit in on a maths lesson. I took Chris Lindup with me to the maths class because maths is one of the areas where he has problems at Lawrence Weston and I had been told that, at Garibaldi, the maths department had achieved great things.

One of the first things Bob Salisbury did when he took over was to appoint a new head of maths, Chris Dickinson. As I watched Chris teach his class I was impressed not only by the fact that he is a hard working and obviously dedicated teacher, but that he has a plan which he has followed through. He realized very early on that the only way to lift the performance of his colleagues and of the students was by targeting a small bunch of students and demonstrating to the school and to themselves that youngsters from this area could be successful at maths. When Chris took over the school's pass rate in maths at GCSE level was 6%, and the subject was one which frightened the students, and even the brightest students felt that maths was too difficult for them.

When Chris Dickinson arrived he realized they would have to prioritize and so for the first year they concentrated on putting extra efforts into the fifth form, Year 11. As a result of endless coaching and encouragement the results went up to fifteen GCSE passes, or 35%, within a year. They split the fifth form into two groups, one of which

105

they felt were capable of getting higher grades and who were pushed hard towards a minimum C pass. They had come in early and worked through lunchtimes and after school until they felt the students were confident. To my amazement the students had taken to this extra attention with real enthusiasm instead of resenting it, since they themselves were anxious to pass. Once they had succeeded with Year 11, they then spread their attention to the other forms, as a result of which the school has now reached the national average for GCSE passes in maths. Every student works for short-term targets (the longest target being a term and many much shorter), and each receives a certificate from the headteacher when they achieve their targets. As a result of this encouragement, respect and trust, the apparent miracle of changing maths from a 'can't do' subject to one of the favourites has been achieved, and Chris was looking forward to some reasonable 'A' level maths results for Garibaldi for the first time. The current 'A' level group were the first to have gone through maths with Chris and his department from the beginning of their time at Garibaldi. Practically all the students wanted to go on to university, even those who wanted to become professional footballers or models, and the difference in aspiration between the youngsters at Garibaldi and those I had met at Lawrence Weston could barely have been more extreme.

During my visit to Garibaldi I went to one of the first British Coal pits to have been leased to Richard Budge, in order to meet some of the parents of children at the school. Although the pit now only employs 150 miners, they were hoping to increase that to 250 in the summer, and they were still producing 150 000 tons of coal a year. They had secured sales for the coal they were producing and had the same management, although many fewer of them. They were knowledgeable about and interested in Garibaldi School and they were determined to do their best for their children's education. It was a tribute to Bob Salisbury's efforts that the parents I spoke to talked about the improvements at Garibaldi since he took over: they felt he'd done a wonderful job. On my way back to the school I briefly joined Chris Lindup and Bob Salisbury, who were fishing at a nearby lake which the school used as a means of introducing their students to the sport, to the general delight of students and teachers! Chris said that he'd picked up lots of ideas from Bob and that he was going to begin implementing his changes at Lawrence Weston in September when everyone was fresh back from six weeks' summer holiday.

Bob's ambitions for Garibaldi are limitless. The school has really concentrated on producing all-rounders and, thanks to Bob's entrepreneurial skills, it has one of the best language laboratories I have ever seen. I visited the technology department and the graphic design department and I ended up talking to the sixth form. These students had very different aspirations from both the students at Clifton College and those at Lawrence Weston. They wanted to become industrial designers, civil engineers and chemical engineers. It was really refreshing to listen to young people with realistic goals who wanted to knuckle down and actually make things. It's not that I think everyone should go into industry, but if we are to succeed as a country, industry has to get its share of the best and the brightest as happens in other countries.

Towards the end of my visit to Garibaldi, Chris Lindup and I attended one of the regular meetings with the parents and found them doing a SWOT analysis. The meeting was totally different from any parent-teacher meeting I have ever been to before and the enthusiasm and commitment of the parents could hardly have been demonstrated more clearly. People were ready to raise criticisms and suggestions and Bob and the staff were not in the slightest defensive: they welcomed all ideas, however extreme. Everyone seemed to be having a thoroughly great time.

Chris and Bob and I had a final meeting at which Chris asked Bob where his vision had come from and Bob replied that it was a combination of experience in several other schools and sheer desperation. Garibaldi would probably have closed had it stayed as it was, so something had to be done and quickly. Bob also said that the hardest part had been the first few months: changing things inside an institution that has been operating in the same way for years is a difficult process and people object . . . but he spoke to every member of staff in quick succession and once the ball began to roll people either left or rapidly threw themselves behind the changes. I said that I felt Chris faced a more difficult challenge than Bob in the sense that Chris had already been at Lawrence Weston for some time without implementing major changes, whereas Bob had arrived at Garibaldi and immediately embarked upon a programme of change. But Chris seemed invigorated by the buzz at Garibaldi and by the visible signs of change and things happening and, I think, left Garibaldi full of renewed hope for Lawrence Weston.

The real lesson from Garibaldi lies in the methodical, organized and carefully thought-out way Bob has managed the whole affair. He refused to accept any limitations, always finding a way round, involving everybody, building up the belief of the staff, the students and the community in the school and what the school was capable of, and he restlessly and relentlessly sought every opportunity to enhance the perception of the school in the area. Bob believes that nothing is impossible and this sends a strong signal to his staff, pupils and the community that Garibaldi is a school on the up. What's happening at Garibaldi shows that it's not all doom and gloom. Garibaldi is by no means at the top of the academic tree, but by heavens they're climbing, and it's all been done within the restrictions that every school in the public sector suffers from. Although the school has not received any particular support or help from the Local Education Authority (LEA), they seemed quite happy for Bob to go ahead with all his initiatives.

I really enjoyed my day at Garibaldi and I left full of the belief that the quality of a school depends upon the leadership of the headteacher, the enthusiasm and motivation of the teachers and the attitudes and aspirations of the students, far more than on political directives or financial solutions. My experiences at Garibaldi also fill me with renewed belief that the only thing that stops any of us is our own lack of confidence in ourselves and our skills. If we are willing to change, we can achieve anything.

The dramatic changes at Garibaldi show that it is possible to triumph even within our current rather unhelpful system. But teachers do have a very tough time coping with shortages of money, low aspirations and a continuous barrage of new government initiatives such as the national curriculum. This, combined with continuous criticism of their abilities, is hardly the best way to switch them on. And so my next call was to find out whether teacher training is giving Britain's teachers the best possible start to their professional life. I also have a personal interest in teacher training because Abigail, my granddaughter, elected to become a teacher and, at times, she's found her training a difficult and painful process.

7. How do we teach the teachers?

Teaching is one of the most important jobs in the country. It is the teachers, at least as much as the parents, who are responsible for growing and developing our young people. But teaching is a lonely job: no one watches the teachers when they teach a class and there can be little in the way of support in the classroom. It is rather like flying solo, you can prepare for it as much as you like, but ultimately it is something you have to do on your own. It is down to you to establish a relationship with your pupils and entirely up to you whether their enthusiasm grows and develops before your very eyes, or whether they become bored and drop out.

At the time that I was making this film my granddaughter, Abigail, was in the final year of her teacher training degree course at Warwick University. I am, as I suppose all grandfathers are, inordinately proud of my granddaughter and it is true to say that I would not have minded what career she chose, providing it made her happy, but I was really delighted when she told me she wanted to study to be a teacher. She has always been very fond of young children and I have seen at first hand how well she gets on with them. The starting point of success in any job has to be that you enjoy it and are enthusiastic about it. It is only when you find your job fascinating and continuously challenging that you can really excel at it, and it is no exaggeration to say that you only need five minutes in any classroom to know whether the teacher is a gifted and inspirational one or is just there for the beer. It was therefore with pride, enthusiasm and hope that I watched Abby embark on her university career. She will graduate from Warwick University's four year course at about the time this book appears, and will then go on to her first real job. Because Abby's training so neatly coincided with the making of this film, I decided to concentrate my investigations into the way we train our teachers on Warwick University's methods, and the embryonic teachers it produces. Besides which, Warwick University has a reputation as one of the best teacher training establishments in Britain.

At an earlier stage in Abby's training, much to my concern, she began to lose her enthusiasm for her chosen career. Her first practical teaching experience had almost broken her. She had been extremely apprehensive and lacking in confidence and there seemed to be very little support for her, either from the teachers at the school in which she was doing her first teaching practice, or from her teaching supervisor at the university. At one time she was so depressed and discouraged I really believe she would gratefully have abandoned the whole course. However things changed when she met Trevor Davies, the headteacher at Balsall Common Primary School. Enthusiasm and enjoyment fairly bubbled from her. The whole family (Abby and her mother live with us) were set to collecting things for her to use in her lessons, and when she was not working at the school she went back several times to see how *her* youngsters were getting on. However until we made this film, I had never seen Abby teaching.

One of the odd things about many state schools in this country is that they all seem to have been designed and built by the same organization: it is as though identical buildings have been dropped down by parachute all over the country. Driving up to Balsall Common Primary School I could, on the face of it, have been approaching any one of a dozen such schools anywhere in Britain. As soon as I arrived at the school I went to see Abby's class and almost immediately hit a real high. When I first saw her in the playground small children were rushing up to her, their faces wreathed in smiles, flinging out their arms for a hug. In the classroom, despite the television cameras and the artificiality of the situation, the children appeared totally absorbed in what Abby was teaching them and I could almost feel her willing them to succeed. It is common practice in schools to exhibit pupils' work, but the walls of Balsall Common Primary seemed more full than most with creative, imaginative concoctions. It may have looked like any other primary school from the outside, but the energy and commitment, smiles, fun and concern gave it a supercharge which was nice to feel: the atmosphere of the whole school was exciting and welcoming. How lucky Abby had been to find her way to such a school.

After watching Abby's class, I had a brief discussion with two of Abby's friends, both named Laura, who were also in their final year on the same primary teacher training course. Sadly, of the three of them, the only one who was sure she would make a career for herself in teaching was Abby. It is a lamentable fact that within five years of completing their training, less than 65% of qualified teachers are actually teaching. There's plainly something wrong when there's a drop-out rate of over one-third. All three of these trainee teachers had the same tale to tell. They found the four year course excessively long and too theoretical. All three felt they needed much more teaching practice in schools. Currently they only spend twenty weeks on teaching practice, the rest of their four-year course is spent at the university.

The first year at Warwick is an overview of the whole course and the subsequent years cover much the same ground, but supposedly in more detail. The girls all said that the practical part of their training happened entirely in the schools to which they were seconded and they all felt it was a matter of sheer luck whether or not they were supported and encouraged in the schools where they did their teaching practice. Before their first teaching practice all three of them had felt ill-prepared, underconfident and therefore extraordinarily nervous of what they described as the awesome responsibility of teaching. All three also said that good supervisors at the university offset any difficulties they encountered during their teaching practice, but it was very much a matter of luck whether they were allotted a good supervisor.

The girls all felt that when they got into the schools where they did their teaching practice, most of what they learned was through trial and error, observation and taking on other people's ideas, so the standards and quality of the schools to which they were sent were absolutely critical. Obviously the university could only utilize schools within a radius of about thirty miles, and only a small proportion of those schools were willing to take on trainee teachers. The girls all wanted more time in the schools and more personal tutoring and support, so that the practical problems of teaching could be better assimilated. All three accepted the need for theoretical backup, but felt that the training was almost 'upside down': too much theory and far too little practice.

The first school Abby went into had a number of cynical teachers who were no longer dedicated to the job and her own optimism and enthusiasm suffered as a result. Since one of the most important tasks for a teacher is endlessly to encourage and motivate the children, the teachers themselves need endless encouragement and motivation. I was far from clear who, if anybody, was doing this. It was time to go and talk to the director of education at the university to find out what her views were. But before that I had a few words with Trevor Davies who was as concerned as I was about the quality of the training of future teachers. He was particularly concerned about the lack of incentives for schools to take on trainee teachers.

Warwick University receives between £5000.00–£7000.00 per student from the government and yet it only spends £100.00 per student per period of primary teaching practice, and even that is relatively recent. Prior to that the schools received no funding at all for taking on trainee teachers. When you compare this with the £4000.00 that a general practitioner (GP) receives for taking on a medical trainee for a year, it's hardly surprising that schools are not rushing forwards with offers of places for trainee teachers. Trevor Davies takes on between twelve to fifteen student teachers a year on extended practice, and for that he would like to receive between £8000.00–£10 000.00 a year in total. He felt that £1000.00 per trainee teacher per year would be a realistic figure, but at the moment it's hardly worth a school's time and effort. However he, like many other schools, takes on trainee teachers primarily as a service to education as a whole. The good side of this is obviously that schools only take on teachers if they actually want to and feel a calling so to do. The bad side of it is that many schools feel it is perfectly reasonable for them to decide that they want no part of the training of the next generation, seeing their primary job as looking after their pupils.

Trevor Davies told me that a big shift in teacher training is planned towards a much more school-based approach and I was delighted to

113

hear it. The DFE plans to double the number of weeks currently spent by trainee primary teachers in schools from eighteen weeks to thirty-six weeks which is good news, but even so he still felt that Britain's teacher training degree courses were too academically based. Although Trevor Davies believes that Britain's education system still ranks with the best in the world, he said that the people who train the trainees at universities often hadn't had recent teaching experience in schools themselves.

I went to Warwick University to talk to Viv Little, the Director of Education, and I asked her whether she thought the right balance had been struck between the practical and the theoretical side of teacher training. I also mentioned my concern that the methods of preparing teachers for their future careers seemed relatively unchanged. Viv thought that, despite the views expressed by the headteachers I had spoken to, the perception in most schools was that teaching and the preparation for it has changed enormously, and that there was a significant shift towards a more school-based approach. Viv thought that studying and learning in a disciplined way was a vital element in the training and education of the teachers and for that reason alone she was strongly opposed to the view I was proposing, that teacher training should be based in schools rather than at universities. Viv also believed that the status of teachers in the community depended to a considerable degree upon the possession of high standards of education themselves, but she recognized the impatience of students with the theoretical aspects of their training. However she claimed that once they were in full time professional teaching jobs they would realize that the balance between the theoretical and practical sides of their training had not been as out of kilter as they thought.

Viv readily acknowledged that there were problems relating to the placing of students in schools. Warwick was currently unable to spare more than the token payment of £100.00 per student, a payment which could not begin to cover the additional work involved for the schools. Moreover universities were dependent upon the collaboration of the schools and had no power over what the students were taught. But Viv believed that the students brought interesting new ideas to the trained teachers in schools because they caused established teachers to question

114

their own methods and also brought them more up to date with current theories. However, the range of schools willing to take students was limited geographically and, while the university did try to move students who had a really bad experience in a particular school, there were limits to what could be done. Interestingly the university had made major efforts to link the theory and practice more closely and were also making major efforts to link a reflective attitude to the process of learning and teaching with the actual problems of doing the job. Viv said she'd like to see the schools partnership schemes – set up under various DFE directives – backed up with more resources that would allow trained teachers more time to work with student teachers in schools, and also give them time to work with the universities in supporting the trainee teacher. But I got the impression that she felt constrained by the DFE directives: she was unable to design Warwick's teacher training courses exactly as she would have liked because so much is prescribed by the government. This means that, in effect, the government is preventing closer links between school-based work and university-based work.

I ended up, as so often, with a depressing feeling of familiarity with the problem. The universities, themselves short of money, did not believe they had any to spare for the schools. The schools, although acknowledging some degree of self-interest in the training of teachers, nevertheless were under ever-increasing financial pressure and needed at least some money to support their trainee teachers. In the middle of all this were the students – the teachers of the future, the young people upon whom future generations would depend for their enthusiasm, ability to learn, aspirations and values. Despite everything that had been said, I still found myself wondering how our teachers were meant to learn the priceless ability to enthuse their pupils, and where they were expected to learn the qualities of trust and respect without which no development of the individual is possible.

In turn the training and teaching of headteachers in these elusive but important skills seemed to be, like so much else in the whole system of selection and training of teachers, a matter of luck rather than of design. As a manager I have always taken the rather cynical view that nothing happens by accident, or if it does it is unlikely to be helpful. The task of managers is to design processes, including human ones, which enable a predetermined result to be achieved. Without question what Britain needs most is inspired teachers who have the ability to develop their students' curiosity, self-esteem and self-confidence, and to foster in them a restless urge to learn more and develop themselves to the utmost of their capabilities. If that is what we are trying to achieve I have an uneasy feeling we have a long way to go before we manage it. It is also a fact that those who train the teachers are often paid less than the teachers themselves, so what possible financial incentive is there for the really good trainers to train the future teachers?

I think that there's still a very big gap between the perceptions of both the schools and the students and the people who are actually teaching the teachers. There seems to be an acceptance of the status quo and an acceptance of what I think is an inadequate speed of response to the challenges. And I don't think it's going to change quickly enough for my granddaughter. It will be down to the luck of the draw for her whether or not she finds herself in a supportive, endlessly encouraging school. There's no doubt that in order to succeed we need the best possible teachers and the best possible teachers require the best possible preparation and training, and that certainly doesn't seem to be happening at the moment.

8. Lawrence Weston revisited; and some conclusions

A year after first visiting Lawrence Weston, I returned. Chris Lindup, the head, had finally launched his Pacific Institute initiative, albeit much later than I felt was desirable, and I was anxious to see whether the school had that pleasant feeling of movement and achievement which is a sure sign of a well-managed outfit. Chris was full of enthusiasm about what had been accomplished and confident that I would be as thrilled and excited as he was. And there *was* a palpable change in the atmosphere at Lawrence Weston. I felt it as soon as I entered the school, and what's more Chris had planned a surprise for me. The whole school was assembled, all wearing their new uniforms, for a school photograph. At one of our earliest meetings Chris and I had discussed both having the whole school in uniform and the idea of a school photograph, and I was delighted to find that both things had been achieved. Despite the cold there was a tangible feeling of excitement and pride as the photographer, perched on the school roof, prepared to take the photograph.

After the photograph I went on a tour of the school and spoke to both students and staff. One of the first things I discovered was that Lawrence Weston no longer featured at the bottom of Avon's academic league tables. They had achieved a 300% improvement in their exam results, although admittedly their results had been so poor before that there was plenty of room for change, but Chris told me later that they were expecting a significant improvement on those results this year and a dramatic improvement the following year.

The pupils had been asked what changes they would like to see in

117

the school and in what order. Their suggestions had ranged the whole way from more lockers to a swimming pool and a sauna, and when the teachers looked at the pupils' list of what they wanted in the school they found that a number of simple things could be done almost immediately. A homework club had been set up within a couple of weeks of the suggestion. The children had also asked for a breakfast club, which had been greeted with real enthusiasm by the cook, who had wanted to keep the kitchen open in order to avoid meals being bought in on a contract basis. Since September the daily messages, which in the past had been only a few lines, were now a whole page of items about clubs and trips, and I was later told that six new clubs had already been set up.

The pupils all believed that things were getting better; although quite a few of them weren't overly keen on wearing a uniform, they were pleased that their uniform was more comfortable and practical than that of St Bede's next door. There was a fund-raising exercise in progress to replace the school's ex-Post Office bus, which they had nicknamed the 'Postman Pat Bus', because its obvious provenance had added to their feeling of inferiority compared to other schools who all had their own school buses emblazoned with their school's name. The minibus fund was doing well and they were full of hope that they would reach their target. All the pupils remarked on the positive effect of the repainting of the school buildings and the youngsters were all keen to field rugby and football teams, but I had to point out that they really needed more pupils before this was a realistic possibility. However there has been a small increase in the school's roll already.

I went to see Julie Coulthard to find out how she felt. A year ago Julie had been looking forward to a new start, but now she had very mixed feelings about the Pacific Institute course. Even though she was the first to admit it had given a kickstart to change at the school, she was concerned that the changes had been much slower than she had expected. She had rather expected that the course at the Pacific Institute would cause an instant change in everyone's beliefs, but now she recognized that it was merely the beginning of a much longer process. However, she did feel that the school had a different atmosphere and was more alive and that both teachers and staff were beginning to

118

believe in themselves again. As she said, unless the teachers had self-belief and self-esteem there was no hope at all for the pupils.

Both staff and pupils had been involved in defining the sort of school they wanted. The teachers had drawn a cartoon which described what they wanted Lawrence Weston to become, and this was on display in the common room and the idea was to tick off each item as it was achieved. They had also published a booklet which had been distributed to all the children outlining the changes they wanted to achieve. This was just the sort of confirmation of movement and achievement which I felt would give everyone a concrete feeling of success. The minibus seemed to me to have been an excellent early initiative because it was such an obvious and visible sign of the whole school pulling together to achieve a common goal. I made a few suggestions about other things they could do to make it all happen more quickly. For instance, Chris could talk to some of the largest car dealers in Bristol, with the aim of getting a substantial discount off the minibus when they bought it. They could then change the name of the minibus appeal to, for instance, the 'Ford minibus appeal', or whatever it might be, and the task of raising the money would be somewhat eased.

I also discovered that Peter Muddyman, Chris's head of maths, had taken early retirement. I went to see the new head of maths, Heather Jones, who had been in the maths department for four years. She was very enthusiastic and said that all the teachers now shared a view of what the school should look like in five years' time, and knew what had to be done to get them there. Heather had set herself the task of ensuring that all her pupils were excited about maths and no longer found the subject frightening. She believed many of the primary schools taught children that maths was hard and considered it a low status subject. The maths department was concentrating on trying to change that attitude and demonstrating that maths was not only fun but was relevant to the children's lives. When I visited the class they were learning about prime factors in a very imaginative way. Heather was also attempting to link maths with science and the humanities, and she had begun this process by reexamining and changing the syllabus for Years 7 and 8. They had now introduced three completely different types of text book for different levels of student, so that those who were really interested in the subject could move on without being held back by the others – the very thing which had worried me so much when I had attended the maths class here a year ago.

Heather believed, in addition to the successes she was having in her own department, that Lawrence Weston was definitely up and coming again. I left Heather and Julie immensely encouraged. They had demonstrated that everything depends upon the self-belief of the teachers and their belief in the children they are educating. Without the confidence of their teachers there is no way that children can believe they are able to learn, or feel comfortable enough to ask questions and receive the support they need.

I was delighted with Lawrence Weston's progress and so, clearly, was Chris. He felt that their main achievement was the clarity of vision about where they wanted to go and the increased motivation of the teachers. For years the teachers had believed they could not succeed with the children at Lawrence Weston and this had become a self-fulfilling prophesy. The 300% improvement in their exam results and the fact that Lawrence Weston was no longer bottom of the academic league in Avon had, in itself, made a tremendous difference. Everyone in the school now believed they could do better.

Chris was generous in his praise of Bob Salisbury and how useful the visit to Garibaldi had been, although he professed to have learned more about the marketing of the school than about the initiatives Bob had taken to ratchet up their performance. He felt that money could be attracted if he was able to sell Lawrence Weston better, but was not really thinking in quite the same entrepreneurial way which comes so naturally to Bob. Chris was also working on the link with the primary schools and had spoken to all of them about the necessity to increase the self-belief of the youngsters. Both he and the primary schools had set a major short-term objective to increase the reading capabilities of the children. Chris was particularly pleased that the staff had taken so many initiatives on their own, without prompting from him. One of the signs of improvement was that many more students were assisting with the pantomime and this was reflected in many other areas of school life. In the same way as every other headteacher I had spoken to, Chris was also anxious to play a more positive part in teacher training and to receive the resources to do so. He felt there was a real eagerness now to find out what the young people wanted and needed, and to tackle those particular areas first. There had been some welcome changes in the aspirations of the pupils leaving the school and the careers advisor had commented that more young people were enquiring about further education.

I admire Chris immensely. He does not find this form of up-front leadership easy and he was pushing himself to take very big risks which his previous training had done little to prepare him for. He was doing all this not because of pressure from the LEA, but because of his deep feelings of concern and responsibility for the young people in his charge. This seemed to me to be exactly what was needed, but I wished there was more obvious support for headteachers like Chris.

I ended my revisit to Lawrence Weston by watching their pantomime, *Aladdin*, which included, as all good pantomimes should, a pantomime dame, who led the youngsters in an exuberant chorus of 'There's no business like show business'. The enthusiasm and the laughter both on stage and in the audience was heartening, and it left me feeling that a new sense of hope had returned to Lawrence Weston.

Some conclusions

The dedication of Britain's teachers is breathtaking and I find it exasperating that Britain is not making better progress with the educational reforms which are so urgently needed. I am sure that student teachers need much more practical in-school training, but to make this work a way has to be found to encourage and promote the schools who really switch on all their teachers.

Both Lawrence Weston and Garibaldi demonstrated to me that, difficult though the current situation is for secondary schools, far more can be achieved if the headteachers are motivated, supported and given some basic training on how to manage change. Recent changes to the curriculum, and other changes, have increased the demands upon headteachers, but little has been done to prepare them to manage the changes in the aspirations of their teachers and students.

I have no doubt that every aspect of the future of Britain depends upon the form of education we provide for all our people. For the privileged few, education in Britain has always been equal to the best in the world, but apart from them, it is a matter of luck and location whether or not you attend a good school. Inspired, dedicated teachers who believe in the children in their care, who believe in giving respect and trust and who continuously demand more of their students can still achieve extraordinary results, irrespective of any other problems with which the students are struggling in their own lives.

Moreover I have yet to meet any parents who are not concerned about their children's education and their future. But parents are as confused about what they can do to help improve their children's opportunities as the teachers are. We simply cannot accept a concept that the best we can do for the young people of the future is to keep them off the streets and teach them to read and write. Keeping young people occupied is not the object of the exercise. Time and again our schools demonstrate that the problems lie not with the intrinsic potential of our people, but rather with the atmosphere in which they are taught, the size of the challenges they are given, and the rate at which they are expected to learn and improve. But it is no use hoping that a whole new generation of Bob Salisburys will suddenly appear to lead our schools. We need to place far more emphasis on supporting and teaching our many excellent headteachers to lead their own schools more proactively and imaginatively into the future, and to ease the bureaucratic burdens they carry. It is the headteachers of Britain who have to give the lead, and this depends much more upon generating self-belief and a sense of dynamism within the system, than it does on responding to the limitless number of statistical controls and measures to which their performance is constantly subjected.

As far as I'm concerned the more you expect from a person the more he or she will deliver. I know that to be true from my own experience. When I trained for the Navy at Dartmouth, we were all constantly expected to achieve just that little bit more and we all rose to the occasion. Teachers with high expectations breed students with high levels of achievement. Britain's youngsters are Britain's future, but since more than half of them are still leaving their secondary schools unqualified, we have a long long way to go.

British education has, I believe, failed the vast majority of Britain's population. It has concentrated on the few at the expense of the majority, but it is the majority who need access to a good education, and an education which is relevant to the needs of Britain, otherwise Britain's economic future will decline further than it already has. In the Navy and at Dartmouth the effort was concentrated on raising everyone up to the same high standard and I don't see why that principle shouldn't be applied in schools.

All schools are different, just as all teachers and all children are different. Plainly the problems that face a school like Lawrence Weston are very different from those that face a school like Clifton College, but we need change in all of them. Garibaldi school is a shining example of what can be done, and if more schools can follow this example then perhaps in twenty years' time we could begin to achieve the higher standards that we all so desperately need. But we are still wasting far too much of our talent, partly due to our divisive education system. We desperately need a new sense of movement and relevance, and a positive belief that no one will be satisfied until every one of our people has the chance to be educated to the very best of his or her ability. This is every citizen's birthright, and if it is not achieved, Britain will be unable to compete on a global basis come the twenty-first century.

PART THREE

9. Back to my alma mater

The Royal Naval College, Dartmouth

It was in 1935, at the ripe old age of eleven, that I made the single most important decision of my life. In those days my reading matter consisted of a perpetual diet of boys' adventure stories, practically all of which focused on life at sea, and so I duly announced to my startled family that I wished to pursue a naval career. This was a surprise to my parents since only one member of either of their families had served in the Navy (I come from a staunch army family), and most of my father's life had been spent in India, many miles from the sea. Even my preparatory school at Deal was out of sight of the water and, apart from liner voyages to and from India, I had absolutely no experience of the sea. Logic, however, does not usually play a prominent role in the decisions of eleven-year-old boys. I knew I detested my preparatory school, and believed, fortunately correctly, that life in the Navy would be more stable and worthwhile.

The headteacher of my prep school had made a number of ill-advised and unsuccessful attempts to turn me into a prototypical public schoolboy with a natural love of cricket and Latin. Indeed, it may well have been the fact that I wouldn't have to play cricket at Dartmouth and that Latin was not taught which proved the final deciding point. I wrote to my father and informed him that I wished to apply to the Royal Naval College at Dartmouth and, in due course, I received an indication of his acquiescence from my mother. I suspect my father's decision was influenced rather more by the fact that I would be self-supporting from the age of seventeen than by any consideration about my suitability for such a career, or even my happiness.

My headteacher judged that I could probably pass the necessary

124

entrance exam with a little bit of specialist cramming, which in the event proved to be invaluable. The exams for Dartmouth were as predictable as the rest of my life in the Royal Navy was to be. The crammers, with whom I spent the holiday before I sat the exam, had done an exhaustive analysis of the limited range of questions which arose at every cadetship exam and predicted, with surprising accuracy, the most likely ones I would have to answer. I sat the exam in the civil service rooms near Great Russell Street and it turned out to be my first and last competitive examination. At the same time every candidate sitting the exams was invited to the Russell Hotel, where we were measured by Gieves, the tailors. In this way they established an iron grip on my sartorial requirements and potential pay packet which was not to be released until I left the Navy some twenty years later.

It was as a consequence of all these activities that I found myself, together with most of that term's forty-four new pupils, travelling from Paddington to Kingswear the day before the winter term began in January 1938. The approach from Paignton to Dartmouth must be one of the most beautiful railway journeys in Britain and we embryo naval officers, dressed in our miniature uniforms, craned out of the windows of the train to catch our first glimpse of the College which was to be our home for the next three years. I can well remember how terrified I was that I wouldn't be good enough to become a proper naval officer.

My naval revisit was to begin at Dartmouth and as I returned, in exactly the same way as I had first arrived so many years before, I experienced, I have to confess, many of the same feelings of anticipation and fear. I have a very sentimental attachment to the Navy and although I knew that the Navy I was returning to would be very different from the Navy I had left, I was not sure what I would find. The train no longer runs from Paddington, and on this occasion I had the pride of the Dart Valley Railway – a privately operated steam railway – entirely to myself (if you exclude the film crew and my producer) but nothing could detract from my excitement as the Dart came into sight and I saw the College standing proudly above the town and the Dart estuary. I saw a pristine white ensign flying from the masthead and at first sight the College appeared to be exactly the same:

there were no signs of any change to the classical lines of the old buildings.

But, of course, Dartmouth has changed. The estuary, which used to play host to a handful of yachts and a substantial number of ocean-going merchantmen is now filled with modern pleasure craft. As we passed the Phillip Boatyard I could see that it was no longer building the tugs, ancillary vessels and small naval ships for which it had once been famous. It was now solely a yacht marina and the only activity that remained the same as in my day was that the Phillip Boatyard still built yachts.

I arrived at Dartmouth to accompany the new intake on their first day of training in April 1994, and it was fascinating to compare what I saw with my own experience back in 1938. Instead of forty-four thirteen-year-old boys who were joining the mightiest navy in the world (larger than the French and the German navies put together), the April 1994 intake was limited to just thirteen recruits from outside the Navy with an average age of twenty-four. They were joining at about the age I had been at the end of the Second World War, during which I had served in surface ships, had been sunk twice and had then been on continual active duties in the Submarine Service. In addition to the thirteen officer cadets who were seeing the Navy for the first time, there were a further twenty-eight non-graduates who had joined and served in the Navy as sailors and had won their way through to officer training. The total intake that April was sixty-six, made up with a further twenty-five international cadets from a variety of countries. British officer training is still widely recognized as being amongst the best, and a number of governments are prepared to pay for the indoctrination of their future naval officers by the Royal Navy. It is a Navy which, despite its pitifully small size in comparison with the Navy I had known (in 1938 the Navy's trained strength was 119 000, today it is 48 500), it is still rated to be, in professional terms, one of the best in the world.

I was visiting the College before the results of yet another defence cost study, *Front Line First*, were known, and the newspapers were full of predictions of further reductions. Since the end of the Cold War the financial pressures on the Navy have intensified and they've drastically

126

reduced the number of ships and shore establishments. And it seemed to me that the size of the intake of cadet officers at Dartmouth that April spoke volumes about what was expected of the officer strength for a navy of the future. Today the Navy has an officer corps of about 7500, but it is difficult to see how they could be planning to sustain even half that number if the intake remained at the low levels demonstrated by these young men and women, nervously starting their naval careers proper. The total number in training for the whole of 1994 was 345; in 1993 it was 489 and in 1992 it was 640.

I was taken round by the Training Commander, Angus Sinclair, a wonderful former submariner, who seemed to me to epitomize the very best sort of naval officer. He was a man whose integrity shone through and who, as well as having served in nuclear submarines, maintained the impeccably high standards and expectations which were such a feature of the Navy in my day and which I was soon to learn had not been relaxed at all. As I began to meet some of the new cadets the changes at Dartmouth became more apparent. They were being kitted-out in the block which in my day had been the hospital and it was quite apparent that the grip of Gieves – now Gieves & Hawkes – on naval outfitting had been relaxed by the imposition of competitive tendering, coupled with the issue of 'slops', as the Navy calls its contract-made clothing. The young men and women who were starting their naval careers were wrestling with the time-honoured problem of naval boots while I was endeavouring to find out what had made them join. The first shock was that most of them had joined for training in careers other than becoming the career seamen officers which most of us had expected to become. There were pilots, observers, air traffic controllers, supply and engineering officers and one solitary career seaman officer (from civil life) whose prospects seemed to me to be pretty bright as long as he could stay the course!

And there was one enormous difference from my days at Dartmouth: the officers under training included a number of women. I was always a great admirer of the women who served in the Royal Navy in my day – indeed I was lucky enough to marry a Wren officer and in a number of my intelligence appointments I had Wren officers working under my command. Nevertheless, we would no more have expected to see a woman officer aboard a ship than to see a pterodactyl suddenly appearing on the quarter-deck. My days at Dartmouth were monastic, not only were cadets not allowed into the town, they were not allowed to mix with girls at all while they were under the care of the Royal Navy. The only exception was the end of term dance, where those of us who had managed to acquire girlfriends in our time away from the College could introduce them, always appropriately chaperoned, for an evening of decorous ballroom dancing. Ballroom dancing was taught assiduously to every cadet during his time in service: it was a well-known part of every naval officers' duty to be able to dance for his King and country in the coastal cities of the world.

Angus took me to see the passing out photograph of my term and our term officer who, in common with over half the other young career officers who were at Dartmouth at that time, was killed during the Second World War. As I stood in front of the photograph, it occurred to me that the vast establishment that comprised the Royal Naval College at Dartmouth was becoming an anachronism. In 1992 the new intake was 465, but in 1994 it was a mere 219. The number of officer cadets starting naval training has more than halved in the last two years and, since the cost of running Dartmouth has remained broadly the same, the cost per officer has roughly doubled. Those employed at the College say that the quality of the training justifies the extra training costs and that the Navy can thus maintain its standards despite the vast reduction in its size. Dartmouth can accommodate 550 cadets, but if the cadet intake remains as low as it was in 1994, the Navy's officer corps will obviously be reduced. In order to maintain an officer corps of 5000, Dartmouth needs an intake of about 340 cadets a year. Despite the lack of recruits, the establishment remained much the same as I remembered it. The sports fields, the swimming pool, the rifle-range and all the other paraphernalia which had been there in my day were still there. In fact the only part of the entire establishment which seemed to have been changed at all was Sandquay where, in my day, engineering instruction was carried out, and where, these days, a commercial contractor has taken over the task of maintaining naval craft.

My initial impression of Dartmouth was of a machine running on to fulfil a purpose which was no longer relevant to the future needs of the Service. Moreover, the motivation of the new entrants was very different from the motivation in my day. It was the attraction of becoming sailors that drove most of us, combined with the conviction that the Navy would always be the prime force for world peace that it was in 1938. When we joined none of us could have envisaged any other sort of career than to serve out our days in the service of our country, preserving the peace in far-flung corners of the globe where the Union Jack was never hauled down. The Navy's role was self-evident then, and anybody questioning the need for a Royal Navy would have received a dusty answer in any pub in the land. But the young people who were joining today were interested in pursuing technical careers and although they do still join to go to sea, and they were all excited by the prospect of exercising command, they had almost all chosen to follow specializations which have fewer sea-going opportunities than seamen officers (who serve continuously at sea). They certainly did not look upon their time with the Navy as a career for life, as I did. When I joined Dartmouth I discovered I had committed myself to a naval career for as long as the Royal Navy wanted me. You could only leave, as I was to find out many years later, with the agreement of The Admiralty Board, who were under no obligation to disclose their reasons for accepting or declining your request. Indeed, the first time I asked to leave the Royal Navy my request was refused and only when the extremity of my family circumstances became clear was I grudgingly given permission. There is a vital difference these days: anybody who feels they have made a mistake can leave within twenty-four hours of writing a letter requesting to do so.

The Navy seems to have become human, they even supply wide, medium or narrow shoes these days, and after kitting out, the officer cadets went for their first naval haircut which also seemed a good deal kinder than in my day. Unlike the aged naval pensioner who cut our hair, there was now a lady hairdresser who also dealt with the women officers' hair. I was interested to discover that less than half of them had ever played competitive sports, something which would have been unthinkable for a cadet joining in my day. Even at the age of thirteen we were all expected to play a wide range of the usual competitive games. In fact Dartmouth was located where it was – instead of on a training ship at Portsmouth as had been the case in the 1850s – partly so that there should be more access to sporting facilities.

However some things remain the same. The task at Dartmouth is to teach high standards of leadership as well as the basic art of seamanship on which survival at sea depends. Modern technology has still not produced a ship which cannot be sunk by the sheer forces of nature if it is mishandled by its officers and men. Cadets are also taught the necessities of drill, the ceremonial handling of a naval officer's sword, etiquette, social behaviour, manners (both wardroom and elsewhere), and the naval history and traditions which it is their duty to uphold. But these days it seems that the new intake of officers is not as competitive as they were, nor so eager to stand out and take charge, despite the fact that many of the cadets select the Royal Navy largely because of the opportunity of early responsibility. Those in charge of training believe it is their job to inculcate this habit and the self-confidence that goes with it. The amount of time put into developing leadership skills has been doubled over the past few years in order to build up the confidence and character of those who are going to sea as officers. In Angus's view, and certainly from everything I saw, the quality and dedication of the trained officer was as high as it had ever been, and all the officers I met at Dartmouth were convinced that it was important to train the officer cadets in a different establishment from that of the sailors, particularly because both groups often came from the same background. I was told that the difference between an officer and a sailor could be just one grade at 'A' level. The training staff believed that in order to increase the confidence of the officer cadets they should be trained separately and allowed to make mistakes without being observed by the men and women whom they were later to lead. However I just don't find this argument about separate training very convincing. Even when I was trained I made plenty of mistakes in front of my sailors and they forgave them. Officers have to earn their positions of leadership by their character and commitment. It's not something, in my opinion, that should be practised in private.

The Navy believes that it can turn out a qualified naval officer in about two and a half years, which is six months to just under a year less than competing training establishments in other countries, although it is still luxurious compared with the wartime training of reserve officers. The young men and women I met on this visit were facing seven weeks of intense physical and practical training, primarily about the principle of leadership, after which they would go on to their professional naval training, and after about eighteen months they would begin to train in their chosen specialization. However the Navy's expectation of these recruits was identical to its expectations in my day. The Navy never was satisfied with an individual who could not give just that bit more to improve his performance, and still it is not. The small number of seamen officers I met were all still as keen as we had been to obtain command of their own ship, despite the fact that their chances were growing progressively less.

I found myself torn between admiration for the keenness, enthusiasm, and smartness of the officers at Dartmouth, and concern that the College was carrying on almost as though it was unrelated to the real, modern world. Britain's economic strength has been so reduced in world terms that it is inevitable that we must examine the amounts we put into defence and the role we play in the world, but there did not seem to be a clear vision of where the Navy was going, and what the country wanted from its Navy, and therefore it was difficult to establish a clear training requirement. However the officers at Dartmouth were very conscious of their responsibilities as custodians of standards, and also of the need to keep the kernel of a Navy so that it could be expanded if the world situation changed. Many of the people I spoke to were concerned about the size of the Ministry of Defence (MOD) with its large numbers of people involved in control and management, and everyone was worried by the lack of clarity about the role of the Navy as defined by the government; they felt that there was a political vacuum in terms of defining what sort of navy the country needed.

I went on to meet Captain Moore, the Commanding Officer at Dartmouth, who had come from the command of FEARLESS, an amphibious landing ship. The captain was very concerned to point out that, despite the unchanged external appearance of the College, almost everything concerned with the training of naval officers had changed and was continuing to change at a frightening rate. In his view he was responsible for maintaining the capability to train the largest numbers they could expect, and he thought that a potential solution to Dartmouth's higher costs was to broaden away from the officer training area into other fields of training, utilizing the scientific educational capabilities, language training and various other skills which existed at Dartmouth. However he felt that it was essential that Dartmouth also remained a military academy, taking young people out of civilian life or rating service and turning them into officers. Like his subordinates he believed that the initial training of officers and sailors should be done separately, although I felt that since HMS RALEIGH near Plymouth, where the sailors are trained, was currently even emptier than Dartmouth, it would surely make economic sense to amalgamate the two training establishments in the same location, even if the training itself remained separate.

Captain Moore assured me that nepotism had gone from the Navy altogether. Very few of the new intake of potential officers came from naval families which was a major change from my own experience. Captain Moore believed that the role of the Navy was being reexamined but, like others I spoke to, he had little idea what the future requirements would be. Meanwhile, the machine tumbles relentlessly on, as far as I could see, producing the same sorts of officers with the same sort of training which was required during the Cold War and before.

Captain Moore believed that although young people were not attracted to the Service by the same rather romantic ideals which motivated many of us, and also did not have the same expectations of a career which would see them through to retirement, the appeal of a practical seagoing life and a sense of adventure still enabled the Navy to attract a fair measure of the type of people they wanted. The research that had been done showed that people wanted to be of service to their country and believed that the Navy would make the most of the talents of anyone who joined it.

When we turned to the financial aspects of the job the captain, much to my surprise, did not know the exact cost of training an officer, either in general terms or in the more expensive circumstances caused by the reduced intake at Dartmouth. The whole accent seemed to be on making quick savings to balance the budget, irrespective of any long-term effects, because of Treasury pressures for a reduction in the Navy's budget. There seemed little doubt that if the College was to be preserved, and certainly the naval officers there were strongly of the view that Dartmouth was the bedrock of standards of the Royal Navy, it could only be justified financially if the College was used to capacity. Even then I suspected the cost would still be prohibitive, but a combination of very high fixed costs and gross underutilization is a recipe for economic disaster.

I was interested to discover that, almost without exception, the officers felt the loss of Dartmouth would kneecap the officer corps, despite the fact that Dartmouth has been in existence for less than 100 of the 400 year history of the Royal Navy. The officers all felt that the Service was becoming increasingly difficult to manage. Generally speaking the commitments of the Royal Navy, post Cold-War, have remained the same, but the defence budget, the numbers of ships and the numbers of service people have been reduced. This means that the frequency of ships' deployment at sea has increased (although the length of each deployment has remained about the same).

The Navy undoubtedly feels itself under unremitting and unreasonable pressures and appears confused about its future role. All agreed that much of the fun had gone out of naval life and if economic opportunities outside were better, quite a large number would leave for jobs where they thought there were stronger prospects. Almost without exception they believed the Navy was reacting to financial pressures and was losing its case by default.

I was to visit Dartmouth again before the end of filming, for the survivors of the term who had joined with me in January 1938 had arranged to hold their seventieth birthday reunion at the College over a weekend. Twenty-four of the forty-four had arranged to attend, which represented all but two of us who were still alive, or with whom we had not lost touch. We had had a reunion about five years earlier but this was the first time we would all revisit Dartmouth together since we had left in 1940. It was fascinating to see where life had taken us all. Even though we were all in our seventies, practically every one of us was still active in some way or another and it was a particular surprise to me how many were involved with their local churches. As

133

well as dining in the College and yarning till all hours, we attended a church service on the Sunday and enjoyed a trip together up the river. It was a marvellous opportunity to see whether my own concerns about the future of the College were shared in any way by my colleagues. Rather more than the usual number of my term had remained in the Navy for the whole of their careers and we were able to muster no less than five former admirals.

Our reunion was jolly but also quite emotional. It pointed out yet again the difference between our expectations as young men about our futures, and the sense of confusion reigning at the present time. Even though the pre-war Navy was undoubtedly short of money, financial considerations had not loomed large in our thinking. Nobody questioned our role or the sense of privilege we had in serving our country as naval officers. Not one of us envisaged following any other career but that of being part of the Service until retirement. Almost without exception I found my colleagues shared my feelings. We all felt pride that naval standards had been maintained but that pride was tempered with incredulity that the fabric of the building and the size of the establishment could still be relevant to the much reduced role all of us saw for the Navy in the future. To all of us at the reunion it was unthinkable that Britain could survive without a Navy, although, regrettably, it was all too easy to imagine the Navy surviving without the Royal Naval College at Dartmouth, at least in its current form. However what is important is to have a Royal Navy which is relevant and apposite to the defence of Britain for the future.

The question before us was what solution could and would be found. Would officer training be relocated with the other two Services (the Army and the Air Force)? Should Dartmouth and HMS RALEIGH be amalgamated so that the initial training of officers and the initial training of sailors would be carried out in the same location, albeit separately from each other? Or would Dartmouth be filled up, as Captain Moore hoped, as a training establishment, utilizing the facilities and the skills of the instructors and teachers for whatever commercial purposes would enable the costs to be defrayed? Again and again we returned to the same conundrum. Without clarity of the role of the Navy from the government, it was impossible to design a Navy for the future. Without clarity of the design of the Navy for the future it seemed impossible to work out in any economic way what facilities would be needed to provide the necessary officer corps. There appeared to be too many questions and too few answers.

10. Back to sea and back to Tyneside

ARK ROYAL

The Navy exists to go to sea and the Navy at sea is quite a different animal from the Navy on land. The Navy comes alive at sea and I was particularly thrilled to be returning to sea myself. I was lucky enough to spend practically the whole of my wartime service at sea and when I was ashore, after the Second World War, I was generally operating outside large naval establishments in my various roles for Naval Intelligence. The whole purpose of shore establishments in the Royal Navy is to maintain the ships and their crews who are actually doing the fighting. When we were on active service we felt sorry for those who had to fulfil that important but, to us, relatively detached role. Since all the training, leadership style and managerial systems were designed for the efficient running of ships at sea it was not altogether surprising that shore establishments (which are still rather quaintly known as ships) have a somewhat unreal feeling about them.

So it was with a feeling of very great excitement that I left Heathrow to visit our flagship, ARK ROYAL, on operational duty in the Adriatic, off Bosnia. Not only was it my only opportunity actually to go to sea again during the making of my film about the Navy, but I had also not been aboard an aircraft carrier, except in harbour, since 1937! During that year I was invited aboard the GLORIOUS to witness the coronation review. The captain, who subsequently became the First Sea Lord, had been a long-standing friend of my parents in India and he invited us and the Maharaja, my father's ward, as his guests to see the review. Although by that time I had already committed myself to joining the Navy, the review would have persuaded me (had I needed any persuasion) that I was fortunate to be joining the most important Service in the entire country.

GLORIOUS could barely have been more different from the ship I was now to visit and nor could my method of joining. We were flown from Rome to ARK ROYAL in a Sea King helicopter which had just delivered one of the visiting admirals in time to catch his return flight to Britain. Courtesy, therefore, of the admiral and the MOD, the film crew and I found ourselves enjoying a low-level flight across Italy for which I would have paid a fortune of my own money. Of course I had flown in many helicopters before but they had always been relatively well-insulated, soundproofed civilian versions. The Sea King, which is still, after nearly thirty years of service, the workhorse of the Royal Navy, provided none of these refinements. The Sea King was first produced for the Navy in 1969 and its design is based on the 1960s American S-61 Sikorsky. The Sea King is the ultimate in versatility; it seemed to be able to perform almost every task one could imagine, from lifting and hauling heavy loads, to air-sea rescue, the detection of submarines or acting as the modern equivalent of a picket boat taking people to and from their ships. However, inside the helicopter it was hot and sweaty and so noisy that it was only possible to communicate through the intercom system. Nevertheless, the flight gave us the sort of wonderful panoramic effect which can only be enjoyed by flying over a country at about 1000 feet at a relatively slow speed. After a flight of about an hour and a half we crossed the coast and we were all eager to catch sight the ship itself.

The ARK ROYAL was one of three aircraft carriers, each from a different country, which were stationed in the Adriatic to provide essential air cover for the United Nations (UN) forces in Bosnia. Each of them had an area of sea about forty miles by ten, around which they steamed endlessly while providing platforms for the aircraft which were operating in Bosnia itself. From the air it was quite surprising how small the ship looked. We stood off for a few moments until the ship was ready to receive us, which gave us an opportunity to enjoy an absolutely first class view of the ARK. From the air she looked immaculate and well-ordered, impressions which were to be reinforced when we landed. I was greeted by the Commander, and by the Commander Air Engineering, Dai Morgan, who was to be my coordinator during my visit. Once I had been welcomed aboard in traditional style I was introduced to the admiral's steward, who would look after me during my stay. The admiral, Admiral Gretton, was the son of one my term officers during my time at Dartmouth who had gone on to become a distinguished wartime captain and subsequently a vice admiral.

I had quite a lot of experience in the Mediterranean during the Second World War, and have passed through it on a number of subsequent occasions. It is a highly deceptive sea. The fact that it is landlocked makes one assume it will be placid and quiet, as it was on the day we joined ARK ROYAL, but the seas can whip up with extraordinary speed and malevolence, and the Mediterranean in an angry mood can test the skills of any sailor. The Mediterranean holds a particular place in my heart: I was sunk twice off North Africa at the beginning of the North African campaign, as well as operating in submarines from Malta. Curiously, despite all this experience, I had never actually been north into the Adriatic before.

You can tell the nature of a ship almost as soon as you step aboard it, just as you can tell the nature of a factory by walking through the shop floor. Happy ships are, almost without exception, efficient ones. As soon as I stepped aboard ARK ROYAL I got the feeling of a truly happy ship. It came from a combination of teamwork, enthusiasm, evidence of mutual respect, and a curious admixture of high professionalism and easy humour. The ship's company were working very long hours in pretty tough conditions, but despite that they all believed in the job they were doing, and were intensely proud of the ship and all it stood for. The extraordinary thing about ARK ROYAL was the mixture of extremely advanced technology with other items of equipment which antedated the Second World War.

I just had time to unpack my bags before I was taken up to the bridge to meet the captain of the ARK, Captain Terence Loughran. The ship was replenishing from its attendant Royal Fleet Auxiliary tanker, the FORT AUSTIN, which meant the two were steaming alongside each other attached by a jackstay to which fuel lines were secured. Stores were also being transferred and under these circumstances both ships are relatively unmanoeuvrable. A replenishing operation in constricted waters almost always seems to attract fishing vessels and others who demand their rights by the law of the sea, rather than understanding the problems of large naval vessels carrying out intricate manoeuvres.

ARK ROYAL had been in the Adriatic from January to September 1993 and was in the middle of a second nine month period of Adriatic service when I visited in July 1994. Naturally enough, there had been an endless stream of senior visitors. The captain stressed how relatively easy life was on real operations because of the visible sense of purpose. However, like everyone else in the Navy they felt themselves to be under continual financial pressure to reduce costs, while still being obliged to maintain the same high standards and meet the same obligations. It was ironic that for the first time since Nelson's day the Royal Navy is now smaller than the French Navy and the ARK ROYAL was dwarfed in size and number of aircraft by the French aircraft carrier operating a little further north. But, despite cutting back, the Royal Navy is still endeavouring to maintain a fully rounded service, with a nuclear deterrent, aircraft carriers, amphibious capability and submarines. Each of the arms of the Service has been reduced to the level below which they cannot effectively cut back any further. Three aircraft carriers are needed if the Navy is to maintain one continuously at sea, and the ARK ROYAL was proud of the fact that, because of their ability to move anywhere, they were able to operate their aircraft continuously, whereas the Italian airfields can be shut down by fog. Moreover the ability to operate at sea meant that the Navy's forces were beholden to no one and, together with their supply ship, were totally independent of the goodwill of any other country.

Somewhat to my surprise, the captain did not know the exact cost of running ARK ROYAL or keeping her on station but, as he explained, he had no control over these matters: the complement of the ship was laid down and dictated by broader considerations than the practicalities of keeping the ship operating at the time. Even if he felt it possible to manage with fewer officers he was unable to take the decision to reduce his complement. This is a big difference from an industrial manager, who is judged by his ability continuously to achieve the same results with lower costs. I've always believed it's important that the people who actually spend the money should have control over it, and I suspected that the captain would agree with that.

However, naval manning is by definition somewhat inflexible because of the specialist in-house training of their people. But nevertheless the more I went around, the more I came to the conclusion that greater flexibility in this area was one of the many desirable changes the Navy would have to face. As things are organized at the present time it takes many years to train a naval specialist. A first-rate nuclear submarine engineer takes eight years to train and therefore recruitment and training is being carried out against an unpredictable forward picture which is continuously changed in response to financial pressures. And it is even more difficult than that: the Navy's determination to produce lean manning of ships after the Falklands War means that ships are now designed to operate with fewer people: ten years ago the average frigate would have had a ship's company of 240. Today the same ship's company averages 160 or so.

When I visited ARK ROYAL, one of the biggest surprises to me was the enormous cost necessary to maintain only seven Harriers on operational duties, and also that, due to the reduction in total Fleet manpower, there are now more senior officers in the modern Navy. The ARK ROYAL alone had, as well as the captain, ten commanders and nine ranks between the captain and the able seamen. But the whole pattern of the manning of ships has altered enormously due to increasingly sophisticated technology. On an aircraft carrier the officer to sailor ratio is one to five; in most other ships it is between one to ten and one to fifteen. On an aircraft carrier the air crew adds to the number of officers but, from a business point of view, hierarchies create more and more work and in the Navy promotion and hierarchy have been substituted for other forms of reward at a time when every other organization is heading for flatter and flatter structures.

I asked the captain what changes he would most like to see in the Navy and he replied that firstly he would like some stability and predictability for the future, and a vision of the future they could stick to and, secondly, that he wished for more recognition from the government and from the British public of the worth and role of the

Royal Navy. It seemed to me that the second would lead to the first and until there was a clear long-term vision of what the Navy could uniquely do within the economic capability of the country, it was unlikely that there would be much stability. On a number of occasions in conversation with senior naval officers I encountered the argument that it was necessary to have the Navy in order for us to retain our seat on the Security Council. This begged the question of whether Britain needs a seat on the Security Council, given the realities of its economic power. It doesn't seem to me that Japan or Germany have suffered too much from not having a seat on the Security Council and, if the cost of a seat is the maintenance of levels of armed forces that Britain cannot afford, it does not seem to be a good argument for the maintenance of a large sea-going force either.

That evening I was entertained to dinner by the captain and three of the commanders, two of whom had just received notification of their promotion. We were entertained in the admiral's quarters, in the style that only the Navy can still maintain. Champagne on the quarter-deck preceded an immaculately cooked and served meal which would not have disgraced The Ritz Hotel. The following day I toured the ship and was able to watch much of it in operation. Many things had barely changed in all the years I have been away. The galleys were still turning out the finest roast potatoes in the world and at last I found out the secret of their preparation. But equally the galleys underlined the whole immutability and rigidity of the Royal Navy. Not only were the officers' and the sailors' meals cooked and eaten separately, but the sailors' messing arrangements were also divided into two separate self-service areas, one for the junior and one for the senior sailors. Interestingly the chief cook was very much more sensitive to the sailors' preferences than had been the case in my day and a lunchtime meal now included salads and vegetarian food as well as the good old Navy stodge which used to maintain sailors at sea. The officers meet and are served their meals in the wardroom, as has happened since time immemorial. They are still waited on at table and change for dinner, even on operations like this. At a time when the trend in industry and elsewhere is to cut out hierarchical differentiation, it seemed that these were the very last things that would change in the Royal Navy.

I was particularly interested in what the helicopter crews had to say. They shed a different light on the motivation and problems of the Royal Navy. The Sea Kings they were flying had been designed in the late 1960s and were now so old that it was only by constant maintenance that the aircraft could be kept flying. Their successor aircraft, the Merlin, has been on the way for seventeen years and so, when it does finally emerge in service, it will already be outdated. The Sea King had been made over so many times that maintenance was even more difficult than when it had originally been designed. Indeed the first helicopter that the current captain of the ARK ROYAL had flown as a junior pilot was still in service, and actually operating from ARK ROYAL at the time I was there.

The squadrons are dedicated to ARK ROYAL for the length of time she is at sea; then they relocate to Yeovilton, one of the naval air stations ashore. The maintenance crews worked round the clock, twelve hours on and twelve hours off, in appallingly hot conditions in the hangars in order to keep the squadron operating, and it seemed to me that the cost of maintenance alone might well have paid for the replacement of the Sea Kings by a newer model. But it did not seem to me that the total costs, including operating costs, played a part in hastening the procurement cycle.

I had not realized that the naval method of selection and training of able air crew was quite different from that of the Royal Air Force (RAF). The initial naval selection was of older, more mature candidates and they have their own allocated maintenance teams and move together as a unit. Moreover, they are trained in a very wide range of activities, from antisubmarine warfare to reconnaissance, air-sea rescue and so on. But, despite the fact that they were rather more confident about the transferability of their skills compared with their non-air crew naval compatriots, they were still worried about the future of the Navy. The air crew in particular were not motivated primarily by pay and, almost without exception, they were in it for the love of flying, however better equipment featured high on their list of priorities.

As with the Sea Kings, ARK ROYAL itself was an old (1970s) design and expensive to maintain. The ARK ROYAL was commissioned in 1985 and although the staff were as enthusiastic about Swan Hunter having built the ARK as it was possible to be, and despite the excellence of its construction, some aspects of the ship had not been able to keep up with the changing demands made upon it. About half the electrical load in the entire ship was taken by running the air conditioning, which was still inadequate to maintain comfortable temperatures in Adriatic conditions. Sophisticated software had been applied to existing hardware, in the belief that total performance would improve, despite the fact that software costs are extremely high. An interesting comment about the differences between the Navy and industrial life was made by one of the engineer commanders, who had recently taken an MBA. He had become very enthusiastic about the idea of empowerment, but it is virtually impossible to empower those at the bottom when you have a very long hierarchy, in his case eight levels between him and the sailors he was trying to empower. Again and again I came back to the problem of multiple heirarchical levels instead of a more flexible reward system. The Navy seems to be preoccupied with planning and controlling events which are, in reality, uncontrollable. Take redundancy, for example. In most naval redundancy rounds the Navy attempts to select a cross section of individuals of every ability in the belief that by so doing the promotion opportunities of the best are maintained. They have also sought to retire those who were over-specialized, but most other organizations facing the need for redundancy today use the opportunity to try and improve the overall standards of the organization by getting rid of the weaker members.

Despite the antiquity of much of the equipment, and the conditions under which the aircraft – and indeed the ship – had been maintained and operated, the enthusiasm was almost tangible, as was the sailors' pride in the ship and their ability to keep their aircraft flying and operating. It is easy to find things to criticize in the Royal Navy but no one can gainsay the incredible acts of front-line leadership of which ARK ROYAL was a first class example. The Navy's ability to train its people and motivate them cannot be denied and there is little doubt that their belief that they are the most professional navy in the world is also true. However to expect those trained professionals to operate near obsolete equipment seemed to me to be a waste of their expertise. I felt that nobody had really thought through what the delay in the new

143

helicopter, the Merlin, was really costing every single day in terms of the extra work the men were having to put in to keep the Sea Kings in the air. It seemed to me to be the wrong way round. The money should be spent on purchasing new aircraft sooner, rather than on the extra expense of maintaining old aircraft. But I left ARK ROYAL full of admiration for the crew and feeling that she was quite plainly a happy ship that was run efficiently, within the limitations imposed upon him, by a good captain. However I was becoming more and more concerned by the number of people I'd met who had expressed the same uncertainty about the future of the Service, the positions The Admiralty Board were taking, and Britain's requirements of its Navy.

My visit to ARK ROYAL left me with mixed emotions. Pride that the Navy I knew and which had brought me up was still maintaining its standards, style and tradition, but also concern that it was not changing fast enough. I felt that too many of the ordinary people in the Navy who have to speak up for their Service were uncertain and confused about the future and how they were going to cope with it. Uncertainty is the greatest destroyer of morale. People always imagine far worse outcomes than reality actually brings forth, and it seemed to me that large numbers of people in the Navy were worrying unnecessarily about what the future might hold in store. But I had one more visit to pay before I drew my final conclusions.

Swan Hunter

When I served in the Navy we had plenty of ships; now we've barely got enough to keep the three key arms of the Navy – the submarine service, the amphibious capability and the aircraft carrier capability – going. Any more reductions and one whole arm might have to go. I wanted to see how the industrial infrastructure which maintains the Navy was coping with these reductions and there seemed no better place to start than in Newcastle at Swan Hunter, which gave me an opportunity to revisit the place for the first time since 1944 when I joined my first submarine, HMS TRUSTY. The name Swan Hunter is in itself the guarantee of a well-constructed ship, but the yard I was visiting today might have come from a completely different world.

I arrived at the Swan Hunter shipyard at Wallsend in 1994 just after it had gone bankrupt and been taken over by the receivers. There is very little sadder or more poignant than a shipyard which is not working. Shipyards, of all industrial activities, are places where you can actually see everything going on, and I remembered something like 30 000 people working in the shipyards on the River Tyne. There was a constant movement of cranes performing an industrial ballet against the skyline, and a shipyard in full flight is a mass of people, rather like worker ants, working in a coordinated manner to complete their own part of the complex mechanism that goes into the building of a ship.

In losing Swan Hunter we have lost the only one of the four existing warship yards which is currently capable of building an aircraft carrier. Any other yard will need to make a special capital investment if another aircraft carrier is required. When Swan Hunter went not only did we lose the physical capability to build an aircraft carrier, but we also lost the experience necessary to put together large and complex warship orders. From a shipbuilder's point of view the problem has been exacerbated by the lack of commercial attractiveness of many of the designs the Royal Navy has ordered. Generally they require more complex and specialized ships than are needed by other navies and thus it is difficult for these shipbuilders to win foreign orders. Until recently, the producibility of the ship has been an afterthought, although the liaison between ship designers and the producers has improved and some broader use of commercial standards has become acceptable. Previously almost every single item used in Royal Navy warships had been specially made for the Royal Navy, with a predictable effect upon its cost.

This sad shipyard, for all its lack of movement, showed signs of money having been poured into it. The cranes were all 1960s or 1970s refurbished cranes, the slipways had been reequipped and there were vast coloured halls for modular construction of large pieces of ships which are now assembled from prefabricated sections. There were about 1000 people still working in the yard finishing the last two firm orders.

When British shipbuilding was privatized the government sold Swan Hunter to the management as a purely naval yard. Having done that, in theory at least, market forces were to decide whether they would obtain the necessary work to keep going. Sadly, however, there was not enough work available to maintain the number of warship yards in the country. Despite diversification and their efforts to obtain business overseas, Swan Hunter finally went into receivership. The yard had simultaneously been bidding for a major contract, which would have employed about three quarters of the workforce then on the books for a further period of three or four years.

The difficulty with running a medium-sized naval yard is that the orders tend to come in once every three or four years, and usually one at a time, although each separate order may be for more than one ship. However, when one order is lost the whole yard is threatened. The fact that the yard had been designated for warship building meant that, until autumn 1993 when they lost the MOD contract, Swan Hunter was precluded from obtaining any subsidy for merchant shipbuilding, which put an added onus on the MOD to have a clear strategy to maintain enough manufacturing infrastructure to meet the needs of the Royal Navy. Swan Hunter's difficulties were compounded because they had spent large amounts of money and effort obtaining a contract to build ships for Oman but, understandably, when the yard went into receivership the Omanis would not confirm the contract without government guarantees, which the government in turn were unwilling to produce. It began to sound very much as though somebody somewhere had marked Swan Hunter as surplus to requirements and was merely interested in hastening the day when the yard would go to the wall.

I was taken round by Alex Marsh, who had been the Joint Chief Executive and who was staying on to assist the receivers while they endeavoured to find a buyer. Alex readily agreed about the need for them to work very closely with the Royal Navy, but complained about the absence of strategy and reality in the forward planning of naval ship building. The Navy, while indicating what they might like to build, never appeared to be in a position to commit to any particular sort of vessel. The forward plans for new ship ordering programmes had altered continuously and dramatically, year upon year, in very much the same way as the intake of future officers at Dartmouth. Alex felt the Navy were trying to keep the Service exactly as it had been and to maintain everything in tip-top, up-to-date fashion, all on a much reduced budget. When the money was not there programmes changed, contracts were not awarded and there was an inordinate delay while new plans were drawn up. If, like Swan Hunter, the supplying industry was undercapitalized and reliant on continuous cash flow, they were doomed to failure from the start. Moreover, in the cushy days of 1944 when ships were needed, and needed in a hurry, most of the work was done on a cost plus basis, whereas now everything is on bidding for fixed prices. Because there are more warship yards than can be sustained in the long term, the effect of competitive tendering has been to drive prices down as the yards scrabble for their future survival.

It was difficult to discern a strategy in this approach for the retention of the sort of industrial base required to ensure Britain could build the warships which would presumably be needed for the future. This appeared to be in marked contradistinction to the approach used in France, Italy and Germany. In Alex's view the lack of any firm forward ordering programme, which made the development of an industrial strategy impossible, derived in turn from a lack of political clarity about the future role of the Navy and the sort of defence industry necessary to support it. The result of the Navy being so uncertain about their role and being unable to follow that role consistently, even if they understood it, is exacerbated by the considerable problems of day-to-day management of the country's finances, which originate from the Treasury. As a result, in Alex's view, everything comes down to the lowest common denominator, which is the least cost option for the year in question which is then disguised as market forces at work.

Alex had actually worked out where TRUSTY had been berthed and to my immense surprise the battery shed into which the submarine battery was off-loaded while she was refitting was still standing there, looking even more sad and decrepit than when I first saw it. When we went down to the berth which I had been alongside so long ago I recognized the tunnel going under the railway track which led out of the yard and, to my amazement, behind it was The Ship Inn – just as I remembered it. Like the yard itself, The Ship Inn had also gone into receivership, having been a tied house in more than one sense. I found it all immensely depressing. I thought back to the days when the yard

147

was building 200 000 ton tankers whose bows overhung the shipyard walls. The work went on night and day and Swan Hunter had to pay compensation to the inhabitants of the houses in the road outside because their daylight was blocked by the gigantic tankers under construction and, as a result, they had to use electric light all day.

It is a sad and ironic fact that since privatization in 1986 the flexibility of the workforce and the productivity of the whole yard increased out of all recognition. Total closure seemed a poor reward for so much effort. But despite these appalling prospects everybody I met at the yard was still totally committed to finishing the work on the last two ships to their usual high standards. Obviously these workers, with their specialist skills, were in many ways tied to the yard for as long as it remained open. Swan Hunter was the last shipbuilder in existence on the Tyne and the area as a whole has high unemployment, so the outlook for both workers and managers was poor. Since the yard was in receivership they would in any event receive minimum compensation when the yard was finally shut down. Despite all this they remained caustically cheerful and they worked at the same pace and with the same attention to detail as if there were tasks lined up ahead of them forever.

Alex was very proud of the flexibility of the Swan Hunter yard and the number of ingenious ways they had found of solving problems. For example they had erected mobile sheds clad in plastic, costing about £250 000 each, instead of building permanent structures which constrained the use of the slipways. Their outfitting sheds were capable of building structures up to 200 tons outfitted with equipment and electrical cables and painted, ready for lifting into position and fitting as a modular unit. But the fabrication sheds were totally empty and everything saleable had already been removed. They had invested in automatic bays to manufacture and strengthen flat panels for ships and had numerically controlled burning machines which would cut out heavy plates automatically. One of their primary problems had been trying to keep too large a capacity against the unknown quantity of future orders.

A visit to the stores was a rapid illustration of the vast number of construction materials which had been made and paid for, only to lie unused in the stores due to changes in intention, all of which ultimately swelled the cost of the end product. Everyone I met, including those in the stores, were loud in their praise of the efforts being made by the receivers to save the yard and seemed to accept with surprising tranquillity the increased responsibilities which had been placed upon the relatively small remaining workforce. One of the first things the receivers had done was to remove large numbers of management, as a result of which people like storemen were doing their own arranging and purchasing of transport and so on. Tom Scott, the Project Manager, and the others were the first to admit that there had been too many managers employed in the yard before receivership and they had been agreeably surprised at the ability of their workforce to take on many of these responsibilities.

Tom took me round the frigate NORTHUMBERLAND, which was in the last week of construction prior to sea trials and was a surprise to me in a number of ways. It was a good example of the Navy's approach to lean manning. In my day the complement of a ship was dictated by the number of people necessary to man all the weapons. This number was in turn so large that there were always more people than were actually required to steam the ship and the problem was largely to find useful employment for all these spare bods – such as cleaning, painting, maintaining and exercising. With modern technology and computerization the fighting complement of a ship is far less and does not provide the surplus cover needed for all these other tasks. As a result, for instance, modern ships are spring-cleaned when they return to port because today's much smaller ships' companies have less time to spend on such tasks while they are at sea. The NORTHUMBERLAND and its sister ship the RICHMOND were the last of the Type 23 ships whose contracts were won by Swan Hunter, and in the event the last work to be undertaken before the yard finally closed down. The Type 23 is universally thought of as a much better designed ship than its predecessors, because it is very quiet and very flexible. To my amazement the yard did not know what the total cost of the ships were, since they had only quoted for 80% of labour costs and materials: the other 20% – for which they had no figures – was the cost of MOD-supplied weapons and suchlike.

149

The manufacturing and construction process for the ships is totally rigid and the shipbuilder has no flexibility for saving money, even if he wants to. In fact I was shown examples of suggestions which had been made to change items which were impractical and would cause future maintenance problems. Since they had been unable to get agreement from any individual they had no option but to go ahead with the manufacture of something they believed to be wrong. In one example it had been decided by the Navy to half panel the mess deck. Tom pointed out that cutting the panelling halfway up the deck meant fitting all the various pipes around it, which would otherwise have been hidden beneath it. The offcuts were unusable for anything else and the whole scheme ended up costing more. Despite Tom's efforts he had been unable to get anybody to take responsibility for changing the original instruction. It appeared that no one individual was responsible for minimizing the total cost of the ship, since the responsibilities for different parts of the vessel were divided amongst a large number of specifiers and suppliers. Any deviation from the agreed drawings constituted a defect which was held to the shipbuilder's account and it was nearly impossible to find anyone prepared to agree to any alteration from the original drawings.

Tom showed me example after example of potential savings if the total cost of the operation had been looked at in an holistic way, allowing for the cost of installation, fitting and suchlike. Although set against the total ship's costs the amounts saved would have been small, but it is by saving small amounts of money the whole time in a variety of different ways that costs are continuously driven down. As far as I could see the MOD requirement was that the cost of the last ship should be just the same as the first, whereas any normal industrial procedure would be continuously to improve the product and reduce the cost. Despite all this the officers and ship's company of the NORTHUMBERLAND, many of whom were standing by the ship, were loud in their praise of the standards and quality that had been maintained.

While I was visiting Swan Hunter a French consortium put in a bid for the yard and government agreement was being sought to enable Constructions Méchaniques de Normandie (CMN) to buy it. Since it was the only viable bid for the yard it appeared that the government was faced with a choice between allowing the yard to go altogether and losing the hard core of skills and potential production capacity, or accepting that a warship yard in Britain would be managed and controlled by the French. The new owners believed they could secure overseas orders in addition to the one Swan Hunter had previously obtained. However, they would need time to set the order book up and were, therefore, looking for some refitting work from the government which in the event was not forthcoming. In fact, because of a delay in the takeover, the MOD cut the price of the last two Type 23 ships by £700 000, contributing to the demise of the Swan Hunter shipyard. The people on Tyneside feel this was a deliberate action to shut down surplus capacity rather than maintain employment on Tyneside with the potential for export orders which would have helped Britain's balance of payments.

We did a brief trip down the river looking at the yard from the riverside and it was rather like progressing through the ruins of Hamburg after the Second World War. There was no sign of activity on the river anywhere – in fact the only sign of life was the dock at Hawthorn Leslie, the now defunct shipyard opposite Swan Hunter's which has been converted into a museum. Whether by design or by accident we now have one less shipyard, one less group of men capable of building warships, and one less opportunity to earn money in the export trade. In addition unemployment has been increased on Tyneside and a highly skilled design team has been dispersed. In the meantime our ships are built in ways which minimize the chances of continual reduction in cost and the organization appears to be one which divides responsibilities so that there is no one who can agree the sorts of trade-off between optimal performance in one area and another, which are the primary ways in which improvements are made. It seems to me that everybody should work together on one site. The MOD should handle things on site so that there is more communication between the contractors and the MOD where the work is actually taking place. A distant bureaucracy cannot see, nor get to grips with, the problems at first hand and that is how communication fails and the wrong instructions are given.

151

There's no doubt this isn't an easy time for the Navy. But in the absence of a consistent and clear vision of what's required of them by the government, the Navy has even more responsibility for charting its own course. And the people who have to do that are the ones at head office, at the MOD. It was time I found out from those at the top what The Admiralty Board felt, and how they thought they were leading the Navy – and into what future?

11. Whither the Navy in the Nineties?

Headquarters

My visits to Dartmouth, to ARK ROYAL and to the now defunct Swan Hunter shipyard had all left me with the same feelings. I had the impression of dedicated men trying to hold back inexorable external pressures for change, which they recognized but were uncertain about. If the argument for a future navy is that it must be flexible, then that flexibility must come from inside the Navy itself, and despite the dedication, goodwill and enthusiasm I'd encountered, I hadn't found much evidence of flexibility. The dilemma that faces every naval officer is how much of the glorious past must be maintained in order to hold on to the ethos, conditions and beliefs of the Service and how much can safely be changed. There is a yearning for careful and cautious change, despite the fact that the cataclysm of the collapse of communism has produced unavoidable pressures for total change.

In the past the Navy designed precision instruments to deal with predictable situations. What they are now faced with is a future which demands simpler but more adaptable solutions to problems which are, by definition, unknown until they actually happen. All of this places even greater emphasis on the need for clarity about the role and necessity of the Royal Navy today, but my overriding feeling after my visits to the various parts of the Navy was one of lack of focus and coordination. The individual parts of the Navy seemed to be run almost independently of each other. Meanwhile the whole organization was continuously reacting and changing in an attempt to meet constant but ill-defined political demands. Faced with these uncertainties, and the obvious need to adjust from their very specific role during the Cold War and before to a role which was uncertain and difficult to predict, the Navy seemed to me to be desperately trying to hold on to everything. This is probably due in equal parts to uncertainty about what might be required, and a desire to protect the force it had once been. Meanwhile, although extremely courageous action had been taken in reducing the manning of the new generation of ships, the tail (the staff, shore establishments and so on) of the Navy, which exists to support those ships, was still larger than I believed should be the case. In many cases it was possible that new equipment would save on running costs. In the case of shore establishments it was still unclear what alternative uses could be made of some of the historic and listed buildings. In the middle of all this the officers and men and women, as always, were magnificent. They were of the same high quality as they always had been, and just as dedicated to the task of maintaining the Navy as the pre-eminent Service of its kind in the world.

As I thought about all this on my way to the MOD I allowed myself a detour to visit the old Cabinet Offices where I had worked in 1947. The Cabinet War Rooms have been opened as a museum and the office where I used to work as a humble naval lieutenant is now an item of interest to numbers of museum visitors! Little has changed in the offices themselves but they looked extraordinarily dated and dingy: everything looked exactly as it had at the end of the Second World War. At the time I was appointed to the Cabinet Offices I had little experience of working on shore and was impressed by working underground in a supposedly bombproof environment. In reality the offices were little more than made-over basements. When we were involved in operations I had to work at night and had dossed down in Winston Churchill's office, which was also unchanged.

At the time the biggest surprise to me was that policy was created so far down the line by such junior people. I remember being told to produce some plans within the first days of my appointment, which eventually proved to be British policy in an area of which I had only the most trivial personal knowledge. To my horror my paper proceeded inexorably upwards through the machinery of government, up to the Joint Development Committee, on to the chiefs of staff and then,

Garibaldi
Comprehensive
School near
Mansfield, in
Nottinghamshire:
Sir John visiting the
language laboratory
(ABOVE), and with a
design and technology
class (LEFT).

ABOVE Pupils and staff at Lawrence Weston School, Bristol.

RIGHT Sir John's granddaughter Abigail doing her teacher training practice at Balsall Common Primary School, near Coventry.

Clifton College, Bristol: a rugby game (ABOVE); Sir John talking to pupils (LEFT).

ABOVE Sir John with fellow old boys at their class reunion at the Royal Naval College, Dartmouth.

OPPOSITE ABOVE Talking to Angus Sinclair, Training Commander at the Naval College.

OPPOSITE BELOW Sir John, with the Royal Naval College in the background.

ABOVE Sir John and Admiral Bathurst, the First Sea Lord, at the Royal Naval College, Greenwich.

OPPOSITE On board the aircraft carrier HMS ARK ROYAL, in the Adriatic, off Bosnia.

ABOVE Sir John revisits the ICI plant at Wilton, near Middlesbrough.

RIGHT Sir John with Ian Gibson, the Chief Executive, at the Nissan car plant in Sunderland.

horror of horrors, on to the Defence Committee. I speedily realized that we were responsible, to a very real extent, for the political directions that were handed back down to us. In those days our whole job was to create government policy. These days I can't make out whether there is a clear government role for the Navy which is not being adequately communicated inside the Service, or whether there is confusion within the government and within the Navy, as to what a modern navy is actually for. I can see that it must be particularly difficult to run a navy when you're not really clear who the enemy is or where the threats may come from. That's been the case since the end of the Cold War, but somebody in the Navy has to decide what sorts of ships we keep, what we build for, how many we have and what their capabilities are. I wondered what I would find when I visited the MOD itself.

The commodores

I met the commodores responsible for the various departments at Navy Headquarters and in many ways they correspond to a management board. I met seven of them, which in turn indicated the way in which the functions of the Navy had been broken down into self-contained fields of decision. I met them in the 'new' MOD building (new being almost forty years old), but for all its splendid exterior the building was definitely showing its age. There was a depressing similarity and symmetry of design which was rather like an airport hotel. Every corridor and every door looked the same, and increasingly the officers behind the doors started to look the same as well.

The commodores had dressed up for the occasion, wearing their broad stripes, but despite endless attempts to get them to talk about what they felt they should be changing, it was almost impossible to move any of these distinguished officers away from the party line, which was that the Navy was already infinitely flexible and doing everything possible within the available money to ensure that money was used for the best possible purposes. I found the meeting a somewhat dispiriting one. I said that one of the most important things was to make sure every sailor and officer in the Navy knew what the Navy's role was and why the Navy was so vital for the future (something which, sadly, I had not come across on my travels). It was difficult to judge how much of the commodores' defensiveness on this subject was due to their fears of being seen to be acting politically and how much represented their own personal views.

Next I said that I felt the Navy was perilously close to reaching the irreducible minimum number of ships below which it would be unable to support the Navy's three key arms, the submarine service, the aircraft carrier capability and the amphibious capability. The commodores did not accept my views on this subject and neither did they share my sense of urgency about this; they felt that if they had fewer ships the only effect would be that they would lose the ability to undertake concurrent operations. I found myself caught in a circular argument: the government is restricted in its choices by the size of its Navy, while the Navy is restricted in its size by the decisions of government.

I said that without exception I had found the standards everywhere to be extraordinarily high which was heartening, but that decision-making and financial responsibility should be pushed down the line so that those who spent the money could also control it. I was told that ships at sea were ring-fenced from this kind of responsibility because they had enough to cope with without becoming financial managers as well, and the commodores strongly contested my view that they were being run by the Treasury. They actually claimed that they had pushed financial responsibility as far down the line as possible and indeed were, in every sense, masters of their own destiny.

The commodores were convinced that the best way of reducing numbers was to reduce the intake, rather than maintain a steady intake and make more redundancies from their trained people. There was little support for my view that Dartmouth was untenable in its present half-empty state, but every time I pressed for facts they were not forthcoming. For example nobody could tell me the optimum number of naval officers they were planning and training for, although they said, jokingly, that no reductions could be made since the chances of promotion to rear admiral had been reduced from one in four to one in eleven already!

I also got nowhere when I tried to tackle the problem of the design of the industrial base to support the Navy in the future, which they saw as being a political matter rather than a professional one and outside their own involvement. While they maintained that everybody was looking for reductions in manning and suggestions for manning reductions could easily be sent up the line, nobody I met saw this as a major part of their job. In most other businesses people not only continuously seek ways of reducing numbers, but also have the responsibility for executing their decisions. And the commodores were not keen on the idea of performance-related pay, although they agreed that the multiplicity of ranks meant that each rank was effectively a pay point, so that in their terms performance-related rewards existed in terms of promotion.

The commodores accepted that the MOD itself was too large but they believed that numbers there were being severely cut. They made the point – several times – that the Navy was in a process of transition and that they had some way to go in terms of deregulation, decent-ralization and removal of layers. But when I asked what specific action had been taken to decentralize, deregulate and remove heirarchical layers I did not receive specific answers. The commodores claimed that defence policy was the result of discussions between the Navy and the Treasury in which the Navy was quite satisfied with the role they played. They actually believed they had at last got a degree of political commitment to the maintenance of a balanced Navy which had emerged from the latest defence cost study, *Front Line First*.

I became more and more convinced that the Navy was overmanaged and underdirected. I also sensed a real fear of publicly presenting their arguments about the Navy's role in case it was seen as an attempt to enter the political arena. They felt that alerting the public to the potential dangers of the current world situation would be seen as counterproductive and sabre rattling in order to justify their own existence.

After my meeting with the commodores, two of them gave me to understand that they were more open-minded than they had appeared in the discussion, but I certainly did not leave my meeting with the Navy's management board with a feeling of a radically-minded group pressing for the sort of sweeping changes I suspected would be necess-ary to produce the best Navy we could have, to deal with the threats which might face Britain in the future. It was time to meet the First Sea Lord and find out what he felt.

The First Sea Lord

It had been arranged that I should meet Admiral Sir Benjamin Bathurst, the First Sea Lord, at the Royal Naval College at Greenwich. This is one of the oldest and most architecturally important of all the Navy's remaining shore establishments, and the first surprise I received when arriving at Greenwich was to find that, in marked contrast to Dartmouth, it was reasonably full. Greenwich runs staff courses and one course – the joint services defence course for mid-seniority officers – is a tri-Service course.

I started by congratulating the First Sea Lord on the maintenance of the Navy's high standards, and then I explained my concerns about the lack of clarity, both in the public mind and down the line in the Navy itself, about the role of the Navy in today's world. I said I felt that the chaps down the line were not getting a clear message about what the role of the Navy is, nor why we need a Navy for the future. I also said I was sure that the general public did not understand the Navy's role either. Rather disappointingly the First Sea Lord started by producing the text-book answer which is that the Navy's role is to support Britain's foreign and security policy. Since I found it a bit difficult to discover what those policies were, his answer did not reassure me.

I said I felt that some of the things the Navy had done had been extraordinarily high risk and very brave. For instance I felt that the lean manning of ships had gone far farther than I would ever have believed possible, but that the rank structure was still the same as it ever was. There appeared to be more chiefs and fewer indians. The First Sea Lord said that although the number of admirals had been reduced by 20%, the Navy was still top heavy, but that an independent review was examining exactly these points at the moment, following on from the findings of the defence cost study, *Front Line First*. The independent review was charged with finding ways to manage the changes identified in *Front Line First*, such as ways to change the hierarchical pyramid and the reward system and make both more flexible. The independent review will report its findings in 1995 and Admiral Bathurst was certain that the Navy would act extremely quickly on its recommendations.

The Navy had been reduced in size by about 65 000 by the end of the 1980s and a further reduction of 30% would be achieved by 1995–96, and the First Sea Lord readily accepted that it had not been possible to maintain a balanced reduction in all aspects of the Service at the same time. An obvious example was the area of information technology, where the decision-making processes are simply not being adapted fast enough to take advantage of the technology presently available. Admiral Bathurst felt the Navy was bound to go down the road of having fewer, but more highly skilled people and that, in turn, this would demand a different approach to their reward system.

Admiral Bathurst agreed with my view that the Navy was perilously close to the minimum level at which maximum flexibility could be maintained, but he believed this point was now accepted by the government who realized the need to change from threat based forces to capability based forces. The problem was to design the maximum amount of flexible capability within the available money, since only the Americans now have the economic strength to maintain capability in every field simultaneously.

I pointed out that the violent fluctuations in officer recruitment, besides the inevitable financial effects on the cost of training officers, gave an impression of uncontrolled reactions and it was difficult to believe that Dartmouth could be maintained. However the First Sea Lord believed he needed to maintain the large number of commanders at sea in order to provide sea experience at commander level and that there could, therefore, be a future need for some 300 officer cadets per year to be processed through Dartmouth. He believed it was still essential to train the officer corps separately from the sailors, despite my objections, but he also thought it would be possible to reduce the cost of Dartmouth and still maintain separate officer training.

Admiral Bathurst saw the split between specification by the Navy of what equipment was needed and the procurement of such equipment by separate organizations as a useful source of pressure on the Navy to reduce the tendency to gold plate their requirements. And he also said that the downsizing of the Navy had affected every part of the Navy, including the procurement executive and that the changes now faced by all those in the Navy were as far-reaching in their effects as the change from sail to steam had once been. But he claimed that he was dedicated to making radical change and, if anything, he was concerned that the rate of change was too fast and stated that there were many shore establishments where the officers were thoroughly enjoying the challenge of actually managing the resources and adopting new business practices.

Although the First Sea Lord accepted that the amounts of money under the Navy's direct control were limited he still felt it was possible to move large amounts of money from one aim to another, provided the government accounting rules on capital and revenue could be changed to accommodate such matters. Yet again I came across the difficulties of making significant economies unless capital and revenue could be interchanged, so that more freedom to deal with pay structures, ranks, numbers employed and so on could be introduced. The First Sea Lord certainly showed himself open to greater changes in the reward system and more flexibility in payment methods, as well as changes in the rank structure of the Navy. He also agreed about the problems of maintaining an adequate incentive to take risks in a situation where everybody was concerned about their future employment. He was looking forward to the completion of the independent review which would enable the Navy, together with the other Services, to look at the whole career structure. In the meantime he was also trying to reorganize the training areas, where the intention was to contract out, and he was working on a major reorganization of the whole medical support area for the Service. (As it turned out, the independent review – a 90 000 word package drawn up by the former deputy chairman of British Telecom, Michael Bett, after a nineteen-month study involving interviews with 14 000 servicemen and women – called for changes in the conditions of staff, including performance related pay to reward the best, without always promoting them. A system of bonuses was also recommended and the review called for the deconstruction of the complicated rank and salary structures in the forces that have evolved over the centuries.)

As the First Sea Lord and I talked, I was very aware of the problems of balancing change and retaining valuable naval traditions. The First Sea Lord told me a story which illustrated the influence of strong naval traditions. Shortly after the Falklands War one of the commanding officers wrote an article in which he said that he had felt a tremendous sense of history as they pushed across the exclusion zone into the jaws of San Carlos water, into what he believed to be certain death for many more naval personnel than actually occurred. He did not claim that he was making history, but he did feel that the generations of naval officers who had gone before him, and who had faced similar situations, encouraged him and reassured him that he was doing all right and that the mission would succeed as long as the Navy kept its nerve. The First Sea Lord said that he wanted to keep that sense of a great naval tradition, but that he also wanted to push through radical change.

I said that we had all been deeply conscious of our great naval tradition during the Second World War, and that it had been a powerful boost to morale, but I also said I was still worried that unless the Navy convinced everybody else that they were making the fundamental changes which would enable the Navy to play an effective part in this modern and unpredictable world, then change would be forced upon the Navy, and when change is forced upon an organization the reaction is always to resist. Change must be managed by those within the organization in the process of change, not forced upon it by outside events. The First Sea Lord very graciously agreed that it was his job, and The Admiralty Board's job, to make quite sure that these messages were communicated down the line and also that those who worked in the Navy were clear about the Navy's *raison d'être.* He said it had been helpful to him to be reminded that these things weren't happening quite as well as they should be at the moment.

I left the First Sea Lord with mixed feelings. He seemed more prepared to think in far-reaching terms than many of the others I had met and I had received some of the answers from him. I felt more convinced than ever that we have an enduring need for a navy in the future. If we're to defend ourselves beyond our shores we need a navy, but since the end of the Cold War the Navy has been under intense financial pressure and its numbers have been radically reduced since my day, so the Navy of the future is, of necessity, a lean-manned Navy. In order to achieve the best from less, it must be a highly flexible Navy with a clear vision which every man and woman, not just in the Navy, but in Britain as a whole, understands. If the Navy is to survive it must be willing continuously to change and to adapt and, while preserving some of its traditions, it must be willing to jettison others.

In terms of quality and professionalism I believe the Navy's claim to be one of the most professional navies in the world is justified. The integrity and ability of the officers are still first class and any firm would be glad to recruit entirely from the Royal Navy's officer corps and would not, I am sure, suffer from the experience. The question is whether these able men and women, who have been trained in a tradition which holds tenaciously to the values of the past, can adapt to the very different needs of the future? Can they do it, and can they do it fast enough? I fervently hope so.

PART FOUR

12. Does industry matter?

My revisit to industry – of all the four programmes in the *Trouble-shooter Returns* series – struck me as the most difficult and was the one to which, oddly, I was looking forward least. I have worked in industry, in one way or another, since it became apparent that my daughter would not make a full recovery from polio and my wife and I resolved that I should find a job which would allow me to live at home, and return there every evening. Despite the fact that I possessed no relevant qualifications, except some facility with languages, I never doubted that I could obtain a job. I wanted to do a job where I still felt I was contributing something to Britain and, like most young men in the mid-1950s, I was strongly imbued with the concepts of socialism and the wish to do something for society as a whole. I also remember rashly promising my wife that, while I could not guarantee that we would be able to maintain our previous standard of living (a forecast which was certainly borne out over the next few years), I was nevertheless confident that we would not starve.

However the situation in industry today, forty years on, is markedly different and I think that difference – the loss of Britain's world share of industry – contributed to my sense of foreboding about the making of this fourth programme. In the 1950s Britain was the second most powerful economy in the world and the world's largest exporter. British cars, motorcycles, textiles and shoes were acknowledged leaders in their fields and we were all confident of a future where industry would go on producing jobs and wealth. But it hasn't worked out like that. We have slid down and down the economic league until we are now one of the weakest members of the European Union and, even worse, many of our homespun industries are now in foreign hands. Looking back, I don't know what it was in my assessment of life which led me, even then, to expect that the country of which I was so proud was going to hit economic problems. Nevertheless I was convinced all was not well even then, and that the prosperity we took for granted, with full employment, growth, investment and new building all around us, the years when 'we never had it so good', were unlikely to last. Because of my fears of economic squalls I decided that the sort of job I would look for would be something in a basic industry, something which would serve the fundamental needs of men and women.

I looked, unsurprisingly, at heavy industry and speedily decided that, if I could get into it, a company like ICI would be ideal. Here the luck which has so often sat on my shoulder played a part. Not only had my brother-in-law recently joined ICI as an engineer, but two members of the Russian section of the Naval Intelligence department in which I was working had recently resigned their commissions and, surprise, surprise, now worked at ICI as well. After they left we used to meet for a pint and they regaled me with tales of how different their lives were: how rewarding, how interesting and how there were no limits to the possibilities they saw ahead. In those days a company like ICI appeared to offer employment from the cradle to the grave to those who worked honourably, and with assiduity, and although I did not expect the scope and freedom for the use of my initiative and imagination I had enjoyed as an intelligence officer in Germany after the Second World War, it was to ICI that I went, and it was ICI of which I was ultimately to become the chairman. I learned my craft as a business manager at ICI, and I continue to be intensely proud to have served in that company. I left the Navy in 1956 and I have played a much larger part in industry in Britain than in any other field in my life, and it is still as much a part of me as my right arm.

However, over the last forty years I have witnessed what appears to be the inexorable decline of Britain's industrial leadership. Whole areas of manufacturing that Britain used to dominate have either died out or been taken over by more successful economies. Some people think that doesn't matter but I think it matters desperately. Others think that we are now on the brink of a major economic comeback, and that all the

164

factors that have dragged us down over the years have at last changed. But have they? I have watched Britain's economy slide further and further down the relative scale while the strengths of countries like Germany and Japan, and now even Italy, have long since surpassed our own.

There are those who have asked, with monotonous regularity, whether industry matters. Indeed in the 1980s there was a fashionable view that, since Britain had been the cradle of the Industrial Revolution, it was natural that the British should blaze the trail towards the future where the making of things would be done by the newly emerging, developing countries, and where the superior and older countries of the West would earn their living by selling knowledge. At one stage in the 1980s this view was so prevalent that, when I was invited to give the BBC Richard Dimbleby Lecture in 1986, I chose as my subject 'Does Industry Matter?' There had been recent statements by politicians that it didn't and that we should cease looking back and start looking ahead; that we were destined for a happy post-industrial life, paying our way by selling knowledge, financial services and tourism. But the problem is that we cannot rely solely on the service industries because our world share of services has declined even faster than our world share of manufacturing.

In February 1986 a key newspaper, *The Times,* published an article entitled 'A Post Industry Year Please', which poured cold water on the necessity for industry and painted a picture of the good life we would all lead when British industry finally disappeared altogether. Nearly ten years later almost everybody says they accept that we need a more vibrant climate for manufacturing, and yet we still do not seem to create the conditions which give our businesses the best chances of competing against the toughest in the world. German, French and Japanese manufacturers do not feel misunderstood by their governments or unsupported by their financial institutions. So why, when our need is so great, do we apparently have this unique problem?

In my lecture I pointed out that, at that time, we made and supplied two-thirds of all the manufactured goods we purchased and that our earnings from the export of manufactured goods were 25% greater than our banking, insurance and oil exports put together. The role of industry

165

and business has been to enable Britain to pay its way. Despite the economic truism that any country can live with a balance of payments deficit (for the deficit has to be made up by borrowing, whatever that happens to cost at the time, and has to be repaid eventually by overseas earnings), in the long term each country has to pay its own way. It has to sell something which others want to buy if its balance of payments is actually to *balance*. While I would be the first to be grateful for the contributions made by the City and tourism to our ability to pay our way in the world, they are not the solution. In some ways the service sector is performing as badly, if not worse, than manufacturing. Britain's share of world exports of services has fallen faster than its share of world exports of manufactured goods. This is not totally surprising because the service sector is heavily dependent upon manufacturing industry. It seems to me stunningly clear, and yet people persist in believing that the near-death of manufacturing doesn't matter. It's enough to make me weep. When you bear in mind that everything we stop making for ourselves has to be paid for by yet more overseas sales of something, the problem becomes horribly apparent.

It seems to me impossible for us to be a successful and prosperous country if we no longer have an efficient capability of earning money from selling our products overseas. None of this means that I believe industry is a superior way of life, nor that I believe Britain should be run for the benefit of industry, and I know that industry alone cannot supply the solution to the problems of unemployment. But the job of industry is to create the wealth without which there is no choice and without which our lives become impoverished. That is what I tried to point out in 1986, and that is what, ten years later, is sadly as true as it was then.

Of course, there are big differences. The world competitive capability of the City is no longer as evident as it once was, and many – too many – of the commanding heights of industry have been taken over by foreign companies. While plainly it is better to have a foreign-owned car industry than none at all, there is no substitute for owning the whole thing ourselves. The substantial repatriation of money from overseas by Britain's successful international companies demonstrates all too clearly the advantages of a totally British company and, increas-

166

ingly, the competitive edge in business lies in design, research, marketing and so on. In most internationally competitive companies the numbers of people involved in these areas far exceeds those involved in manufacturing.

We in Britain are told by our government that we are on the brink of a golden age, with more competitive industry, the best economic circumstances for forty years, and so on. I hope it is true. The purpose of my revisit to industry was to try and see whether I thought we really were well poised for the future, or whether we were going to see a repetition of the not so distant past in which our decline would continue. I've just turned seventy-one and, of course, I'm slowly but surely falling to pieces. But it feels to me as though Britain is doing the same thing. Now in my case it's probably inescapable, but Britain does have some choices, and if this country is to prosper, every part of it has to become more efficient, and it must do so in world terms. Not only do we have to earn more money, but we also have to make the money we have available for education, or roads, or infrastructure, go further if we are to achieve more of what we, as a country, want and need.

ICI

I began my revisit to industry by returning to Wilton, near Middlesbrough, which was where I began my ICI career. I learned most of my industrial skills at Wilton and this is the place where I rose, metaphorically speaking, from tea boy to head boy, so it has a special place in my heart. I haven't been back to Wilton since I retired as chairman in 1987, but I worked at Wilton during the whole time the site was being built and developed. I progressed through every level of job to chairman of the division which ran the plant. I left Wilton when I was appointed to the main board of ICI in London in 1973.

In the 1960s, together with its sister plants north of the River Tees at Billingham, Wilton comprised the largest chemical factory in Europe. The whole thing was ICI-owned, and the site was designed as an integrated one, each factory supplying another with essential raw materials. The main products of the site were based on oil, and on the simple ingredients that go to manufacture chlorine. Working in the petrochemical industry was a bit like being a pork butcher. You started with the whole animal (a gallon of oil) and then broke it into the smallest chemical constituents before reassembling it in a whole variety of complex chemical ways. You ended up with almost everything you could imagine, from nylon and terylene man-made fibres, to polythene and polypropylene.

The pace of development was frenetic. In 1946 there was no plant at Wilton at all but by 1970, when I became chairman of the division, we employed 15 000 people and what we made represented a significant proportion of Europe's production. We considered ourselves to be leaders in every respect, but for some years now ICI has been in retreat. It has become difficult to stay up with the best in the multiplicity of areas in which we used to operate. When I took over as chairman I believed we would still be able to make a virtue of necessity if we could learn to use the sheer spread of our activities in more imaginative and creative ways. I believed the ability to present any new material either as sheet, granules, film or fibre was, in itself, a competitive source of strength. But the industrial world is hard on anything but the winner. Once leadership is lost in a particular area it becomes increasingly expensive and, in many cases, impractical to catch up. The intervening years have seen ICI focusing down on to a smaller and smaller range of products. The process had begun in my day when it was apparent we had lost the race to keep up in polythene by backing our own technology rather than moving on to new methods of production. We then exchanged the whole of our polythene business with BP, and took over their PVC business, which meant that we both ended up with a real chance to get out in front in our chosen fields and to stay there.

It was with mixed feelings therefore that I revisited the site I had loved so dearly and whose birth and upbringing had taken up so much of my early management endeavour. We approached the site down Wilton bank, which is the same route I had taken every day for fifteen years from my home on the Yorkshire moors. I felt the familiar thrill of excitement as I looked down across the broad panorama of the works and saw plumes of steam disappearing into the cool winter air. To me, perhaps because I was involved in its birth, Wilton has always been an object of sheer beauty and a tribute to human skill and hard work. Just as when I see a really beautiful bridge I marvel at the magnificence of the engineering, so for me a well-designed and functioning chemical plant has a wonderful symmetry, power and strength: a beauty all of its own. Where other people see nasty, dirty plants, producing products they think they can do without, I see massive monuments to human endeavour, creating things which make life better for everyone.

At first sight everything looked exactly as it had in the past, and once on the site I discovered they had laid on a treat for me. One of my earliest jobs with ICI (in the late 1950s) was driving round the country conducting a work study into the pay and conditions of ICI's drivers and designing an incentive scheme for them. I drove with the men for nearly two months then, and when I remet one or two of the drivers I had known in those days, I remembered what it was like sharing long trips with them. Those trips instilled in me an immense regard for the drivers, and an understanding of what a hard, harsh life driving a long distance lorry is, even when working for a paternalistic and good employer like ICI. Now, to my amazement, I was face to face with one of the original Scammel tankers in which I had done so much of my early work. Of course it is an antique now, and suffers from lack of speed and comfort by comparison with its younger, more up-to-date competitors: I felt a good deal of sympathy with it.

As we drove around the perimeter I got my first shock. Plant after plant no longer bore the ICI roundel, in fact the trip became more and more like a brief tour of a United Nations of the world's large chemical companies. The ethylene oxide plant now belonged to Carbide; the polypropylene plant to BASF; the nylon plant to Dupont; the polythene plant to BP; and so on. Each of the plants which ICI had sold represented an entire business in which now, with the exception of BP, there was no longer a British champion leading the world. The British have moved out and the foreigners have moved in. It was a graphic sign of the unbelievable changes which have occurred, even in the short time since my retirement in 1987. When I talked to the general manager of the site, Arthur Dicken, who I remembered well from my own days, I got another rude shock. In their heyday Wilton and Billingham together provided 30 000 jobs. When I asked him how many people ICI employed on Teesside today the full time number was down to

6000. Practically everything which is not the actual operation of the chemical plants is now contracted out. This process began during my time as chairman, and reflects the inevitable concentration of business on the things it does best. However, ICI's departure from many of the fields in which we once operated has occurred almost entirely over the last few years. The situation across the river at Billingham was even more stark: there, many of the plants had been razed to the ground and there were great areas which looked like bombsite clearances after the Second World War. This, however, was not the result of an enemy armed with bombs, it was the result of our failure to defeat the enemies of international competition; a graphic example of what happens when the horrendous challenges of survival and adaptation – that are necessary if old established businesses are to move fast enough to retain a leadership position – are not met.

The other feature which I found very striking was that there had always been a buzz of excitement, a sense of growing and new plants being built, but there was little such activity visible now. No large new plant has been built at Wilton for five years and the problem with this is that, while it is a very quick job to get out of something, it is a very slow, painstaking, expensive and patient process to build up a world leadership position and, as Wilton exemplified all too clearly, nothing but world leadership is good enough. None of us who were involved with Wilton in the past, and none of the people there today, have any doubt about the tremendous advantages that Teesside has to offer as a world competitive production site for chemicals, but in the future will the plants be British owned? Will the jobs in research, selling, development and technology, which are associated with the ownership of a business, still be based in Britain I wonder? Wilton's shrinkage is mirrored by the reduction in size of the steel industry on Teesside, and by the total disappearance of the shipbuilding industry. When I started in 1956 these industries, together with heavy engineering, provided the prosperity on which the development of the river and of the surrounding area was based. What had come to take their place? If the bright new world, the golden age we are promised, is to happen, where is it being born? The impression I had throughout the day was of a slightly desperate business hanging on by its finger tips, rather than a self-confident one, leading the way into the future and forcing its competitors to respond to it.

One of my last tasks as chairman of ICI was to initiate the selling off of ICI's tanker division: it was no longer part of our core business. When we decided we should concentrate on the jobs only we could do, we invited the people running the ancillary operations such as gardening, tankers, canteens and so on, to set up their own independent businesses, with an initial supply contract from ICI. The tanker businesses at both Wilton and Billingham became Imperial Tankers but, although the relevant decisions had been taken in 1987, the business was not actually set up until 1989. Imperial Tankers has retained ICI's business, albeit a diminishing quantity in tonnage terms, but it's bloody tough being a service industry when your main customer starts to shrink quite as fast as ICI is shrinking. I remembered John Robinson, Imperial Tankers' Chief Executive, well from my own ICI days. He used to be on the industrial relations side of things at ICI, and he led Imperial Tankers' buy out. The majority of the drivers had come with him, many of whom had been driving for ICI for much of their lives.

The business of transporting chemicals and petroleum products by road is not an easy one. The primary consideration always has to be safety rather than price but, because safety is tied up with the cost of maintenance, the age of the tanker, the skill and care of the drivers and so on, it is not an easy thing to measure. One of the aims John and the much reduced management team had set themselves was to reduce their dependence upon ICI to less than 50% of their business within five years, and they had pretty well managed to do so. Although they worked for other types of businesses, it was still very largely the chemical and oil businesses who understood the necessity of paying for a quality service. The difficulty is that the tanker business is so cut-throat that you only really make money if the tankers are running the whole time. On the one hand you have to have the capacity to handle anything which is thrown at you, but on the other you cannot afford to have tractors and trailers sitting on the park and not earning.

After meeting John I went for a quick run with Colin, one of the drivers I had remet earlier, in a Scammel tanker. He told me he'd never had the slightest doubt about wishing to move over from ICI to Imperial

Tankers, because, like most long-distance drivers, he was totally dedicated to the road. Colin has been with ICI for twenty-four years, but, in the event, it was his dedication to the work of driving that tipped the scale. Almost all the drivers had moved over to the new company and became shareholders. They were in no doubt whatsoever that they had to make their own futures and couldn't rely upon anybody else. The difficulty with service industries is that, while efficient ones are essential for large businesses to survive, they do not have an independent existence. Ultimately they are dependent upon the growth or failure of their customers. All the drivers at Imperial Tankers were worried about the decline in the chemical industry on Teesside and it was this concern which was leading them to try to develop businesses in other areas. In view of the competition, they were having great difficulty increasing their prices. At the same time the cost of new tractors and trailers was going up steeply, with a new vehicle now costing over £100 000.

I explained to John Robinson that I was concerned about Imperial Tankers' business. Their profitability wasn't high enough and yet they were thinking of borrowing more money to expand further. Since they were not earning a return which would pay for the additional borrowings, they were digging themselves into deeper trouble.

I urged them to look for some export and import business, and one of the areas they told me they were already looking at was edible oils. It seemed to me that if this was what they wanted to do they would need to have a different brand name. I didn't think too many people would be anxious to transport edible oils in tankers which were primarily used for chemicals! I urged John also to look at the idea of trying to develop his factory space as more of a trading area and to ensure he didn't take on more full-time drivers, but filled the gaps with part-timers. I wondered whether Imperial Tankers could act as an administrative centre and booking agency for owner drivers in the tanker business.

John and his company are in a tight situation, but it was good to see everybody involved and understanding what was needed. I certainly felt that they had a reasonable chance of pulling through. But Imperial Tankers showed how difficult it is to start up and run small businesses in Britain. Margins are often not high enough to enable reinvestment and finance is hard to come by, and expensive.

172

13. The foreign invasion

I spent nearly fifteen years working in the north east, and it was one of the happiest times of my life. I formed a deep affection for the area and its people. They are proud, industrious, humorous, realistic people who don't expect handouts but get stuck in to help themselves. They are people who are totally unimpressed by position, or affectations of power, but who value the individual for what he or she is worth. However the economic picture in the north east in 1995 is very mixed. On the one hand traditional industries like the chemical industry and the dockyards have either shrunk, or gone altogether. On the other hand, foreign-owned companies like Nissan have arrived and are making a huge success of things. I have very mixed feelings about this. There's no doubt it's better to have Nissan here than to have no car industry at all, but nobody should make the mistake of thinking that a car assembly plant is the same as having a complete car company. In the first place it doesn't have all the ancillary bits like design, research and worldwide marketing and in the second place, foreign ownership tends to attract foreign-owned suppliers. However it is a fact that one of the brightest spots on Teesside is Japanese-owned, and so it was to the Nissan plant near Newcastle that I travelled next.

I have visited Nissan and its suppliers on earlier occasions, and I know the chief executive, Ian Gibson, well. He and I have much in common. Ian has followed his career for many of the same reasons as I have, and he also began at ICI. Although the Nissan plant was set up on a greenfield site ten years ago, it has only just begun to make a profit. I asked Ian whether his Japanese bosses were worried about this very long period before their massive investment began to pay off. His reply pointed up an interesting contrast between the Japanese and the

British approach. He explained that the Japanese would not have expected to break even in under eight years. They had always believed it would take that amount of time for their employees to acquire the relevant skill levels to succeed competitively. For the Japanese, business is a journey, not an event. Ian's approach has been to try to get his people to like and feel comfortable with learning, and then instil in them a massive sense of pride in their achievements. His own experience has convinced him that nothing stops us achieving world leadership in manufacturing again except ourselves, and our willingness to accept the position into which we have drifted.

The irony of the Nissan experience is that they are not doing anything that could not have been done by a British company. They started with a clean piece of paper and a clean piece of land, but with very clear principles about what they wanted to achieve, and a realistic expectation of how long it would take. Ian pointed out that, in the bad old days, most British firms expected to hire a line worker on Monday morning at 8.00 am, and have him running a full job, building a car, after four hours induction. At the Nissan plant in Sunderland they expect to train new employees for a minimum of nine months before they are fully accepted on the assembly line, and the percentage of payroll costs devoted to training varies between 7% in a really poor year to 14% and 15% in a year when they were expecting major changes.

The idea of *keizen* (or continuous improvement) applies not just to every operation in the factory, but to the factory itself. During the week I visited they had completed their one millionth car and were planning the introduction of a new model later in the year, and everything was aiming at continuous change and improvement. In terms of competitiveness in the Nissan group Ian reckoned they were at present in the top three. They had overtaken, in effectiveness, three of the original Japanese plants and were ahead of all the rest in the world. Their aim was to be the best plant in the Nissan group within a year. Nissan, in turn, considered themselves to be, with Toyota, the finest car producers in the world.

I asked Ian to what he ascribed the success of Nissan by comparison with British firms who had found it impossible to remain in the inter-

174

national race. He said firstly that he believed there was a national culture in Britain that disdains making things. Both Ian and I enjoy the fun of making things and seeing the things we've made being used by people all over the world, but our enthusiasms are seldom shared by others. The basic belief that making things is a part of making Britain great seems to Ian (and to me) to be missing, and this is compounded by British amateurism. Ian feels there is a contempt for training in Britain and that our education system leaves much to be desired. He feels that by the time people leave the state system they are often glad to be rid of learning, looking upon education as a necessary evil rather than the gateway to a life of excitement and interesting work. He also thinks, as I do, that there is a gulf between the media and academia and people like him and me in our understanding of the excitement and worth of manufacturing. In addition he does not feel the financial institutions are particularly helpful to the goal of making manufacturing better or easier but, like me, believes the basic responsibility for overcoming these difficulties lies with industrialists like ourselves. He also believes that the responsibility for instigating change lies with us and thinks it is up to us to try to ensure that stable, long-term funding is available for small businesses. Also like me, he does not believe very large companies share these problems: it is much easier for them to get access to money anywhere in the world.

Ian is concerned at the very short term pay backs which are expected of people trying to expand and grow small businesses in Britain, in particular people who need, say, £100 000 to £300 000. Most genuine new businesses, and practically all manufacturing businesses, take time to grow and need patient money. Ian felt the strength of Japan lay not so much in the big world names represented in the north east, like Nissan and Sony, but in the thousands of small businesses supporting ten to fifty people, which have the same efficiency and enthusiasm about what they are making, and the same wish to have big world names as customers. The Japanese experience, derived from their own history after the Second World War, led them to expect to spend a prolonged period building up their knowledge and expertise before they could hope to be the best in the world. Being nearly best is simply not good enough. All this is allied to the Japanese cultural belief that everything can always be made better. Even if they believe they have reached 100% of what is possible, they will still look for ways to improve.

I found Nissan's production lines impressive, not so much for the speed of everyone's reaction but because of the quiet methodical order. The workers were involved, but not frenetic. I have seen production lines moving faster, but there was an unmistakable enthusiasm about the whole activity which produced a feeling of confidence. Training clearly pays off for Nissan. These guys are making high quality goods and are one of the most efficient car plants in the world. The people working here have been carefully chosen, and even more carefully trained and developed. Ian told me that he felt the key is training. When training stops people don't only lose existing skills, but flexibility for the future is reduced and the motivation of the staff is reduced. Training people tells them that management and the business value them. When training becomes a matter of routine in a company, when it is seen to be happening all the time, then the attitude switches from the (mostly British) idea that training is for those who can't do the job to the idea that training is an investment being made in people. I had been told that many in the north east did not like the Nissan way of working, and considered that their individuality was diminished by working under these tightly controlled conditions. If that is so I certainly did not meet those sorts of people on the plant and fortunately, perhaps for the north east as well as for Nissan, there still appear to be more than enough people queuing up for every available job.

I was given an opportunity to find out what Nissan's training is really all about, and how difficult it is to acquire the skills which are needed in order to do a reliable job on the production line. Anyone who thinks of workers on the line as unskilled, simply doesn't know what they are talking about. It was a fascinating insight, not only into my own cack-handedness, but also into how the whole thing is organized. I started with some hours learning to use an air tool to wind nuts and bolts, how to locate them, how to start them without cross-threading them, and using just the right amount of air. It sounds deceptively easy, and I'm sure it must be relatively easy for a youngster, but I found myself growing increasingly scared of trying it for real, on the assembly line. They then moved me on to learn how to fit a throttle assembly to one particular type of engine, and I'm sure it must have been one of the easier ones! The operators have to be able to fit the correct bits and bobs to a whole array of engines which pass, unstoppably, down the line. Just learning this tiny fraction of the whole array of skills which was needed on the line would have taken me days of effort in order to get the certainty and dexterity needed. Mind you, that may well have been because I was so utterly hopeless at it in the first place! The whole way of doing the job had been worked out to a standard system by the supervisor and his people – moreover they were continuously chipping off a second here and there.

The pressure for workers to perform to a set standard on the line came from the other nineteen operators in the twenty-man team, rather than from the supervisor, who is coach, spare hand and troubleshooter combined. The best speed I ever got up to – for a job which had to be accomplished in thirty-five seconds – was a minute and a half. My torturers then insisted that I try my so-called skills on the line itself! Bob, whose work I effectively screwed up, seemed relaxed and unhurried. Indeed, the supervisor kept on telling me to relax. Fat chance, as the line rumbled on and I rushed further and further down it trying to tighten up the last nut!

This is why Nissan expends so much time on its training and why it is such a struggle to be multi-skilled. Not only do you need dexterity, but any lapse in concentration shows up immediately. The two lads with me, Charlie and Andy, were already being trained for the new engine, which is not expected to be introduced until 1996. If everyone realized how much effort it takes to acquire these skills, and gave them the respect they deserve, I feel that we'd have a very different attitude to industry across the whole community.

Nissan seems to me to be a clear indicator that we *can* do it, if we set ourselves the right aims and the right managers are given the right training and the right incentives. But why does it take foreign ownership and foreign aspirations to persuade British workers and managers that they can work to these world class standards? What stops Britain doing it for herself? Having Nissan in the north east is like having a heart transplant: it's better than being six foot under, but it's not as good as having your own heart, and one of the problems of having foreign-owned assembly companies in Britain is that, inevitably, they choose suppliers with whom they are already familiar, which means these suppliers are often also foreign. One such example is the Ikeda Hoover car seat plant which is just three-quarters of a mile away and whose sole current customer is Nissan.

The thing that really delights me about the Nissan plant is that their British managers are not content merely to copy and keep up with the best. In a most un-British fashion they are only satisfied when other factories are copying them and the pace is being set by them in the north east. They are aiming to be the best in their group, worldwide, by 1996 and their achievements so far leave me with little doubt they will attain their self-set goals within the next year. However, no business can be better than its customers or its suppliers and the Japanese approach to their customers and suppliers is quite different from the British approach. The Japanese develop relationships with their suppliers over a period of time and are willing to spend money where necessary to help a supplier change or update the equipment supplied. This doesn't seem to me to happen very often in Britain.

Nissan showed that with the right levels of aspiration, and patient financial backing, it is possible to set up a new business which has every chance of becoming a world leader. However, in our aims for the future we British cannot rely solely on new companies coming in from other countries and starting afresh on greenfield sites. We have to develop our own new businesses, and the old established businesses have to adapt faster and ensure that they are always in front. Sadly, I am uneasy about the British ability to adapt, and to do so fast enough.

14. The British resistance

One of the sad realities of life is that over the last fifteen years Britain has barely expanded its manufacturing capability at all. Today Britain is making, in essence, almost exactly what was made in the late 1970s, but with far fewer people. While this is welcomed, and indeed without fewer people we would be in even deeper trouble, the true sign of success must be that we are *increasing* the amount of wealth we are creating as a country. Business and industry are a bit like the human body: to survive and prosper, old cells have continuously to be replaced by new ones. In the case of business the replacement won't take the form of an entirely new type of cell, it may merely be a modern version of the old, but unless this process of industrial renewal is continuous and is aimed at the right areas for future growth, our standard of living in Britain will inevitably decline.

I do not believe the problems of Britain can be solved by the large companies. Indeed for many years I have felt that their days are numbered, largely because of the difficulty they have in adapting to changing conditions fast enough. The process of renewal of Britain's business base requires a dynamic private sector which aims at being the best in the world, but which is continuously producing tens of thousands of new enterprises – even though only a few will eventually make it all the way.

One of the undoubted successes of the past fifteen years has been the very large number of small companies which have started up. If it were not for this achievement, our current problems of unemployment would be even more horrendous, but this increase in small businesses also highlights the need to provide conditions in which small businesses can prosper. By any statistical analysis Britain has rather more than its share of large companies for the size of our population and gross domestic product (GDP): forty-three of the world's 500 largest industrial companies in terms of turnover are based in Britain, compared with thirty-three in Germany and thirty-two in France, but the difficulty is that not all of them have managed to maintain their pole position in the world competitive league. Effectively there is no longer a British-owned car industry and the areas in which the British lead the world are becoming fewer and fewer. Those areas in which we *are* successful are clear indicators of our ability to be world beaters. The success of the British pharmaceutical industry and the domination of the worldwide alcoholic drinks industry by British firms are welcome signs of these areas of vitality. But we cannot hope to survive merely by being a sort of offshore aircraft carrier which the Koreans, Japanese, or even the Americans, see as a good launching pad from which to attack the European market. We have to ensure that our small businesses have an environment in which they can grow, and indeed it is good to know that we can still do so. Companies like Paul Smith, Mulberry and Dunhill show our ability to establish world positions in luxury products dependent upon design. Design is still a subject which is outstandingly well-taught in Britain and a most surprising number of European company successes are based upon British design ability. The sad thing is that so many of our industrial designers are forced to seek employment outside our country because of the lack of a lively internal demand for their skills.

Plainly, the most important single factor is the entrepreneurs and managers who have the aspirations to establish globally successful businesses. But if you have the people with ideas who are willing to take the risk with the technology or the skills, how easy is it for them actually to develop a business through all its stages, with the heavy demands on capital involved? My friends at Imperial Tankers showed very clearly the problems of boot-strapping up a business on its own earning capacity. It can be done but it is, inevitably, a slow and painful process. There have been endless debates about the short-term approach of British businesses and the responsibility for this has been laid successively at the feet of the business people themselves, the financial institutions, the government, and almost anybody else I can think of. There is no doubt that, by comparison with the Japanese who enjoy very low interest rates, our business people are required to achieve results in time periods the Japanese themselves would consider quite impossible. If Nissan are prepared to carry an investment for seven or eight years before they expect to breakeven, what chance do we have if we require a payback period of two or three years? If the pressures and requirements of high rates of return in order to pay high interest rates and dividends are worse here than elsewhere, is it really possible to grow British businesses and to enable the acorns to become oak trees which will shelter us all? To find out more about this I headed south into the Midlands to a company in that part of the world which seemed to be bucking the usual depressing trend.

The Triumph Motorcycle Company

The Triumph Motorcycle Company has been rescued by an extra-ordinary entrepreneur named John Bloor. John is a modest, slightly shy man who started life as a plasterer and built up a very successful house-building business. This business prospered to such an extent that it generated amounts of money far beyond John's own requirements and it was at this stage that he decided to put his money behind his dreams. As he explained to me, his belief is that in order for Britain to prosper, manufacturing must become dominant once more. Unlike most people who enter the motorcycle business, John has never been in love with motorbikes. He approached the idea of relaunching the Triumph Motorcycle Company through a strict and logical process. He wanted to make an end product which could be sold to people from many walks of life, with a well-spread, diverse market. To minimize the risk he wanted a product which would sell worldwide and would therefore not be reliant upon the rise and fall of one economy only, and he believed that automated machinery and greatly improved labour relations would enable more consistency of manufacture, so that quality would be truly competitive. Lastly, but perhaps most sig-nificantly of all, he realized the market was totally dominated by the Japanese, whose fortunes are highly dependent upon the valuation of the yen. John believed the Japanese would become victims of their own success and therefore production which was based entirely in Britain, and on the pound, would enjoy an increasing competitive advantage in his chosen niche market. Like me, John believes in the capability of British working people, providing they are well-managed and well-led.

The Triumph name went into receivership in 1983 and there were no grants, help or investment available to assist John in building the business back up. He had to do this entirely from his own resources. I find this astonishing when you consider that non-British companies who set up subsidiaries in Britain, like Nissan and Ikeda Hoover, *decide* to invest in Britain precisely *because* they qualify for government grants. John Bloor could have got some money from the Department of Trade and Industry (DTI), but he would have had to buy British equipment and he felt that British equipment wasn't up to the standards he required, so he invested £70m of his property company's money in the Triumph Motorcycle business. Because of the risk and the timescale there was no way he could have taken on the task with borrowed finance.

John's enterprise began in 1984 but the first motorbikes were not produced until 1990, and the first profit appeared in 1995. Indeed, it will be 1996 before the level of production and sales, combined with the expertise of the workforce, will be sufficiently high to ensure they are making a reasonable profit. However the expected future profit margins seem to me to more than justify the total investment. But John Bloor stumbled upon a serious British problem when the Triumph Motorcycle Company went back into production under his stewardship: on the whole British subcontractors don't deliver on time, make promises they cannot, or will not, keep, and they fail to make parts to the required standards. John explained that his original confidence in the quality of manufacturing technology in Britain had caused him severe problems. However the lack of quality, service and competitive pricing by the subcontractors upon whom he relied had eventually forced his company to manufacture for themselves and John Bloor has made a virtue out of a necessity. Instead of buying in crankshafts and crankcases, frames etc., all these have now been set up in-house from scratch, in most cases using Japanese equipment. Many of the problems they have with the supply industries arise because those industries are unwilling to make the necessary investment in the specialized machinery, and they are not well-managed. I was told that Triumph had spent nearly £10m on processing equipment in order to make, in their own factory, what they should have been able to buy off the shelf from outside suppliers. Even now, shipments from Japan arrive on time, while only 20% of British subcontractors are able either to deliver on time, or to meet the quality and standards upon which the whole operation depends.

The high-quality manufacturing standards Triumph have set themselves have given them an edge and a major selling opportunity as component manufacturers in their own right. Triumph manufactures 40% of its components, double that of most companies, who tend to buy in around 80% of the necessary components – but I would not be surprised to see this factory selling components in its own right on a large scale soon. They are already selling crankshafts to Toyota and the difference in quality between what they are able to manufacture themselves and what they can buy in is mind-boggling. For example they have been unable to buy crankshafts to closer tolerances than seventeen microns but were manufacturing their own to tolerances of five. The frame assembly, which is carried out by robots in-house, is so accurate that there is only point two of a millimetre tolerance between the centres of the frame, making all the subsequent assembly that much easier. John and his manager, Alan Heard, believe they have the most highly robotized manufacturing plant in Europe and from my observation they are probably right.

John Bloor believes that setting up the factory on a greenfield site has been a tremendous advantage, and as I was shown around I was bound to agree. One of the plus points is that everybody was able to start from scratch together which, in my opinion, facilitates the process of change which, in Britain, we find so difficult. People in Britain cling to the habits of yesterday, so if you want to change things it is much easier to set up anew like this.

An interesting feature of John's management style is that his house-building business was based upon groups of seven people, a number which I also believe to be a very effective one for group working. The whole Triumph factory is organized on the same concept: seven men working to a team leader, who in turn respond in groups of seven to the next stage up and so on. The average age of the workforce is twenty-seven, and the engineering workshop actually preferred to take on unskilled people and train them up to their own standards. The team leaders work closely with their people and I noticed a number of them taking videos and operating stopwatches. When they have taken a video they all sit down together to analyse how they can do the job better. The team leaders have considerable discretion over paying a fairly substantial bonus to their people and all the workforce are multi-skilled so that it is possible for each man to acquire a range of six or seven skills over time. The ultimate aim is for each of them to be flexible enough to turn their hands to almost any job. The total manpower in the business is now 370, and the factory works on a two shift basis but has the capacity to increase to three shifts on its existing investment once demand builds up further.

I was surprised at the amount of stock they were carrying and plainly there is room for significant improvements in that area once the supply chains are further developed, however part of the reason for their high levels of stock is the fact that they have had to manufacture so many parts themselves. John was painfully aware that the lack of British infrastructure represented a major hazard for his whole operation, but there was not very much he could do about it. He pointed out that they have always been in the position where the success or failure of the Triumph business would not jeopardize the whole group, but there cannot be many companies which are so fortunate. Eighty per cent of production is exported, despite buoyant demand in Britain, and to meet this they have set up subsidiaries in Germany, France and America. Triumph now holds 15.3% of the large bike market in Britain and they are producing eleven different models, at a rate of about 15 000 bikes a year and are aiming to hit 40 000 by the end of the century which would put them on a par with BMW and behind Harley Davidson. As usual the problems lie in getting the price low enough for them to be fully competitive with the competition, despite lower volume. Harley Davidson prices start at about £5500.00 for a basic model and go up to £14 000.00. The retro bike – the 1970s bike that the Japanese produce –

retails for around £6000.00, and Triumph's Thunderbird retails in Britain for around £7750.00.

The same meticulous care and high standards that have been applied to the development of the original bikes have been applied to every other aspect of the business. The bikes are tested on a rolling bed at up to 150 miles per hour before being shipped in batches of thirty and the bikes are aimed at the part of the market dominated by BMW, for which the largest single European market is Germany. The first models have been sold in Germany and the dealer network in Britain has been built up with tremendous care and attention to detail. The total British market at which Triumph are aiming is small compared to the potential German large bike market of 100 000 per year. Their consistent aim has been to sell into the toughest markets and to take BMW on their own ground. The bikes themselves are only supplied to agents, who provide demonstration models for their potential purchasers, and the pricing is carefully pitched to enable agents to make a living from a reasonable level of sales. I was amazed to find that providing demonstration models is not normal practice: I wouldn't have thought anybody would fork out the £6000.00–£10 000.00 necessary for a luxury bike of this type without having actually ridden the thing first.

Triumph are aiming to produce a classic bike using the most modern technology and engineering. The Japanese, who are never frightened of competition and want the market to open up, have been generous with their advice. But despite all John's efforts they found they are still unable to buy aluminium castings in Britain to the standard they require, and much of the steel they need still comes from Japan. Unhappily, from the point of view of Britain's prosperity, this is because the British steel suppliers John approached said they would supply 50 000 tons of steel, or nothing, whereas the Japanese approach was far more flexible. As I've said before Japanese suppliers take care to develop relationships with their customers, and in this case they agreed to supply a small amount of steel at first, believing that Triumph's demand would build. Although less than 15% of the components for the bikes are still being bought from Japan, these amount to 40% of total material costs and include the components which are the most sophisticated and critical.

Triumph are already applying for outline planning permission for a new factory four times the size of their original one. If the present sales build up can be maintained they will be working three shifts by the end of the year. While I was there, a new engine was being set up every nine minutes. John and Alan would be the first to admit they had used very much the same approach as the Japanese. A sign of this was that there were only twenty-five managers and superintendents in the entire factory – all the responsibility has been pushed down the line.

The visit to Triumph was really inspiring but I could not help wondering about the degree to which others would have had the patience of John Bloor. Companies which have £70m of their own money to invest and leave for a period of ten or twelve years before getting a return do not exactly grow on trees in Britain. Triumph showed both what was possible but also the difficulties of achieving it. The irony is that soon after John bought the Triumph name and started his long odyssey, Triumph's main British rival, Norton Motors Limited, also came up for sale. I'd made a *Troubleshooter* film about Norton in 1992 and it really made my heart bleed to see the difference between the two approaches. The future for Triumph bikes looks hopeful: the future for Norton bikes, unless they've made some radical changes since I last visited, does not. Triumph offers hope for a way ahead and demonstrates, yet again, that we can succeed if we wish. But it also demonstrates the enormity of the change in attitude that is required. We need the same high standards of professionalism on the part of a myriad of suppliers, but in business, as in so much else in life, nothing succeeds like success. With the initial investment John has made he could have started almost any kind of new business, none of which would have represented the enormous exposure of financial risk which is such a feature of the Triumph company. I shall watch with interest to see how close they get to the aims they have set themselves, but I would put quite a lot of money on their chances of success as long as they retain the existing team. I left Triumph to revisit Norton.

Norton Motors Limited

At roughly the same time that Triumph was bought by John Bloor (a man who obviously believes in making things), Philippe Le Roux, a merchant banker, purchased the Norton brand name. He recognized the potency of the Norton brand name, and the stock market backed him with £20m, which was promptly spent acquiring many strange and, in some cases, quite unrelated businesses. While John Bloor slowly, steadily and methodically built his business up and pushed every penny into design and onto the shop floor, the money which was raised for Norton, on the back of the Norton name, went on what might be described, perhaps a little unkindly, as speculation.

When I visited Norton in 1992 the company was in a bad way. Philippe Le Roux had gone and David Macdonald, the new Chief Executive, was endeavouring to restructure and save something from the wreckage. As well as the brand name, Norton possessed something which Triumph did not. It possessed the rights to the Wankel engine, a German invention which dispensed with normal cylinders and gave a very high power-to-weight ratio for a high-revving lightweight engine. Yet the whole thing was a mess and it was almost impossible to discover how many bikes they were actually making. I could never reconcile the figures that David Macdonald kept on referring to as sales of bikes, engines etc., with what seemed to me to be the potential market. Sure enough, when we went to visit the Norton factory this time we discovered they were closed and production of motorbikes had virtually ceased. It was extremely sad.

Last time I was at Norton I'd felt that unless they went into receivership and were thus able to lose the heavy shackles of debt they were carrying, there was no chance for a revival of the company. I also had real doubts about whether the salvation of the business lay with the motorbikes. I believed that the future of Norton Motors lay in the development of other outlets for the engine, and my belief was shared by David Garside, the Director of Engineering. Last time I visited David had been endeavouring to put together a management buy out in order to continue developing the engine for the unmanned aircraft market, but he was not an entirely free agent since he had been asked to go into the business by the banks, who held the largest amount of the debt, and although I understood that he had managed to wrench the unmanned aircraft business away from Norton, it was now going through yet another metamorphosis. The Norton company had been taken over in lieu of a bad debt by a Sicilian who had little interest in the Norton engine business, and David Macdonald was making yet another attempt to revive the company, but as yet without much success.

David Garside's own attempts to raise the money to buy out the Norton unmanned aircraft engine business had not been wholly successful. He had been unable to raise the necessary money to buy the business from the banks, and the venture capitalists David approached required a 40%–50% return on their capital, a crippling price there was no way they could have paid, and David received no help from the City, who had in turn played a role in the disappearance of Norton. So, 80% of the business had eventually been bought by Alvis UAV Engines, the British defence contractors, with a 20% shareholding retained by David Garside and two of his colleagues. But Alvis had not achieved the results they had hoped for with the business because, as for all defence contractors, business comes in large chunks or not at all and is heavily dependent upon political and other considerations which the business itself is quite unable to affect. So, in turn, Alvis had sold their 80% of the business on to Silver Arrow. Silver Arrow is 50% owned by Federman Enterprises Ltd., and 50% owned by the Elbit Group, both of which are large Israeli companies involved in aerospace. The Israelis are actually the largest manufacturers of unmanned aircraft in the world and so at least there is now a reasonably steady demand for the product.

David told me they were hoping to sell 300 units (worth about £1.4m) during 1995 and that elusive but important item, profit, was at last in sight. The engines for target drones sell for about £2000.00 each, and the engines for surveillance UAVs (unmanned air vehicles) sell in a range between £10 000.00 and £15 000.00. The annual world market, including engines for target drones, is between 4000–5000 engines. In the meantime, just as when I had first met David, despite the lack of money and almost as an act of faith, they had still continued development work on the engines. But despite this development work there was no chance of raising the money required to apply the engines to other uses. Their primary difficulty is, obviously, that they are very short of cash. I still believe that the best uses of the engines would have been in mobile fire pumps, generators and so on but it looks as though this is not to be. Norton shows what happens when the desire for a short-term killing takes priority over long-term investment.

Triumph showed that new companies can rise and thrive in Britain, but they need to be allowed time to become profitable. Britain needs companies like Triumph, but they are only possible because they have substantial committed finance behind them, and enough time to develop and grow. The far more common story of many small British businesses is a sad story of missed opportunities. In the 1950s British motorbike companies held the majority of the world market. But due to lack of investment and far too much short-termism, disastrous results have been sustained and today's abysmal subcontracting standards have not helped Britain's loss of market share either. Naturally enough my next call was to a subcontractor.

Velden Engineering

My visit to Triumph highlighted the serious problems of obtaining high quality components delivered on time in Britain. The irony is that this was once exactly the sort of jobbing engineering that provided the backbone to Britain's engineering industry. What has gone wrong?

Velden Engineering is a private limited company whose core business lies in precision subcontract machining. They make parts for anything from cars to 'planes, from trains to milk floats to the bits needed for hip replacements. They rate themselves as the most dynamic, fast-moving, forward-thinking outfit in their field and their ultimate long-term ambition is to become the premier subcontract precision machining company throughout Europe and the world.

However the physical environment in which the company operates is not yet, in my opinion, ready for such a challenge. Velden Engineering is based in a former cotton mill in Bolton. They rented the building for many years before purchasing it for £125 000 about three years ago. They have assets of over £1.5m, and for the last few years their turnover has been stuck at about the same level. They employ about ninety people and have been badly hit by the recession. They finally returned to a very low level of profit last year and are now hoping for rather better margins. However they have not been reinvesting the money which has been set aside for depreciation, so in reality they have been moving backwards over the past three or four years.

The company is run and 90%-owned by Alex Kitchen. He is a dynamic engineer who bubbles with enthusiasm. His attitude to management issues is one in which he enthusiastically tries to embrace every new concept. Despite the unlikely circumstances under which they operate, his firm was one of the first to obtain BS5750. (BS5750 is the British Standard mark established in 1979 as part of the government's national quality campaign.) No matter how hard the going has been, Alex has continued to develop his people through assiduous and imaginative training. His personnel policies seemed to be everything one would hope for and the whole place hums with activity, enthusiasm, laughter and commitment. The staff he was forced to lay off during the recession have unhesitatingly returned to him, and almost all his managers started in the company as apprentices and have been trained by Alex.

Alex's ambitions lie genuinely with the success of his company rather than trying to make more money for himself, but he has massive problems. While they have all the sorts of things one would expect of a highly successful company, such as total quality management, barcoded production scheduling and controls, cell technology and manufacturing, preventative operator maintenance and a surprising emphasis (for so small a company) on integrated computer systems, they are bedevilled by some major difficulties. In the height of the recession they lost confidence in their core business of engineering and sought escape by manufacturing a range of well-engineered golf trolleys and buggies. The range was marketed under the name 'Eagle' and, with typical flamboyance, they claim to be the number one manufacturer of trolleys and buggies in Britain, despite the fact they have barely made any sales. They have a tiny development department of two or three people who are encouraged to develop new ideas of every sort, utilizing spare time and capacity as it becomes available. All in all it sounded exactly the sort of company which ought to have been able to supply the likes of John Bloor at Triumph, and which should have been expanding solidly over the years.

Almost as soon as you enter the factory, however, you discover why things have not worked out. No new machine tools have been purchased for five years and the majority of the original machine tools are old and a long way from contemporary state-of-the-art machining. The basement of the building was like an archaeological museum, full of card control and hand managed machines, and ancient pieces of machinery made by Alfred Herbert, once one of the leaders of the British machine tools industry. The equipment might as well have been operating in a Third World country. However, without exception the people were bright, committed, intelligent and enthusiastic. Alex is a skilled publicist and utterly committed to the revival of the fortunes of his company. He has always had a forward plan and has enjoyed the support of a host of different organizations from the DTI to British Coal Enterprises to the Training Agency and so on. His involvement with Bolton and its people is sincere and total, but the reality of his business has been one of survival rather than growth and, despite the excellence of his people and the sincerity of Alex's ambitions, the factory simply cannot work to the extremely tight tolerances demanded of high value added machining. Nevertheless his customer base includes companies like British Aerospace, although the machining done by Velden Engineering tends to be of the less critical type which obviously does not command the high margins which they really need.

As I went round the factory I was struck again and again by the air of irrepressible optimism. However, it seemed to me that there were a number of fatal omissions. There had been no really sustained marketing effort and little attempt to sell the company's services to a wider range of customers, or to optimize the scope of the business they were obtaining. Their reactions to the bad times had been to cut costs rather than reinforce their efforts to obtain more business. Alex and his company have made the classic British error of not continuously investing in (a) their core business nor (b) in modern machinery and, despite Alex's enthusiasm and good personnel policies, he has not employed a sales director at Velden. They believe – another classic British mistake – that if they invent a better product, it will sell itself. It seems to me that Velden Engineering is unfocused and their diversification away from their core business into such things as golf trolleys and bednasiums (as you might guess, a bed which converts into a miniature gymnasium . . .) was, I felt, ill judged.

It seemed to me the first and most important step to be taken was to produce a proper marketing organization. The second problem appeared to lie with the machine tools stock. They were all obsessed with the fact that the machine tools had cost them so little, but they didn't seem to realize how much the high level of manning required on the outdated machinery was costing them. Even their computer controlled tools were of an age where it was difficult for any operator to manage more than two machines at a time. Although they do not pay their employees highly, their wages and salary costs still represent nearly 45% of their total costs. Combined with their imaginative personnel policies and commitment to trying to hold on to their people, this placed an almost impossible burden upon their margins. Wages in Britain are among the lowest in the European Union and have been for a long time. Some people see this as a huge advantage but I see it as a trap. High wages force manufacturers to invest in automation; low wages discourage investment in machinery. But the only way we can remain competitive is to invest in automation because we can never hope to compete with the sort of wages being paid in parts of the Third World, and nor should we. I also happen to think it is appalling that people should be used to do a job that could be done better by a machine.

Velden's capital investment over the past few years amounts to under £10 000.00 per year, and all the managers claimed there is no way they could have managed more. Despite this they have managed to find nearly £200 000 to develop the golf trolleys and buggies. I must confess that I found them most attractive, representing as they do a sort of 'big boy's dodgem car', with surprising power from their electric motor and modern battery, and quite amazing stability on rough terrain. But despite the appeal of the buggies, I felt they were entering a fiercely competitive market without any real idea of what and where they were going to sell.

A trip around the design and development department confirmed my worst fears. They were certainly bursting with ideas – a fascinating range of objects lay around in various stages of development: I saw a

192

version of the electrically powered addition to an ordinary bicycle (of the type which Sir Clive Sinclair appears to be selling so well, although to my mind Velden's was greatly superior), and there was a well-engineered weight training centre. In another corner lay an electrically driven four-wheel drive cross-country vehicle, each wheel independently powered. The difficulty is that none of these products have a marketing plan or a potential marketing outlet.

I tried to point out that they were grossly underestimating the cost involved in bringing this multiplicity of well-engineered products into profit. At the same time they were not investing in the core business. Sadly, the whole output of the factory could probably have been supplied by three machine centres operating round the clock, manned by a grand total of ten or twelve people. As they have built up their business on old-fashioned and secondhand equipment it is difficult for them to break out, despite the undoubted skills of their operators. There was no way they could have competed for the Triumph Motorcycle business, for instance, and, until they are able to buy more modern equipment, I fear they will find it very difficult to push the margins from where they are.

Before I left I recommended to Alex that he should do three things. As well as setting up a proper marketing department as a matter of urgency, he must hive off the golf trolleys as a separate business. If he does not, the golf trolleys will inevitably suck all the money away from the core subcontract machining business, which would then inevitably slide further and further down the line. I also believed he badly needed to invest in much more modern machinery. As long as he believed the old machines were still contributing I didn't think he necessarily needed to get rid of them, but he did need to have a much greater high-precision machining capability if he was to achieve his very ambitious aims for his company.

In the afternoon we went out to the golf course. Golf is not a game I've ever played and I was somewhat surprised that I did eventually manage to hit the ball once, albeit in the wrong direction and not very far! However, what I did find on the golf course was the astonishing ability of Alex's little three-wheeled golf buggy to cope with the steepest inclines and the roughest terrain. I don't know the market well enough to know whether there are opportunities out there for him, but I am certain he has to develop the core business and keep his eyes on that ball if Velden Engineering is to prosper.

Churchill

Churchill is a company I visited during both the 1990 and the 1992 *Troubleshooter* series, and it is one with which I have remained in touch. I was looking forward to seeing my old friends there and finding out how they were faring. The pottery industry has had an incredibly rough time and, although it is still a British success story, the successes have been achieved at horrendous costs in terms of companies and of jobs. However, it is still a business where nearly 80% of the home market is supplied by British manufacturers, and the industry as a whole has a tremendous export record.

When I first visited Churchill, it seemed to me to have a whole range of problems which I discussed very frankly with the three Roper brothers who own the company, all of whom are involved in its operation. The business was set up by their father and all three brothers have been trained in some aspect of the business. Stephen, the chief executive, specializes in selling. Michael, the middle brother and chairman, is an absolutely first-class potter and loves the production and quality aspects of manufacture. The youngest brother, Andrew, trained as an accountant. From a situation where the tableware division had been a drag on the whole company's performance, the Ropers have transformed the entire business. Six years ago I thought Churchill were too occupied with simply feeding the kiln and they were not investing nearly enough either in their core business, or in design. However now their tableware division has become the largest manufacturer of earthenware plates, cups and saucers in Britain, with nearly 80% of all production exported. The test of the competitiveness of any business is its ability to sell its products overseas at a profit, and this the Ropers have triumphantly achieved.

The Roper brothers are certainly amongst the most open-minded businessmen I have dealt with and they took many of my suggestions on board, and went much further. They have delegated more responsibility for performance to their managers and have transformed their

194

attitudes to design. They have developed a whole range of relatively cheap and ingenious robots to produce individual pieces of crockery, and they have continued to invest steadily and heavily in the business. Despite my fears that my recommendations would result in a reduction in jobs, the reverse has happened. So successful have Churchill been that they have taken over another pottery factory and have also bought out a failing bone china business.

Now the Roper brothers are facing twin problems. On the one hand, sadly, none of the brothers' children are interested in entering the family business. This does appear to be a peculiarly British problem. In France, Germany and Japan businesses stay within families for generation after generation. Each generation believes they are holding the business in trust and that they have a duty and responsibility to hand over the company in even better condition to their successors. If the direct members of the family do not wish to pursue the same careers, businesses seem to move out to cousins or in-laws, but always reverting ultimately to members of the same family. Typically, in Britain, businesses tend to be grown and then sold on for immediate financial gain. In the case of the three Roper brothers, who have toiled mightily to develop and expand their company, only a relatively small reward has come their way. Almost all the money they have made has been ploughed back into the company and nobody could accuse the three of living ostentatiously. However, they now felt the time had come when they and their families wanted to see some greater reward, in terms of capital, for all their labours. In any case they wanted to ensure that the company itself would continue as an entity once they all retired.

The other problem is the perennial one facing private companies. Private companies can only grow at the rate at which they can generate profits for reinvestment. This puts a clear ceiling on the amounts they can invest and their ability to acquire other businesses. Of course they can borrow money from banks and institutions, but the interest payments impose a drag on any but the most profitable businesses. Moreover, obtaining long-term financial loans from banks has proved in the past to be somewhat difficult. An unusually large amount of the financing of companies is done through overdraft facilities secured all too frequently, in the case of small businesses, on the owners' personal possessions. Since overdrafts are repayable on demand, the recession of the late 1980s saw a frightening number of small business people losing both their businesses and their personal possessions at the same time. The way round this is to float the company – to take on outside shareholders and become a public limited company. The shareholders' investment constitutes risk capital on which dividends will be paid when the going is good, but who will share the bad times with the owners of the business. The Churchill business has reached a stage where the potential future opportunities were beyond the brothers' ability to finance.

Last time I visited Churchill, the brothers were thinking about floating their company, but the climate was pretty unfavourable, so they held off. Now they were seriously contemplating selling at least some of their shares and going for a public quotation. I have talked to them about this subject over the years and pointed out some of the pitfalls. I have also advised them that, since you only float a company once, and the opposite of float is sink, it is vital to obtain the best advisers for this highly technical operation. Even I, however, had not realized the full extent of the cost of the operation which would have to be met from any money raised by selling a part of the brothers' holding.

I started my visit by going to see their recently acquired bone china company. The brothers had looked at the Queens China Company three years ago and been impressed with the product portfolio which covered tableware, mugs and giftware. However, although the products and design were excellent, the factories were a nightmare, built on many layers like factories of the 1950s. Because of the success of the brothers' basic business they had purchased a new factory site at Wealdon Road. This proved fortunate as it gave them the opportunity to move the Queens' production facilities into a more suitable location, and also to apply their own particular brand of production expertise to the process. However, none of this came cheaply. The total cost of the Queens acquisition was £1.7m which included debts, but one of the advantages of the purchase was that Queens sells to 1500 independent retail outlets which obviously gave Churchill the opportunity to supply earthenware through the same channels. Moreover, Queens added significantly to Churchill's export record, as 55% of their sales go to over fifty countries. Unfortunately, making the Queens production lines more efficient is going to cost Churchill £400 000 and is planned to take about three or four years, but they have big plans for the business. They are aiming for a minimum turnover of £10m with a net profit of over £1m in a relatively short time.

The pottery business is a curious one because, as on my first visit, I saw hand operation which was faster and, from a quality point of view, better than any robotic handling methods that have, so far, been developed. Nick the Dipper has been dipping pottery in its glaze for twenty-seven years and has perfected a technique and a wriggle which the managers claim make him the fastest and the best hand dipper in the business. They have tried an automatic spray glazing machine and yet Nick, with his years of skill, is able to produce better yield and better productivity. However, their preference for hand operation is tempered with a willingness to try new technology in any area they think might be of use. They showed me with pride their cast conveyors, which enable them to have multi-speed belts, allowing them to cast a wide range of different products side by side.

I then revisited the tableware division. What a transformation! The brothers had put Paul Deighton in charge of production and he in turn had hired a development engineer to put in simple automation. I had already heard from one of the linear electric motor manufacturers that Churchill were well up in this area. They were developing their own simple robotic operators in order to reduce manning, speed up production and improve quality. What I saw thrilled me. Even Linda, the fastest bottom-stamper in the West, had been replaced by a simple robot which could at last compete with her dexterity and speed in stamping out the logo! The robots were unique to Churchill, had cost typically under £20 000.00 and, as well as releasing people, had enabled sequential operations to be linked and consistency of quality improved.

Everywhere I went the same sense of dynamic change prevailed. The warehouse, which had once been such a black hole of lost stock, was equipped with up-to-the-minute computer and laser gun-driven technology. The design team had the most modern CAD (computer-aided design) computers, the whole outfit was design and market led, and every department was moving the right way. The sales office had all the numbers bang up to date, including the return on sales of all their exports at well over 20%. Production was up by over 5% per annum and work in hand had been reduced by over 20%. Lead times were reducing almost as I watched. I was thrilled. This was a business where everyone, everywhere, was striving to change, improve and grow.

I ended the day by talking with the three brothers. They were disillusioned about the support they were receiving from the government, pointing out that Britain was the only country which had voted against quotas on Chinese imports of pottery and porcelain. For a company which exports almost 80% of its tableware, 35% of its hotelware and 65% of its bone china, facing competition from Chinese factories which are government subsidized and manned by cheap labour is not easy. We also spoke about the problems they have been having with the enormous variability of exchange rates. From their point of view leaving the ERM (the European Union's exchange rate mechanism) was the best thing which could possibly have happened. One of the difficulties of being a major exporter is that fluctuations in exchange rates can remove your profit overnight, but as a private company they are able to face large fluctuations in profitability without having to worry about how this will affect external investors. They have therefore maintained their key customers in export markets through thick and thin and are benefiting from this policy at the moment.

The brothers have thought very hard about the risks involved in losing their private company status, but felt that the pressures for expansion, plus the need to reward their management team with share options if they were to continue to attract the brightest and best, gave them little option but to go ahead with a flotation. I tried to point out that, in my opinion, the stock exchange is very much like a casino and would place pressures on the way they ran the business for which I felt they were ill prepared. I pressed them to think extremely carefully about whether they went ahead. I felt it would be better to accept the limitations on growth and wait for better external conditions, but they still felt themselves driven by the pressure of the capital expenditure they wanted to make over the next year. The brothers were also concerned because they believed the industry was still rationalizing, and the ability to use shares to purchase other businesses was very attractive. I urged the Ropers not to go ahead with the flotation and I pointed out to them that once the company had floated they would find great difficulty in selling their own shares. It is extraordinarily difficult for principals in a company to benefit from share movements, because the markets will always be watching what they do. Share sales by company principals are often interpreted as a lack of confidence in the future of the company, which inevitably drives the share price down, even though such sales might well have been motivated by the necessity to fund a legitimate expenditure.

How, I wondered, would this business fare? Rather like Triumph, the business seemed to me to be a model of what Britain as a whole needs. They take a long-term view, they invest heavily in people and new plant and they export over half of all their products. Surely this is the very sort of business the City and the financial institutions should be looking for?

In the event the Ropers half followed my advice. Instead of the £15m they had been looking for, the flotation terms they were offered were so unexciting that they reduced the number of shares they sold, ending up by disposing of 25% of the company. This raised £7.5m instead of the £15m originally proposed, but £600 000 of that went in fees to the City, so ultimately the business raised less than £7m.

Churchill seemed to me to fall between two stools and, in some ways, one could argue that they have ended up with the worst of both worlds. They did not get the substantial sums they wanted for reinvestment, but they have got the exposure to the marketplace and all that entails. The company now has to be run with a shorter-term view, aiming at consistency of dividends and earnings. There are virtually no limits to the valuation which can be placed on the shares, either upwards or downwards, and the Ropers' personal wealth is now on the stock market casino table. Because the three brothers between them still control 75% of the company, at least they are not in any danger of being taken over by a predator like Philippe Le Roux. The brothers love their business and have dedicated their lives to being professional potters and businessmen. They feel a deep responsibility to Staffordshire and their workforce and realize that to survive they have no option but to become ever more efficient and to grow. The business is built on traditional British skills, and these skills are a particularly underutilized national asset. As long as pottery manufacture still involves personal skills which cannot yet be replicated by machines, people like Nick the Dipper are a source of real competitive advantage, but the pottery industry is a mere shadow of its former self. It is only the fleet of foot, the highly professional, and the dedicated who can hope to survive, let alone prosper.

The Roper brothers demonstrated that, given the right approach, professionalism and aspirations, British firms *can* grow, despite all the difficulties they face. But the question is, why do they face difficulties from which others are more sheltered? Why do the manufacturers feel that the City and the financial institutions don't think they matter? Why do they feel that the government does not understand the forces their policies unleash upon the manufacturers, who ultimately enable Britain to pay its way in the world? It seems to me that too little has changed in this respect: the north has always made things and London has always made money, and still that hasn't changed. When I used to go to London from Wilton I would look at the Rolls-Royces and think about the people back at Wilton and elsewhere in the north, upon whose hard work these things depended. I mean for each Rolls-Royce, several of ICI's workers were making other – in my opinion far more useful – things. So I decided to visit the City to find out whether they recognize these and other difficulties. Do they understand the desirability of encouraging small new businesses and helping them to grow so that they can take on all comers? Whether we like it or not we are all dependent upon one another. No matter how great our natural financial skills, I find it difficult to believe that, as a country, we in Britain can live off them alone.

15. Making money make money

There is no doubt in my mind that the primary responsibility for Britain's relative economic failure must lie with us, the business men and women of Britain. We are, after all, the people at the sharp end who face competition from the rest of the world and who know from bitter personal experience the sorts of changes which would enable us to have a better chance. Nevertheless, to turn the present situation round from years of decline and begin to rebuild our position needs a tremendous amount of support from the other people upon whom our industrial success relies. Somehow we have to convince the ordinary man and woman in the street that business and industry play a vital role in improving their lot. We need them to be proud of our successes and impatient with our failures.

The City and the financial institutions play a part in this, but their international success, particularly in foreign currency trading, has given them a degree of detachment from ordinary, muddy-booted industry, an approach which differs considerably from that of our major competitors. Bankers in Germany and Japan move effortlessly in the corridors of industrial power, and industry is accorded a position and standing very different from that which we find in Britain. I have long believed our problems lie in our inability, first of all, to have enough business leaders who recognize that there is no substitute for being the best in the world, and secondly to produce the infrastructure and support which enables small companies to grow and expand. In this respect both Germany and Japan have well-established systems to help. Germany in particular has a bewildering array of support systems for small businesses, all of which are, interestingly enough, administered by the banking organizations. The seeds of a very close relationship between the financial and manufacturing communities are thus sown right from the beginning. We certainly don't have anything to match that in Britain, and part of the cause of this is, I believe, that disproportionate numbers of people from British public schools move on to positions of power either in government or in finance. They control the purse strings, but they fail adequately to fund industry because they do not consider industry important for Britain's economy. (See my discussion with the 'A' level students at Clifton College on page 96.)

Thus the City arouses very mixed feelings in me. It is a big contributor to our balance of payments and certainly needs all the help it can get and I have never thought that we are intrinsically so rich that we can afford to forego any opportunity of paying our way in the world, but in Britain particularly the worlds of finance and of making things seem to be totally divorced. The problems of British business stem partly from the short-term attitudes of the City which are getting shorter, not longer. Business can only develop if a long-term view is taken, as Triumph and Nissan have shown. We need finance which will reflect that and which will actually support risk-taking, but most City activities are risk averse.

What is also disturbing is the increasing power of foreign banks in the City. We used to think we were particularly good at banking and insurance in Britain and that we led the world in these fields, but more and more of our proud organizations and institutions have failed to measure up to the best champions from other countries. Even the big clearing banks, which once seemed so large and powerful, have joined the trend of overseas takeovers. The Midland Bank has recently been taken over by the Hong Kong and Shanghai Bank, and so I decided to go and see them next. After all, nobody could complain about the financial success of Hong Kong, and most people believe that Hong Kong's financial institutions have played a significant part in that island's success. They would at least be looking at the British scene through rather different eyes.

The Midland Bank

I arranged to visit Keith Whitson, who recently took over as chief executive of the Midland and who has instigated a very interesting study on the differences between the financing available for small businesses in Britain and in Germany. I wondered how he would see Britain's prospects and whether he had identified what was holding Britain back. Keith's background and experience could barely be more different from that of most people in British clearing banks. He served in Hong Kong and in the USA and is therefore conversant with these fast moving economies. I started by asking how the Midland saw the overall situation and what more could be done to help companies such as the budding Triumph Motorcycle Company and Churchill Potteries.

Keith began by telling me that the Midland's comparative study on financing for small businesses had rather depressingly concluded that the German model was not one which could easily transfer to the British environment, largely because it required changes of attitude on the part of so many people – particularly in the relationships between government, industry and the banks. The prolonged criticisms of the banks during the recession, when many customers believed their banks were looking after themselves rather than their customers, (by, for instance, calling in overdrafts at a moment's notice and thus creating a climate of fear amongst small businesses) led to uneasy relationships between banks and businesses that have not yet been completely reversed. However it was a learning period for the banks too and after the huge losses they sustained in the early 1990s, it will take time to rebuild the necessary confidence that banking staff need in order confidently to lend money to businesses. During that difficult period, I always believed that the Midland Bank acted with great courage. Unlike many of the other clearing banks the Midland decided to leave responsibility for decision-taking with the bank managers themselves, believing that they were the ones with the detailed information and the understanding of difficult situations.

Keith Whitson is committed to the Midland's strategy of working within communities with responsible managers working alongside their customers; managers who are able to take decisions on the ground and to cut out much of the bureaucracy. He told me that in the USA there is a saying that if, when you stand on the roof of your building, you can't see the customer to whom you plan to lend, then you shouldn't lend to that customer. Keith believes, as I do, that head office

203

should set certain fundamental procedures and controls, but that these should not interfere with the ability of the manager on the ground to do his job properly.

Keith feels under the same sorts of pressures for financial performance which face most of industry and are such a potent force on industrial decision-taking. The Midland Bank provides facilities for something like 500 000 small businesses, so their ability to take a long and balanced view of their customers' needs is pretty fundamental to any change. However, he felt that they needed more training and understanding of what industrialists require.

I raised two problems with Keith which seem to me to differentiate Britain and Germany. The first was the considerable reliance in Britain upon equity financing. Since 80% of equities are held by the institutions – who are precluded by statute from financial risk-taking – that money is no longer risk capital. The institutions have pushed for more stability of dividend policy and as a result companies are extremely fearful of the results of a decision to reduce the dividend. My second worry was the reliance on overdraft facilities, particularly for financing working capital. Keith pointed out that the Midland Bank had been actively pushing a fast growing subsidiary named Griffin Factors. In addition to providing financing of working capital they were trying to provide trade finance and trade services operations. It is still very difficult to borrow long-term fixed-rate money, and Keith believes nothing can be done about this until the government maintains the right macro economic conditions of stability and low inflation. Low inflation should, in theory at least, allow lower interest rates, which would encourage spenders and borrowers to borrow on longer-term rates. What is needed is a mixture of short-term finance (for example to build up stocks for Christmas orders) combined with the ability to borrow at affordable rates for businesses with low profit margins.

Keith wants to build the levels of confidence between banks, industry and government. The government plays a major role in providing stability at the macro level, but banks and industry must be willing to talk much more purposefully about longer-term financing. The banks are in a competitive situation with each other and Keith is convinced that banks which devolve decision-making closer to their customers and use a wider range of financial instruments will ultimately be the winners. He is pessimistic about the possibility of having the sort of quasi-state investment banks which do so much for fundamental investment in small companies in Germany and Japan and which I think would be a good idea, and he did not feel Britain could hope to emulate the IKB in Germany until stable long-term interest rates were well established. (The German IKB Deutsche Industriebank AG concentrates entirely upon businesses and is the leading provider of assisted funds. Fifty per cent of the IKB's new lending goes to German manufacturing businesses in the middle market sector — or *Mittelstand* – whose turnover is usually between £10m–£100m.)

Although the Midland has a very large portfolio of successful small businesses, the average loan is only about £20 000 and Keith said that people borrowing that sort of money seldom had the business expertise to develop substantial businesses. He felt that many of the small businesses with which they dealt did not have the right sort of financial acumen, or sufficient training. The Midland is endeavouring to pioneer more training for their small business customers and they have recently taken part in a project in East Anglia, together with one of the other major clearing banks, to run joint training courses for their managers and selected customers. The customers who attend are awarded an interest rate concession for their first three years in business. Sadly, however, the Midland have not had much success selling this service.

Keith is as concerned as I am that Britain's businesses are under particular pressure for short-term performance: institutional investors look at the next quarter or half-year's results in ways which do not necessarily encourage healthy long-term decisions, and Keith felt there was no chance of raising the sort of long-term patient capital necessary for greenfield investments like Nissan unless there were major changes in all the institutions.

However I left the Midland Bank feeling cheered. Keith's background in international banking gives him a very different perspective and he sees the changes and developments on the international banking scene as a guide to what can be done in Britain. Devolving more responsibility to the branches, getting closer to the customer and developing joint initiatives between the government, banks and small businesses, all seem sensible, and the idea of offering training to small businessmen (if he can get them to take it up) seems a very go-ahead concept. But, when it comes to raising long-term finance for investments like Triumph and Nissan no one seemed to have a solution. Everything depends upon everything else: the government must produce stable long-term macro economic conditions before the banks are able to offer long-term loans on low interest terms, otherwise Britain cannot invest as other countries do.

The Treasury

Next I visited the Treasury, which was a real turn up for the books. I was never once invited to the Treasury during my five-year term as chairman of ICI and the only time I did visit them was when I felt they were showing such blatant favouritism to foreign-owned competitors that ICI's petrochemical operations suffered commercial disadvantage. So strongly did I and my colleagues feel that we took the government to court and won the case. The irony was that we were only forced to pursue the case after endlessly attempting to explain our position to the Treasury. Indeed we actually told them that they left us no option but to pursue the matter through the courts if they persisted with their actions. I well remember how I felt that there was a total absence of understanding of our position.

Now, just like every other business, the Treasury is being forced to change, and I had been invited to talk to the staff about the problems of managing change. The necessity for change in Britain's economic management seems to me to have been beyond argument for many years, but the fact that the Treasury was now interested in hearing other views, particularly from an ageing heretic like myself, was, in my opinion, nothing but good news.

One of the perennial problems of management in the public sector has always been that revenue budgeting and capital budgeting are done quite separately, and management is subject to the tyranny of never being able to project further than a year ahead. The ability automatically to use savings from revenue to fund capital expenditure is taken for granted in the private sector, and nobody would even try to run a business unless they were able to do so, however the pressure on saving money in the public sector has grown greater and greater and the Permanent Secretary at the Treasury, Sir Terry Burns, seems determined the Treasury should lead by example. After a spell as chief economic advisor to the Treasury, Terry was appointed to the top job about three years ago and he almost immediately started to change things, attempting to make the Treasury more open and more accessible, particularly to the people who are affected by its decisions. Just over six months before my visit a fundamental revue of the whole way in which the Treasury operates, and how it relates to the external economy and departments of state was put in hand and it was towards the culmination of this process that Terry asked me to talk to the Treasury's civil servants.

After my talk I had a discussion with Terry who readily acknowledged the difficulties the Treasury has always had in taking account of rates of exchange when setting future policies. Britain is the centre of such an enormous capital market, with such a vast amount of trade passing through London in foreign exchange, that government is always open to the accusation of paying either not enough or too much attention to the exchange rate. Terry's defence of the mistakes of the past is that it is fantastically difficult to judge these things accurately. He pointed out that, despite the very strong showing of sterling in the early 1980s, many people would argue that Nigel Lawson's attempt to hold down sterling's value in the late 1980s was a contributory cause of the subsequent recession. Terry did acknowledge that the Treasury is isolated and works too much through other people and other organizations which means that communication, both from and to the Treasury, is all too often confused, and frequently the views of those who are affected by Treasury actions are not heard until it is too late.

My own relationships with the Treasury have been somewhat chequered. Like many other people in Britain I place quite a lot of blame for the difficult conditions we all endured during the recession upon the economic policies which were pursued at the time, and in particular the overenthusiastic introduction of monetarism in the early days of the Thatcher administration. In my view this was done without a full understanding of the implications for manufacturing industry, which obviously contributed to the ensuing calamitous result. Controlling inflation by increasing interest rates has the inevitable side effect of making the currency more desirable to international speculators. The value of the currency therefore rises but it is driven not by its natural competitiveness, but by the policies being pursued. Of course this is exactly what happened in 1981 and 1982, and this was the time when, despite having the most efficient petrochemical plants in Europe, ICI found itself losing money on every pound of product produced.

In 1982 I went through ICI's British customer list and found, to my horror, that one-third of all the firms we had been supplying had disappeared during the year. Of course this did not mean that every one of them had shut down – some had been taken over, amalgamated or joined with others – but a considerable number of those customers had disappeared forever. The trouble with industry is that it is like a house of cards. Each card rests upon others and if you remove one, others inevitably fall with it. ICI was able to survive because Britain represented under 30% of our total business, albeit a very profitable percentage, and it also had the financial strengths to do so. But it caused the company tremendous pain and required massive reductions in our workforce; the closing down of older, less efficient plant and a tremendous effort to increase our overseas sales.

I find it hard to believe that the government and the Treasury fully understand the consequences of their policies. The Treasury has a reputation for not listening to people in the 'real' economy and, despite endless efforts to communicate my concerns, I seemed continuously – in my ICI days – to be appealing to deaf ears. But, to be fair to them, life in the Treasury must be very difficult. Everyone is constantly looking to the Treasury for more money for one thing or another, and now the Treasury is trying a different approach. They want to push responsibility outwards and make the Treasury itself more concerned with the long-term view of the policies pursued. However, this process involves changing methods of public expenditure control which have existed for over 100 years. The Treasury are now trying to move towards three-year rolling capital projections and looking at ways in which the relationship between capital spending and revenue spending can be more blurred. The aims of the current changes are first of all to be sure that the Treasury is doing only those jobs which are essential

208

and that they are doing them well. The second aim is to make the Treasury a better place to work, because of the reduction in hierarchical and bureaucratic levels, and the third is to improve relationships with the outside world.

Interestingly enough, many of those amongst the junior ranks at the Treasury welcomed the idea of reducing the numbers of layers, feeling that their jobs might well become more interesting. Unfortunately the changes had been presented to the staff at the Treasury in a way which suggested that the prime objective was to reduce the costs and the number of people. This is unfortunate, as I believe their primary aim is to run the Treasury with less bureaucracy and make better relationships with the outside world, which would automatically lead to an improvement in the speed and relevance of decision-taking, and a reduction in numbers. The Treasury is attempting to give more power to the departments, and to set clear objectives so that the work is done closer to the decision points. In the past the Treasury's system of controls has been very detailed, entailing telling other organizations exactly how they could spend relatively small sums of money.

I left the Treasury more optimistic than I have been for some time. Changes do seem to be taking place, but my inherent cynicism remains, despite Terry Burns' courage in putting these undoubtedly necessary changes into operation. I wondered whether he would be able to move fast enough and far enough to help solve the sorts of problems which my visits to industry in Britain have shown up. And will these changes be enough? Will our successors in ten or fifteen years' time be thanking the good Lord that they have a flexible, non-bureaucratic and sensitive system? And will that system be one which allows every activity, be it the armed services, education or the wealth creators of business and manufacturing, continuously to change, adapt and be better in a world sense? What will do the trick, in my opinion, is when it becomes evident that the Treasury are not only *hearing* what is being said in the 'real' economy, but that they're actually *doing* something as a result of what they hear. But plainly we cannot wait until the politicians and the Treasury change their economic approaches. We all need to change in our own specific fields, hopefully in some sort of harmony, and much, much faster than we are moving at present.

Epilogue

This opportunity to look back over my life has been a unique chance to pause, and to reflect. One of the delights of my life and career is that it has always been concerned with the future. I know that sometimes the only way to see the present clearly is by the perspective afforded by the past, but this is something I seldom do. I tend to believe that the only thing you can usefully learn from the past is to avoid making the same mistakes in the future. Therefore it is the future, and how one can influence that future in order to make a better world, which has absorbed me from my very earliest days. My journey through life has, however, been a bit of a helter-skelter ride. In my early years in India I was surrounded by people with an unshakeable belief in the right of the people of Britain to enjoy the privileged position their forefathers had won for them. British values, institutions and traditions were almost unchallenged, even in a country which was so vastly different and had an even longer history. Moreover it seemed entirely natural that I, a child from a middle-class background, should enjoy the ludicrous pomp, position and respect which was granted to British people in India in the early part of this century.

At that time it was inconceivable that Britain should find herself in the position she is in today. However, I am an unshakeable optimist. I believe that, in general, life gets better for most people most of the time, and certainly many of the changes in Britain have brought benefits which we could barely have dreamt of in the 1920s and 1930s. Even after the Second World War, when our country lay exhausted and impoverished, our capital stock of plant and machinery old and worn out, our managers and leaders tired and almost at the limit of their exertions, we still believed everything would be all right. Today I see friends, and the sons and daughters of friends, believing they may never work again at an age when life was just beginning for me. I grew up in a world where, until recently, every university graduate believed that the possession of a degree, any degree, would ensure employment.

What a difference in 1995. The prevailing mood appears to be a combination of fear, anxiety and uncertainty. Our young people view life as a battle for survival in which even the fittest may not succeed. People of my own generation worry incessantly that their pitiful incomes and hard won savings will run out before they die, and they wonder what will become of them. Old age pensioners scrimp and save in order just barely to exist. Managers worry about where the next redundancy will fall. Part of the problem facing us all is a devastating lack of self-confidence. We fear that we will be unable to adjust and benefit from the changes which lie in wait for each and every one of us. It is all too easy to see the difficulties, and yet every problem represents an opportunity and every difficulty offers the satisfaction to be gained from overcoming it.

Everything seems to be changing at once, and we are all adjusting at different paces and different speeds to create a new world, a world whose shady outlines we can only just make out. However the optimist in me never fails to find rays of hope, and almost all the men and women I met on this journey refused to accept that things can only get worse. They are determined to work as hard as they can to ensure that things get better. And there is no reason why Britain should continue to be looked upon as a bad joke of a country: a country that disrupts international football matches and whose economy is in continual decline. Britain has the platform and the background to become, once more, the envy of other countries.

My visit to India served to put so many other problems in perspective for me. Whenever I have visited India I have always been led to question the values by which I lead my life. The ability of people with so little to retain their dignity and self-respect never ceases to amaze me, and the way that spiritual matters have a natural place in their everyday lives has much to teach us.

The reform of an entire educational system is a long-term project which involves horrendous change. Despite the fact that we are at

211

last getting more of our people into further education in Britain, their numbers still do not equal those in our major competitor countries. But one has to bear in mind that the entire education cycle is fifteen to twenty years long and the whole cycle has to be completed before the benefits can be seen coming through. Change is not something you do *to* people. Change is something which you have to embrace yourself, and I have long recognized this painful lesson in my own business and professional life. I therefore honour teachers like Bob Salisbury and Chris Lindup who, with very little encouragement, barely any support and no specialist training at all, have set out to achieve the impossible. Obviously the impossible can only be achieved if somebody actually tries to do it. And the impossible, when asked of one by others, will always be described as what it is – impossible. It is determined individuals who have a vision who try, no matter what the difficulties, to achieve that vision and it is they who will show us the way.

I will always feel warmly about the Royal Navy, to whom I owe so many of my basic values, my ideals of service, my belief that every job can always be done better and my belief that there are no limits to what the ordinary men and women of Britain can achieve and aspire to, if they are just given a chance. At present the Navy is making Herculean efforts to retain the best of its traditional features and yet produce the defence our country needs from woefully inadequate funds. It seems to me yet another sign of our overall economic problems that, for the first time since the Battle of Trafalgar, the French possess a larger Navy than we do, arguably with less need. I have every sympathy with those who say it is impossible to design a defence force when you have no obvious enemy. But it seems to me to be blindingly obvious that, living in a small crowded island, we have to retain the ability to defend ourselves far from our shores if we are to have any defence at all – and this surely means that we still need naval power. Changing a proud historic service like the Royal Navy is an horrendous responsibility. What man or woman wants to go down in history as having been responsible for abandoning the Navy's time-honoured traditions? And yet, just as in every other aspect of our national life, we change or we perish.

So to industry and the world of business. When I joined ICI I believed I was turning my hand to the only activity which could actually help to reverse the decline which, even then, was already apparent. The problems are vast. For too long we have accepted that some post-industrial miracle was going to come to our salvation, but whilst we are an inventive nation, and our science and technology can keep pace with the best, time after time we fail actually to bring things to fruition. Our most brilliant inventions and our best-designed products seem only to go to make others rich: we fail to build for the future. Over and over again I have seen the need for long-term investment in our country, both in our people through the education system and in our businesses. Yet we appear to be rather like a whirling dervish pursuing short-term gain and short-term profit ever more energetically. But there are exceptions. Look at John Bloor, with his incredibly patient and skilful building up of an entirely new business in an area which others, who had the custody of the sacred flame, allowed to become extinguished. The Roper brothers are pushing steadily and energetically on and refuse to accept that their business cannot prosper. I have many other friends in industry and I am lucky enough to have many valuable insights into the not inconsiderable number of areas where, despite everything, we still represent world leadership in our chosen fields, be it alcoholic drinks, pharmaceuticals or certain aspects of computer software. There is no question that, even given the current difficulties in Britain, we can take on and beat the best in the world, but at present there are simply not enough people making the effort. There are only a few areas in which we have managed to build up that mutually reinforcing diamond of competitors and infrastructure that Michael Porter describes in his book, *The Competitiveness of Nations*.

Everything is indeed changing. Everything and everyone has the opportunity to contribute to this change if they would just raise their sights. Our aim must be not merely to match the best in the world, but to actually *be* the best in the world, to set the pace which others have to emulate and, if we do finally get there, to understand that it only gives us the right and opportunity to run faster than those who are chasing after us. For our country and fellow countrymen this means continued exertion, continued change, continued travail. But the alternative is to be unable to achieve all the things that we all wish to accomplish for our children and for our children's children. There is no plateau that we can hope to reach, there is no miraculous promised land where everything will be certain and comfortable and like it was in the 'good old days'. In reality the 'good old days' were good only in as much as they projected a picture of certainty. It is the 'good old tomorrows' that we must all fight for now.

Yet again I hang up my troubleshooting boots in a curiously optimistic frame of mind, albeit a subdued one. Even seven years ago I would have had more doubts about our ability to adjust to the demands upon us than I have today. It is not difficult to find examples of individuals who are not waiting for the institutions to change, but are charting tomorrow's course. Every institution, even the Treasury, is committed to change. Let us pray that these changes are fast enough and that they go far enough. Let us pray also that we can regain the initiative, and that young people like my granddaughter (to whom this book is dedicated), who are just entering their working lives, can see years of improvement ahead in the lot of every man and woman. Improvement is not only a matter of material things. We must make this improvement in the way we relate to each other, the way we respect each other and the way we utilize the skills and capabilities of every man and woman in our island. It is not difficult to draw ourselves a picture of how this can happen, but the burning question is, can we really make it happen? Only the men and women of this country can answer that question. Only they can decide whether they are willing to face the discomfort and struggles which will be involved in changing our current situation. There are plenty I have met who believe that it can be done and are doing their bit to achieve it. I only hope there are enough of them.

Index

TROUBLESHOOTER

Department of Trade and Industry (DTI) 12, 182, 191
Dhar 9, 45–51
Dicken, Arthur 169
Dickinson, Chris 105–6
Dunhill 180
Durga Das, Major 34

education 80–135, 175
educational system, reform   211–12
Elbit Group 188
English language 16, 74
equity financing 204
European Union, wages 192
Evans, Robert 13
exchange rate mechanism 198

Falklands War 140
Federman Enterprises 188
First Sea Lord (Admiral Bathurst) 158–61
Foreign Office 12
French navy 139
Fullbore Motors 63

Garibaldi School 99–109, 123
Garside, David 187–8
GATT signatories 13, 31
General Motors 62, 69
Gibson, Ian 173–5
Gieves 125, 127
Gretton, Admiral 138
Griffin Factors 204
Gulf States 17

Harley Davidson 184–5
Harvey-Jones family 70, 90, 122, 136, 163
  father (Mervyn) 9, 32–6, 41–2, 45, 47–50, 78–9
  granddaughter (Abigail) 11–12, 94, 110–13, 16, 214
  mother (Eileen) 9–10, 81
  wife (Betty) 10, 21
Harvey-Jones, Sir John
  Dartmouth days 60
  ICI days 21, 32, 68, 80, 213

Second World War 164
Hawthorn Leslie 151
Headlamp 100
headteachers 99–100, 115, 122
Heard, Alan 183
Herbert, Alfred 191
Himalayas 70–1
Hindustan Motors 51–69, 78
HMS
  ARK ROYAL 136–44
  FEARLESS 131
  GLORIOUS 136–7
  NORTHUMBERLAND 149
  RALEIGH 132
  RICHMOND 149
  TRUSTY 144, 147
HMY BRITANNIA 12–18, 32
Honda 19
Hong Kong & Shanghai Bank 202
Hong Kong's financial institutions 202
Hurd, Douglas 13

ICI 164, 167–73, 206, 208, 213
Ikeda Hoover 178, 182
Imperial Tankers 171–3, 180
India
  agriculture 13–14, 76–7
  and the British 16, 70–5
  bureaucracy 10, 13, 15–16, 73
  economy 16–17, 74–6
  education 73
  exit strategies 14–15, 19
  families 75–6
  family businesses 23, 31, 59–60
  foreign investors 15–16
  industrial education 29
  international competitive standards 77–8
  liberalization 15, 18–19, 78
  licence-raj 15, 51
  literacy rate 17
  manufacturing 13–14, 77
  problems 17, 32, 76–7
  redundancy 17–18
  telecommunications 13–14
  twenty-first century 75–8
  women's position in 77
  world markets 75

216